VOICES of the SPIRIT

Sources for Interpreting the African-American Experience

Denise M. Glover

AMERICAN LIBRARY ASSOCIATION
CHICAGO AND LONDON, 1995

Managing Editor: Joan A. Grygel

Cover design: Richmond A. Jones

Text design: Dianne M. Rooney

Composition by Impressions,
a division of Edwards Brothers, Inc.;
typeset in Sabon, Gil Sans Medium and Gil Sans Bold
using Penta Masterpage

Printed on 50-pound Glatfelter,
a pH-neutral stock, and bound in 10-point C1S
cover stock by McNaughton & Gunn

The paper used in this publication meets the
minimum requirements of American National Standard
for Information Sciences—Permanence of Paper for
Printed Library Materials, ANSI Z39. 48-1984.∞

Library of Congress Cataloging-in-Publication Data

Glover, Denise Marie.
    Voices of the spirit : sources for interpreting the
African-American experience / by Denise M. Glover.
        p.   cm.
    Includes index.
    ISBN 0-8389-0639-7
    1. Afro-Americans—History—Bibliography.   I. Title.
Z1361.N39G56   1994
[E185]   94-29139
016.973'0496073—dc20

Printed in the United States of America.

99 98 97 96 95   5   4   3   2   1

CONTENTS

Contents

ACKNOWLEDGMENTS

A LTHOUGH THIS BOOK HAS ONE AUTHOR, IT HARDLY REFLECTS the work of only one individual. The idea for the book was planted in 1989 when Marian Moore, the director of the Museum of African-American History in Detroit, requested that I do some consulting work to help establish the museum's new library. As I conducted the research required to compile a bibliography of reference and secondary materials for the library, it became clear that a similar publication was needed for high school and undergraduate instructors, students, and the general public.

It would have been difficult for me to complete this work if I did not live in the Washington, D.C., metropolitan area, where researchers have access to some of the best collections of African Americana in the United States. I was able to use the black collections of the Moorland-Spingarn Research Center at Howard University, the Library of Congress, and resources in the University of Maryland Library System and the Montgomery County Public Library System.

I am deeply indebted to Simona Simmons-Hodo, head of reference at the Albin O. Kuhn Library, University of Maryland–Baltimore County—a most user-friendly and pleasant library—for bringing to my attention new works I might have otherwise overlooked and for applauding my early efforts. Jessie C. Smith and her staff at the newly renovated and expanded Frederick Douglass Library, University of Maryland Eastern Shore, were kind, helpful, and gracious. Jessie eagerly granted me unlimited access to the library's growing black collection; I could browse the shelves at my leisure and immerse myself in the works of eminent nineteenth- and twentieth-century African-American scholars and historians. I am grateful not only for her hospitality but for her encouragement, leadership as a library director, and commitment to a profession that too often is taken for granted.

I want to express my gratitude to my family and friends who constantly queried me with such questions as "When are you going to finish this book?" or "How is the book coming?" These questions served as evidence of their faith in me—a steady reminder that I was a woman with a mission. I often feared I would never complete the mission, but they trusted my commitment to this important project. I owe special thanks to Jon Michael Spencer for reviewing the third chapter, and to Herbert Bloom at the American Library Association for his patience.

A special word of appreciation and love goes to my parents, who have always expected the best from their children, who instilled in us a positive self-image, and who demonstrated, by their example, that we are here to make life better for others; and to my sister and brother who, without even saying the words, consistently expressed their pride in me. The real heroes and "sheroes" of this book—however modest it might be—are my grandparents and great-grandparents and all the countless African Americans whose names are not mentioned in these pages. Their collective voice lives in those of us who are here now and those who are yet to be.

INTRODUCTION

D IVERSITY, MULTICULTURALISM, AND AFROCENTRICITY MAY BE the buzz words or politically correct terms and concepts of the 1990s, but they also reflect reality. The face of America is changing rapidly; as we approach the year 2000, we have and will continue to become a more colorful and varied mix of people, lifestyles, religions, languages, races, and ethnic groups. Our challenge is in many ways what it has always been: to understand, respect, and value individuals who appear very different from us—a challenge that historically America has faced with reluctance and often under great duress. Parents, employers, teachers, college instructors, policy makers, social and health service providers—indeed all of us—share equally the responsibility and the opportunity to motivate, teach, serve, live, and work within a heterogeneous population if we are to survive as a peaceful, productive nation.

The voices of the men and women that reverberate through these pages speak to the whole African-American experience: despair and hope, sorrow and joy, struggle and victory, desolation and inspiration. From slavery to the slave community, from slave rebellions to revolts, through emancipation, migration, urbanization, segregation, and civil rights, to the struggle for equality and economic equity, these voices tell of a past and present of oppression, racism, and violence. Yet, these same voices—inspired by the indefatigable spirit and faith of their ancestors—record the lives of a people with the stalwart determination to be free, to transform a culture that was not theirs into one that was, and to produce a community of survivors, fighters, and leaders. The stories unveiled by these voices—expressed through the written word, oral history, and moving and still images—deserve to be heard in classrooms and homes for the lessons they teach about American history and the endurance of the human spirit.

Voices of the Spirit represents a modest effort to assist secondary and lower-division college-level teachers and the general public to move themselves and their students beyond the prevailing stereotypes of

African Americans they encounter in most print and electronic media. It is hoped that this text, used creatively, will breathe three-dimensional life into the faceless, nameless victims we passively read about or encounter in our daily routines. The goal is to help transform the historical events, laws, movements, statistics, and facts into personal experiences that are indeed relevant and significant to our present lives. Perhaps this is, in part, what Thomas Holt means when he says in the introductory essay to *The State of Afro-American History* (1986) that "minds are shaped for action based on our understandings of the past."

Background

This book annotates standard, classic works by nineteenth-century pioneers in African-American history as well as contemporary resources. These works provide readers with a historical context and demonstrate that the current study of African-American history is not without precedent. A cursory review of the foundations for the study of African-American history is useful here.

The bibliographic seeds for the growth of special black collections were planted in 1808 when Henri Gregoire wrote the first book recording the names of African-American writers and their works. The book was entitled *An Inquiry Concerning the Intellectual and Moral Faculties and Literature of Negroes Followed with an Account of the Life and Works of Fifteen Negroes and Mulattoes, Distinguished in Science, Literature and the Arts*. It was not until 1905 that the first substantial record of African Americana, *A Select Bibliography of the Negro American*, was compiled by W. E. B. Du Bois, a black Harvard graduate and an early advocate of African-American history and studies. Indeed, several of Du Bois's works are annotated in these pages.

Efforts to educate African Americans about their history began in the early 1900s and concentrated on the teaching of black history, literature, and culture in historically black institutions such as Howard and Fisk Universities and Hampton and Tuskegee Institutes. Many of the major collections of African Americana were established in the late eighteenth century and early nineteenth century: Tuskegee Institute's Booker T. Washington Collection (1881), Hampton Institute's George Foster Peabody Collection (1905), Howard University's Moorland (1914) and Spingarn (1946) collections, and Fisk University's Negro Collection (1929). This text builds upon the resources located in these famous collections and provides an annotated guide to basic resources for a wider audience.

Scope

Voices of the Spirit annotates classic and more contemporary resources in African-American history, as it is narrowly defined; resources in other disciplines are excluded, with a few exceptions that are noted and explained in the chapter introductions. Sources published from 1883 to the present are annotated and discussed. When available, reprint information is provided for these early works.

General reference books such as encyclopedias, handbooks, yearbooks, atlases, biographical dictionaries; collective biography, genealogy, historiography; general historical surveys; and historical works by chronological period are annotated. A special effort was made to include resources by and about African-American women whose history has for too long been omitted or ignored. Annotations of bibliographies are excluded, although some key bibliographical works consulted appear in the selected bibliography at the end of the book.

Voices of the Spirit focuses on the following types of resources: general history books, including collections of primary documents and historical photographic books; traveling exhibits; and videotapes. Books by African-American photographers offer powerful and enduring visual images of families and individuals, renowned and obscure, at work and play in urban and rural settings. These images invite students and the general reader to envision a life that is in some ways far removed from his or her own, but in other ways, very similar. It is hoped that these exquisite portraits might inspire younger readers to consider photography as a viable career option.

Institutions, organizations, and schools may rent traveling exhibits in African-American history from the Smithsonian Institution Traveling Exhibition Service (SITES) in Washington, D.C. These exhibits provide students and the general public with an opportunity to experience the past through all the senses and, therefore, to understand it as a living history. Readers may contact SITES for a free catalog of exhibits at:

SITES
Quad 3146, MRC 706
Washington, DC 20277-2915
phone (202) 357-3168

The videotapes described in *Voices of the Spirit* are representative of the scope and quality of resources available in this format. There are many more high-quality historical and documentary videotapes appropriate for school and home viewing. It is hoped that by including a variety of formats, teachers, curriculum development specialists, and college professors will be encouraged to combine media, methods, and source material (e.g., oral and family history assignments, historical debates, historical reenactments, and field trips to local historical societies, museums, and sites) to reach students at all levels of interest and ability and with all learning styles.

This text aims to be comprehensive but not exhaustive. Each classic historical and seminal contemporary work listed was selected based on the historian's reputation and whether the work represented a new school of historical thought or theory, an application of new historical methods, or a reinterpretation of a previously existing historical paradigm or perspective.

Arrangement

The six chapters are arranged by genre and historical period. Chapter 1 includes reference books, chapter 2 covers collective biography and genealogy, and chapter 3 annotates historiographical works. General historical surveys are included in chapter 4. Chapters 5 and 6 present historical works by chronological period: chapter 5 covers the period prior to and including emancipation, and chapter 6 includes post-emancipation sources up through the present. Within each chapter, the books and other resources are alphabetized by the author or producer's last name. Books of selected primary documents appear toward the end of each chapter in a separately alphabetized section.

Each chapter is divided into parts, and each part is preceded by an introduction that describes the scope, purpose, and focus of the resources in the chapter. When appropriate, the introductions include an essay on relevant historical works of the period or genre covered.

Each source is assigned an entry number. The first number in the entry represents the chapter number. Each item is then numbered beginning with 1 (the first entry in the book) through 179 (the last entry in the last chapter). For example, the designation **4.97** indicates that the item is in chapter 4, and it is the ninety-seventh entry in the book.

An added letter in the entry is provided for photographic books, exhibits, and videotapes. Following the last numeral for the entry, these resources are assigned a *P*, *E*, and *V*, respectively, to alert the reader to a format other than a book. Entries for books are not designated by an additional letter.

The annotations vary in length, depending on the type, significance, and level of the resource. The aim was to provide enough detailed information to help the reader decide whether an item would be appropriate for inclusion in a course or curriculum. The following information is provided in each annotation: bibliographic entry, scope and purpose of work, number and arrangement of chapters (if appropriate), usefulness of work, comparison with similar works, unique contributions, audience level, and special features.

Finally, at the back of the book, readers will find a list of sources consulted and an author-title index and a subject index.

CHAPTER ONE

General Reference Books

B OTH VALUABLE OUT-OF-PRINT AND IN-PRINT TITLES ARE annotated and included in this chapter for their timeliness and accuracy. The chapter is divided into three parts: Encyclopedias and Encyclopedic Surveys (entries 1.1–10); Yearbooks, Directories, Handbooks, and Chronologies (entries 1.11–22); and Biographical Dictionaries and Directories (entries 1.23–32). Reprint information, when available, is provided in the entry.

Particularly significant are the several nineteenth- and early-twentieth-century publications that illuminate and describe the lives, conditions, aspirations, values, organizations, and work of the newly emancipated slaves and their children. For example, books by James T. Haley and Clement Richardson and yearbooks and handbooks researched and written by African Americans provide sociological, economic, agricultural, as well as historical data and perspectives on early-twentieth-century African Americana. Reference books by Monroe Work and Jessie Guzman can be compared with more-contemporary works represented by Harry Ploski, W. Augustus Low and Virgil Clift, and Gerald Jaynes. By including the earlier publications, it is hoped that these uncelebrated treasures will be rescued from obscurity.

In the final section of biographical dictionaries and directories, many works are indexed in Mary Mace Spradling's comprehensive two-volume *In Black and White: A Guide to Magazine Articles, Newspaper Articles, and Books Concerning More Than 15,000 Black Individuals and Groups* (Detroit, Mich.: Gale Research, 1980). Items with an asterisk (*) are *not* indexed in Spradling's work or the 1985 supplement.

1

Encyclopedias and Encyclopedic Surveys

The ten books included in this first section are primarily one-volume encyclopedias. The earliest book by James T. Haley was published in 1895 and provides a valuable perspective on the lives and aspirations of African-American men and women at the turn of the century. Although not a full-length book, Thomas Holt's article in *The Harvard Guide to American Ethnic Groups* serves as an excellent introduction to the major themes and significant events and personalities in African-American history. Recent one-volume encyclopedias that are affordable, reliable, and handy for both quick reference and general-topic overviews include two classics: Harry A. Ploski and James Williams's *The Negro Almanac* and W. Augustus Low and Virgil A. Clift's *Encyclopedia of Black America*.

The only multivolume work, *The International Library of Afro-American Life and History*, is perhaps the most comprehensive encyclopedia on African Americans for junior high and high school students published to date.

Subject encyclopedias on black women, edited by Darlene Clark Hine, and on civil rights, edited by Charles D. Lowery and John F. Marszalek, are referenced here due to their thorough coverage of two topics of increasing interest in African-American history.

Together, these reference books provide both the general reader and the history buff a full range of books to expand the breadth and depth of their knowledge of the African-American experience.

1.1 **Gibson, John William.** *Progress of a Race or the Remarkable Advancement of the American Negro from the Bondage of Slavery, Ignorance, and Poverty to the Freedom of Citizenship, Intelligence, Affluence, Honor, and Trust.* Naperville, Ill.: J. L. Nichols, 1920. Reprint, Miami, Fla.: Mnemosyne, 1969.

Progress of a Race was first published as *The Colored American: From Slavery to Honorable Citizenship* by John William Gibson and W. H. Crogman in 1902. In the introduction, Robert R. Moton, principal of Tuskegee Institute in 1920, described the purpose of this volume: ". . . not only to record stories of Negro Progress but place them before the public . . . [and] inspire future generations of the Negro as well as enlighten children of other races as to the history of colored people."

The sixteen chapters of the book are arranged topically and chronologically to include a general overview of black history, slavery, Negro involvement in all major wars, migration, club movement among Negro women, the National Negro Business League, educational improvement, religion, and biography. Each chapter is further separated into brief subtopics, which are interspersed with biographical sketches of prominent and obscure individuals. For example, chapter 3, "The Negro in the Revolution," is divided into "Slavery Population," "A Great Mistake," "The First Blood of Liberty," "Crispus Attucks," etc. The information provided on each subtopic is concise and contains little historical background. Both African-American and white men and women are briefly profiled within each chapter. Excerpts from speeches, letters, sermons, and other primary documents are also provided.

Several chapters incorporate information not contained in other sources discussed in this section of the bibliography. The chapter on Negro women in the club movement written by Mrs. Booker T. Washington is especially noteworthy. The work of renowned women—Fannie Jackson Coppin, Mary Church Terrell, Josephine St. Pierre Ruffin—and lesser-known women such as Anne M. Pope Malone, Maria Baldwin, Elizabeth Carter, and Lucy Thurman who founded and contributed to the club women's movement are featured. Useful background information on the members and activities of the National Negro Business League, founded by Booker T. Washington in 1900, is also provided. Additional black-owned businesses prominent during the 1920s can readily be identified in the chapter "Progress in Industries."

The biographical chapter contains more than 160 sketches of primarily renowned Negro men of the period—only eleven women are included. These entries are arranged alphabetically; the reader must scan the entire entry to ascertain the occupation of the person.

This work features many important photographs and sketches of individuals, organizations, buildings, and institutions built or owned by Negroes, pictorial information that is particularly useful to museum curators.

The 1969 reprint of this classic work was revised and enlarged by J. L. Nichols and William H. Crogman. Unfortunately, no bibliography or footnotes are included. An index of proper names is included. This volume should prove an invaluable addition to college or university libraries and history museum library collections.

1.2 **Haley, James T., ed.** *Afro-American Encyclopedia.* Nashville, Tenn.: Haley and Florida, 1895.

This classic historical encyclopedia "teaches every subject of interest to the colored people, as discussed by more than 100 of their wisest and best men and women."

The author's intent is to address the scarcity of books by Negro authors by compiling a reference book of facts, "not opinions," on the Negro race. Written by Negro authors only thirty years after emancipation, and distributed through "subscription only," this book now serves as a compendium of information on Negroes in America.

The book is alphabetized by topic and reflects the educational and social aspirations of a people who were locked out of participation in American life. Selected chapters contained in this volume are "Africa and Africans, an Address to the Colored Bar Association," "Mortality of the Colored People and How to Reduce It," "The Colored Man in Medicine," "Virginia's First Woman Physician," "The Negro in Dentistry," and "Booker T. Washington." Other topics of note include "Opportunities and Responsibilities of Colored Women," "The Future of the Negro," "Advice to Young Ladies," "The White Man and the Colored Man as Christian Citizens," and "Afro-American vs. Negro." Also included are a list of newspapers and magazines edited and published by and for Afro-Americans and biographical sketches and photographs of famous Negroes of the day, with particular emphasis on ministers, educators, physicians, politicians, and musicians. For a book published during this period, there is a surprisingly large number of profiles of women.

Although the book has no index or bibliography, this does not diminish its usefulness. This obscure gem is out of print, but high school teachers and undergraduate faculty in history, journalism, and African-American and American studies will want to resurrect it from the stacks and special-collections rooms of major academic libraries.

1.3   Hine, Darlene Clark, ed. *Black Women in America: An Historical Encyclopedia.* 2v. Brooklyn, N.Y.: Carlson Publishing, 1993.

This long-awaited and much heralded comprehensive encyclopedia on African-American women is the first reference book of its kind to include extensive biographical sketches, topics, and subjects. Of the 804 entries, 641 are biographies of individual African-American women.

Topical entries represent a broad and eclectic range of subjects— from Alpha Kappa Alpha, African Methodist Episcopal preaching women of the nineteenth century, the Baha'i faith, the birth control movement, the Civil War and Reconstruction, domestic women in the North and South, education, Federal Writers Project slave narratives, feminism, and gospel music to National Association of Colored Women, National Council of Negro Women, radio, science, slavery, and the Young Women's Christian Association. Hine includes mainly African-American women's organizations. The exceptions to this rule are those organizations that, while not strictly run by women, involve the work of numerous African-American women, such as the National Association for the Advancement of Colored People, the National Urban League, and the Baptist Church.

Biographical entries focus on women about whom little information can be found in other sources. Biographies of four men who were critical figures in the fight for women's rights are included here: W. E. B. Du Bois, Frederick Douglass, Marcus Garvey, and Booker T. Washington. A useful classified list of biographies, referenced by field of endeavor, is also provided.

The entries vary in length from a half-page article on blues singer Alberta Hunter to a twenty-five-page article on slavery. Biographical entries provide information on the early life and influences of the woman; birthplace and date; elementary, secondary, and college and graduate or professional education; professional and personal accomplishments; contributions to the community; and quotes. Subject entries describe the historical context for the topic; founders or women associated with the organization or event; significance to African-American history and women's history; and controversial issues surrounding the topic.

The authoritative entries are arranged in alphabetical order. To ensure accuracy of information provided, background information included in each entry was confirmed in two sources. Each article concludes with a bibliographical note on the sources consulted. The contributors as well as the twenty-one-member editorial board are scholars in their respective fields. Listed among the editorial board members are Mary Frances Berry and Paula Giddings (entries 4.76 and 4.82) and historians Sharon Harley, Daphne Harrison, Jacqueline Jones, Deborah Gray White, and Nell I. Painter.

Additional features include a chronology of African-American women in the United States from 1619 to 1992; a briefly annotated bibliography of basic resources on African-American women by Janet Sims-Wood, a reference librarian at the renowned Moorland-Spingarn Research Center at Howard University; a list of biographical entries classified by field of endeavor; a biographical note on contributors and editors; and an index.

This source serves as an important companion to the *Encyclopedia of Black America* (entry 1.6), which provides minimal coverage of women and topics related to women. No high school, public, or academic library collection would be complete without this reference book, and no teacher of American history or women's studies should develop a course without consulting it.

1.4   **Holt, Thomas.** "Afro-Americans." In *The Harvard Encyclopedia of American Ethnic Groups*, edited by Stephan Thernstrom, Ann Orlov, and Oscar Hadlin, 5–23. Cambridge, Mass.: Harvard University Press, 1980.

Holt's extensive introductory article, which covers the African-American experience through the 1970s, is an eloquent overview of African-American history and culture. Holt uses a chronological and thematic approach to his historical narrative that weaves together major events, personalities, and statistics in an engaging style. This article serves as a prerequisite to more specialized monographs in the field. A detailed bibliographical essay is included. Holt's article is essential reading for senior high school teachers and college-level students and faculty in history.

1.5   *International Library of Afro-American Life and History.* Washington, D.C.: Association for the Study of Afro-American Life and History, 1976. These works were published under separate titles:

Vol. 1:   Wesley, Charles *Afro-Americans in the Civil War, from Slavery to Citizenship.*

Vol. 2:   Morais, Herbert M. *The History of the Afro-American in Medicine.*

Vol. 3:   Patterson, Lindsay. *Anthology of the Afro-American in the Theatre, a Critical Approach.*

Vol. 4:   Robinson, Wilhelmena S. *Historical Afro-American Biographies.* (See entry 1.29.)

Vol. 5:   Patterson, Lindsay. *The Afro-American in Music and Art.*

Vol. 6:   Wesley, Charles *In Freedom's Footsteps: From the African Background to the Civil War.*

Vol. 7:   Romero, Patricia W. *I, Too, Am America: Documents from 1619 to the Present.*

Vol. 8:   Henderson, Edwin B. *Black Athlete: Emergence and Arrival.*

Vol. 9: Wesley, Charles *The Quest for Equality: From Civil War to Civil Rights.*

Vol. 10: Patterson, Lindsay. *An Introduction to Black Literature in America: From 1746 to the Present.*

The editor-in-chief of this important ten-volume library of African-American history and culture is the late, renowned historian, Charles Wesley. Each volume in the set includes an introduction. Numerous illustrations (with credits supplied at the end of each volume), maps, and reproductions of primary documents are presented in an attractive, easy-to-read format. An extensive bibliography and an index are included in each volume. This set is designed for junior high and high school students and represents the most reliable, comprehensive work of its kind.

1.6 Low, W. Augustus, and Virgil A. Clift, eds. *The Encyclopedia of Black America.* New York: McGraw-Hill, 1981. Reprint, New York: Da Capo Press, 1984.

This comprehensive one-volume encyclopedia is one of the most valuable, authoritative reference books available on African-American history and culture. The contributors are scholars in their respective fields, the articles are extensive and fairly current (through 1976), and references are included at the end of all major articles. As an example of the breadth and depth of this work, there is a fifty-one-page article on African-American history, as well as entries on agriculture, banks, cosmetology, and education. Biographies of renowned African Americans (about 1,400 in total) and historical information on most major and minor institutions and organizations are covered. The text is arranged alphabetically, and the cross references and index are extensive.

High school through college-level students and teachers will refer to this work to define terminology and to locate accurate historical information on major and minor events, topics, and personalities in African-American history. This encyclopedia represents the definitive single-volume encyclopedic history of African Americans published to date.

1.7 Lowery, Charles D., and John F. Marszalek, eds. *Encyclopedia of African-American Civil Rights: from Emancipation to the Present.* Westport, Conn.: Greenwood Press, 1992.

According to the editors, this reference book presents an accurate and convenient overview of the century-long struggle for civil rights.

This encyclopedia contains more than one hundred short articles on individuals, organizations, events, and court cases since emancipation. The scope of this source is limited to persons and events that made a significant positive contribution to the advancement of civil rights; therefore, persons who opposed the movement are omitted. Also omitted are presidents of the United States, members of Congress, Supreme Court justices, sports figures, and military personnel.

The entries are arranged in alphabetical order and include significance of event, topic, or person to the Civil Rights movement, and the date of the event or birth and death dates of the person. A selected bibliography follows each entry. The entries are signed, and a note on the contributors is provided at the beginning of the book. Most entries are concise, ranging from one-quarter page to just over two pages long.

Sample topics contained in the encyclopedia are the Harmon Foundation; African-American suffragettes; Boley, Oklahoma; Arna Bontemps; Detroit Race Riot (1967); affirmative action; the Civil Rights Acts of 1968 and 1990; Angela Davis; direct action; Frederick Douglass; St. Clair Drake; W. E. B. Du Bois; the Emancipation Proclamation; Free Southern Theater; Freedmen's Bureau; *Meredith* v. *Fair*; Mississippi Freedom Democratic Party; Paul Robeson; *United Steelworkers* v. *Weber*; and Henry McNeal Turner.

Other features include a useful chronology of events from 1861 through 1990, a selected bibliography, and an index. Students, teachers, civil rights enthusiasts, and the general public will find this an invaluable compendium on civil rights.

1.8 **Murray, Daniel.** *Murray's Historical and Biographical Encyclopedia of the Colored Race.* Daniel Murray Papers, 1881–1955. Madison: State Historical Society of Wisconsin. Microfilm.

This reference book by the first African-American librarian at the Library of Congress was never completed or published. However, the primary materials from which Murray planned to write the encyclopedia are included among his papers that were microfilmed by the State Historical Society of Wisconsin and are available on microfilm from many manuscript collections in the United States.

Murray, an authority on African-American history, biography, and bibliography, devoted twenty-five years of his life to researching, collecting, and compiling documents and information on African-American life and culture. He acquired much of his knowledge while working as an assistant librarian in the reference department at the Library of Congress. At the request of Herbert Putnam, the Librarian of Congress in the 1890s, Murray began researching books written by African-American authors in preparation for an exhibit that was to be shown at the 1900 Paris Exposition. By the time of the exposition, Murray had uncovered more than 1,100 titles. These helped him to form the idea for the encyclopedia.

The encyclopedia was intended to be a single authoritative source on the lives and accomplishments of African Americans from the earliest times to the twentieth century. It was to include twenty-five thousand biographical sketches, titles of six thousand books and pamphlets, five thousand musical compositions, and plot synopses of five hundred novels by white authors on subjects related to African-American life. Murray conceived of his encyclopedia as a six-volume work to be sold in monthly installments for $24. However, there were not enough subscribers to make publication possible.

W. E. B. Du Bois, who was working on his own *Encyclopedia Africana,* was aware of Murray's work since Murray asked Du Bois to serve as one of his associate editors. Du Bois asked Murray to consider publishing parts of his encyclopedia in *The Crisis,* the official organ of the NAACP, which Du Bois edited. Murray refused; he wanted his encyclopedia to be published in its entirety. Tragically, Murray died in 1925 with the encyclopedia unpublished. His widow unsuccessfully attempted to find a publisher. In 1966, Murray's surviving son, Harold Baldwin Murray, donated his father's manuscripts and some of his personal papers to the State Historical Society of Wisconsin.

According to the *Guide to the Microfilm Edition* of the papers by Jane Wolff and Eleanor McKay, Murray's papers do not include a finished draft of the encyclopedia. They do include correspondence with eight publishing houses concerning his work, as well as invitations to prominent African Americans requesting them to serve as associate editors of the encyclopedia. Also included is a 1911 draft of the foreword, drafts of a preface, an inventory of biographical sketches, drafts of the sketches, notes, annotated clippings, photographs, and miscellaneous papers. The biographical sketches and the notes contain research data and completed or almost-completed encyclopedia articles.

Undergraduate and graduate history and African-American studies majors will find Murray's precocious work an important collection of documents. For comparative purposes, students can study the material found here with data found in contemporary reference works on African-American history. It also serves as historical evidence of early African-American intellectual activity.

1.9 Ploski, Harry A., and James Williams, eds. *The Negro Almanac: A Reference Work on the African-American.* 5th ed. Detroit, Mich.: Gale Research, 1989.

First published in 1967 under the title *The Negro Almanac: A Reference Work on the Afro-American*, this reference guide has improved in quality and accuracy with each edition. Gale now publishes this volume, which was voted by *Library Journal* as "Outstanding Reference Source of the Decade." Thirty-three chapters cover a broad range of historical, social, economic, and cultural subjects including: "Historic Landmarks of Black America," "Black Capitalism," "Blacks in Films," "Growth and Distribution of the Black Population," and "The Black Religious Tradition." Numerous charts, graphs, statistical tables, and illustrations are included. The text also contains an extensive index and bibliography. High school and college students will want to consult this source for the vast amount of information covered. For more in-depth information, they should consult *The Encyclopedia of Black America* (entry 1.6).

1.10 Smythe, Mabel M., ed. *Black American Reference Book.* 2d ed. New York: Prentice-Hall, 1976.

Although currently out of print, this reference source provides a valuable historical perspective on a broad range of topics relating to African Americana. Each of the thirty chapters is written by an authority in the field, including John Hope Franklin (history), Constance Baker Motley (law), and Harry Richardson (religion). The chapters present lengthy essays that serve to introduce, define the scope of, and present the issues on the topics covered. Especially noteworthy is the twenty-five page article on African-American women. Other topics covered are politics, African-American participation in U.S. foreign relations, the popular media, the African-American professional, and the African-American worker. Footnotes are included at the end of each essay and an index is provided.

This source is particularly appealing to senior high school and college students who need to compare and contrast issues and topics presented here with more current perspectives offered in *The Negro Almanac* (entry 1.9) *or A Common Destiny* (entry 1.17).

Yearbooks, Directories, Handbooks, and Chronologies

This second part of chapter 1 includes a variety of reference books that can be consulted to verify and locate specific facts, statistics, dates, places, and events in African-American history or to review the economic and social status of the African-American population at various points in time.

The historical atlas edited by Molefi Asante and Mark T. Mattson is a valuable overview of the social and cultural history of black Americans. Chronologies by Peter M. Bergman and a more recent one by Alton Hornsby Jr. provide a framework for students and teachers to place important events on a historical time line. Two sources on black organizations, agencies, businesses, and colleges and universities allow prospective employers and companies to identify professional black organizations for purposes of advertising jobs and marketing products.

Several statistical sources—including a historical text compiled by the U.S. Census Bureau and a more contemporary one compiled by Carrell P. Horton and Jessie C. Smith—provide a compendium of vital statistics on the social and economic status of the black population. Handbooks edited by Florence Murray and Monroe Work provide readers with a panoramic view of the quality of life for black citizens from 1912 through about 1952.

Historic Landmarks, by George Cantor, assists travelers to identify often-neglected historic black sites through which they can gain firsthand understanding of black American life and a more complete knowledge of American history. Books by Gerald Jaynes and Robin M. Williams and the National Urban League analyze the current status of African-American life in America, reminding readers how far we have come as a nation and a people and how far we have yet to go to achieve full equality for all citizens.

1.11   **Asante, Molefi, and Mark T. Mattson.** *The Historical and Cultural Atlas of African Americans.* New York: Macmillan, 1991.

This beautifully illustrated atlas provides "spatial representation of the most important events, personalities, and facts about African Americans." The authors provide selected information and events on cultural and historical maps from an Afrocentric perspective. According to the authors, an Afrocentric perspective includes viewing the African continent holistically rather than looking at sub-Saharan Africa as separate from the rest of the continent.

The arrangement of the atlas is topical within loose chronological periods. Maps are integrated with text, charts, statistical data, and cultural information to such an extent that the atlas resembles a handbook or compendium of related topics on African-American culture and cultural transformations.

The titles of the thirteen chapters are borrowed from spirituals, an effective metaphor for the African-American experience. Chapters 1 through 3 include an introduction to the diversity and complexity of African geography and cultural groups. Charts, time lines, and photographs of African artifacts supplement the text and cover the slave trade, principal slave ports and major cities, and principal African settlements in colonial America. Chapter 4 describes the nature of enslavement and includes valuable information on religious survival in America. Themes of resistance and abolition are explored in chapters 5 and 6, including a lengthy chronology of Nat Turner's famous uprising, biographical information on well-known African-American freedom fighters, and founders and explorers of the American West.

The Civil War, emancipation, and Reconstruction are discussed and represented pictorially in chapters 7 and 8. Also provided are maps and charts of significant Civil War battles engaged in by African-American regiments and a list of Union and Confederate states and the years of secession. Chapter 9 focuses on lynching and murders, antilynching crusader Ida B. Wells, and early orators and writers. Chapter 10 documents the achievements of African Americans during the Harlem Renaissance period, as well as African Americans in the military, literary, and entertainment worlds.

The leaders and organizations of the civil rights period are profiled in chapter 11. Chapter 12 includes information on an eclectic selection of African-American achievements through a series of maps, charts, and graphs. Selected topics include historically black colleges and universities, departments and programs in African-American studies, African Americans in medicine and the arts, selected inventions by African Americans from 1871 to 1900, and African-American newspapers and radio and television stations. The final chapter presents 1980 census data that portray the social and economic status of the African-American population.

Special features include a chronology of important dates in African-American history and culture, a list of selected references, and an extensive index. Although much of the information contained here can be located in a variety of different sources, the authors bring much of the data together into one visually attractive source. It is, therefore, a worthwhile addition to any high school, public, or academic library.

1.12 Bergman, Peter M. *The Chronological History of the Negro in America.* New York: Harper and Row, 1969.

Covering the years 1492 through 1968, this useful source is divided into four chronological periods: "Slavery" (1492-1864), "Reconstruction" (1865-1877), "Separate but Equal" (1878-1954), and "With All Deliberate Speed" (1955-1968). Each section is preceded by a short historical introduction.

The entries under each date are meticulously detailed and include demographic data and economic, cultural, political, historical, and biographical information. For example, an entry under *1864* reports the locations of schools for African Americans operated and founded by the American Missionary Association; the life of George Washington Carver, the renowned African-American scientist; and the recognition by the United States of Haitian sovereignty.

The book also contains a bibliography and a comprehensive index. This is a valuable reference tool for high school and college libraries that is updated and expanded but not replaced by Hornsby's *Chronology of African-American History* (entry 1.15).

1.13 *The Black Resource Guide.* Washington, D.C.: Black Resource Guide, 1981-1994.

Updated annually since 1981, this national African-American directory also lists regional or state organizations and institutions. Information for entries is obtained through questionnaires. Agencies and organizations included here but *not* covered by Darren L. Smith's *Black Americans Information Directory (BAID)* (entry 1.19) include separate sections on the topics of adoption agencies and services, bookstores, church denominations and organizations, political officeholders and organizations, embassies and consulates, and executive recruiters. Within each section, the entries are arranged alphabetically by title or, if listings are too numerous, by state.

Data under each entry is basic: addresses, names, and phone numbers only. There is also a section on statistical data. Addresses of organizations included in this guide can be purchased as mailing labels. No index is provided. Although there is considerable overlap between this source and *BAID*, the latter is more comprehensive. When the two sources are used together, they provide complete coverage of African-

American organizations. This inexpensive source is an important addition to public and academic libraries.

1.14   Cantor, George. *Historic Landmarks of Black America.* Detroit, Mich.: Gale Research, 1991.

According to its author, the purpose of this book is to "help the history-minded traveler locate and experience a facet of this country that is often overlooked." The criteria for selection include public interest and historical significance. Approximately three hundred African-American historic monuments, museums, colleges and universities, libraries, cemeteries, battlefields, forts, birthplaces, houses, archives, parks, theaters, and churches are described. Also listed are selected sites related to African history and forty-six sites in Ontario.

The book begins with a brief history of black America written by Robert L. Harris Jr., a professor at Cornell University. Each of the six chapters is arranged by geographic region and alphabetically by state within that region. Each chapter begins with a map of the historic sites of that region. Each numbered site corresponds to a numbered legend that names the site. The information on each site includes a historical overview, address, admission charge, telephone number, hours of operation, and handicap accessibility. When possible, a photograph of the site or person associated with the site has been provided.

Other useful features are a time line of African-American history from 1539 to 1989, a bibliography of further reading, and an index. Travelers, students, or teachers will find this book a useful tool for identifying and visiting the plethora of African-American historic sites in the United States and Ontario.

1.15   Hornsby, Alton, Jr. *Chronology of African-American History: Significant Events and People from 1619 to the Present.* Detroit, Mich.: Gale Research, 1991.

Hornsby's book updates and expands upon Bergman's chronology (see entry 1.12) by presenting a detailed chronology of the people, places, and events that had a major impact on African-American history and culture. In particular, Hornsby focuses on gender, region, and class patterns and trends; cultural innovations; and race-relations issues. Biographical information on representative African Americans; depictions of significant events; legislation; court decisions; programs; manifestos; and data on social, economic, political, and educational milestones are also detailed.

Each entry is referenced by year, month, and day and ranges in length from 25 to 250 words. In the book's introduction, Hornsby discusses significant events in the history of African Americans, from the early days before their arrival in the New World through contemporary times. Also useful is an appendix of selected speeches, documents, and other primary-source material, including excerpts from the Emancipation Proclamation; *Plessy* v. *Ferguson*; the Thirteenth, Fourteenth, and Fifteenth Amendments; and Martin Luther King's renowned "I Have a Dream" speech. A detailed index and an extensive bibliographical essay, in addition to the other features, make this guide a valuable source for high school and college students.

1.16   Horton, Carrell P., and Jessie C. Smith, eds. *Statistical Record of Black America.* 2d ed. Detroit, Mich.: Gale Research, 1993.

This reference book, which is published biennially, is a comprehensive statistical source on African Americana. Drawing on both published and unpublished statistics from a variety of government and private sources, Horton and Smith's work replaces the outdated *Social and Economic Status of the Black Population in the United States, 1790–1978* (1979) (see entry 1.21) for current statistics; however, for historical perspective, the 1979 publication remains the best source.

Arranged in broad subject categories, the *Statistical Record* includes approximately one thousand statistical charts, graphs, and tables. A sampling of topics covered includes population; vital statistics; the family; social services; health and medical care; housing; business and economics; education; politics and elections; income, spending, and wealth; and the professions. Within each chapter, statistics are presented under more specific topics. Comparative data on majority groups are included as well.

All graphs, charts, and statistical data are presented here without comment or evaluation. Also omitted is any introductory information on how the tables or statistics are organized within each chapter. Each graph includes the basis of the figures, which enables the reader to find the original source. A detailed subject index makes the information easily accessible.

In spite of this text's limitations, the general public and students and faculty in the social sciences, health-related fields, and religion will be able to use it to find answers to most of their statistical questions. This book is the best single-source statistical tool on African Americana published to date.

1.17   Jaynes, Gerald, and Robin M. Williams Jr., eds. *A Common Destiny: Blacks and American Society.* Washington, D.C.: National Academy Press, 1989.

This study was heralded by historian Robert Harris Jr. as "the most comprehensive review of black America since the Myrdal report in 1944." *A Common Destiny,* according to the editors, "reports the progress and continuance of conditions of poverty, segregation, discrimination, and social fragmentation of African-Americana." More comprehensive and historical than the National Urban League's *The State of Black America* (entry 1.20), this study describes and analyzes the last fifty years (1935–1985) of the position of African Americans in American society.

Arranged by topic, the volume examines participation in social institutions, racial attitudes, political participation, economic conditions, education, health, crime and criminal justice, and children and families. A group of eminent scholars wrote the articles and conducted the research. References at the end of each section also include seminal works by well-respected specialists. An extensive index, charts, graphs, and statistical data contribute to the authoritativeness of this source. Senior high school and college students, faculty in both history and sociology, and public policymakers will find this an indispensable tool for assessing the current status of and future outlook for African Americans.

1.18   *Murray, Florence, ed. *The Negro Handbook, 1946–1947.* New York: Wyn Publishers, 1947. (First published, 1942/43; 1943/44; 1946/47; 1949 by various publishers)

This source is similar to and perhaps even patterned after Monroe Work's classic *Negro Yearbook and Annual Encyclopedia of the Negro* (entry 1.22). Murray, a newspaper reporter and researcher, notes in the foreword that she compiled the book to address the lack of a "convenient source of reference on current facts and figures about the American Negro" (although Work's *Negro Yearbook* [entry 1.22] was first published in 1912). Murray's book provides important factual data on the status of the Negro during the 1940s, a decade in which only one edition of the *Negro Yearbook* was published. While Work's book tended to include more substantive articles, Murray stated that her intention was to present the facts, with no attempt to analyze or evaluate them.

---

*Not indexed in Spradling's *In Black and White.*

Topics chosen for review in the *Negro Handbook* are not unlike those contained in comparable recent sources: population, civil rights, health and vital statistics, labor and industry, education, religious denominations, crime, sports, housing, organizations, business, newspapers and periodicals, government and politics, etc. For each section, the editor identified the source(s) of the data compiled (e.g., Bureau of the Census, Federal Public Housing Authority, U.S. Office of Education, National Association of Colored Graduate Nurses). For several articles, Murray solicited the expertise of authorities in the field: Thurgood Marshall contributed "Teachers Salary Cases" and John A. Davis and Cornelius Golightly offered "Negro Employment in the Federal Government."

Murray's efforts result in a valuable overview of segregated African-American life during the 1940s that can be compared and contrasted with African-American life in previous and subsequent decades. An index is included, although the editor did not compile any bibliographical references. This handbook serves as a convenient and accurate source of facts that will be important to history and African-American studies students at the high school and undergraduate levels.

1.19   Smith, Darren L., ed. 1st ed. *Black Americans Information Directory*. Detroit: Gale Research, 1990–1991.

The purpose of this directory, as described in its introduction, is to "provide a comprehensive source of information on organizations, programs, facilities, publications, and other resources for and about African Americans." Compiled from previous Gale publications, questionnaires, and federal and state government publications, the directory includes approximately 4,500 organizations, agencies, institutions, and programs.

Each of the seventeen chapters focuses on a particular type of institution or organization, including national, regional, state, and local associations; religious organizations; museums and other cultural organizations; businesses; publishers; and producers of videos. Within each chapter, entries are alphabetized by the name of the organization. Each entry consists of the following information: name, address, phone number, contact person, and annotation (when possible). There are no annotations provided for the regional, state, and local organizations; and the video section omits information on the distributor and audience level that would be useful in the selection process. The master and keyword indexes are thorough and include cross references. This directory is a valuable reference tool for the general public and high school and academic libraries. Special government, business, and corporate libraries will find it indispensable for recruitment and advertising purposes.

1.20 *The State of Black America.* New York: National Urban
League, 1976–1994.

Originally founded in 1910 as an organization to help African-American migrants adjust to urban life in the North, the National Urban League now focuses on securing equal opportunities for all minorities. *The State of Black America*, an annual publication, summarizes and analyzes the present conditions of African Americans, while making recommendations for improving their social and economic status.

Each essay is written by an expert in his or her field; separate biographical notes on the contributors are provided. A sampling of topics covered is "Black Americans and the Court," "Budget and Tax Strategy," "Housing Opportunity," "Health Status of Black Americans," "Preventing Black Homicide," and "Understanding African-American Family Diversity." Appendixes center on special interests, including unemployment, teenage pregnancy and parenting, and education. A chronology of the previous year's news events and extensive footnotes serve as useful supplementary material to the essays. Social studies, sociology, and history students and teachers at the high school and college levels will use this book for its accuracy, timeliness, and thoughtful recommendations.

1.21 **U.S. Bureau of the Census. U.S. Department of Commerce.**
*Social and Economic Status of the Black Population in the
United States.* Washington, D.C.: Government Printing Office,
1979.

Although published a number of years ago, the historical data conveniently compiled and presented in this government publication are still useful. The book presents a historical view of the changes in demographic, social, and economic characteristics of the African-American population in the United States. More specifically, the introduction states that the historical profile focuses on changes that occurred in population distribution, income levels, labor force, employment, education, family composition, mortality, fertility, housing, voting, public officeholding, armed forces personnel, and other major aspects of life.

Unlike Horton and Smith's publication (entry 1.16), this book includes for each section a narrative that describes the chapter and statistics presented in the tables. The book is arranged in two parts:

historical trends, 1790–1975, and recent trends, 1973–1978. The tables and graphs are easy to read and present striking data that enable historians and demographers to see migratory patterns, the effects of the slave trade on population and family composition, the influence of civil rights legislation on educational and employment opportunities, and so on. In most cases, comparative data on the white population are provided.

For example, statistics show that between 1910 and 1940 the African-American population in the North grew from 10 million to 22 million. For this same time period, the African-American population in the South dropped from 89 million in 1910 to 77 million in 1940. Also during this period, the white population increased in the South by 2 million but decreased by 5 million in the North. These data help explain the migratory patterns of African Americans that occurred during the Great Migration, and further indicate that the pattern was very different for whites. The statistics comparing income, education, housing, and other characteristics are equally worthy of thoughtful interpretation and explanation.

Although no index is provided, three appendixes provide reliable references for the tables, definitions, and explanations. This authoritative source should be on the shelves of every public and academic library for use by high school and college history, sociology, and American studies instructors and students.

1.22 **Work, Monroe, ed.** *Negro Yearbook and Annual Encyclopedia of the Negro.* Tuskegee, Ala.: Tuskegee Institute, 1912–1915; 1918–1919; 1921–1922; 1924–1925; 1930–1932; 1937–1938; 1947 and 1952 edited by Jessie Guzman.

One of the earliest and most established yearbooks of Negro American life, the introduction to *The Negro Yearbook* describes it as a "compact, comprehensive statement of historical and statistical facts" on the Negro. Founder and editor Monroe N. Work, director of the department of records and research at Tuskegee Institute from 1908 to 1939, also edited the first bibliography of books and journal articles on African Americans in the United States, Africa, and the West Indies. That work, entitled *Bibliography of the Negro in Africa and America* (1928), is still a classic bibliography in the field.

Serving as the voice for the Negro community, which was neglected by the press, the yearbooks addressed a wide range of subjects and issues of the day: economics, racial cooperation, education, riots, lynching, civil rights, Negroes in the military, agriculture, inventors, literature, and so on. The earlier volumes encapsulated these events in short news articles, but later editions included longer, more substantive articles as well as charts and graphs. A bibliography and index are included at the end of each volume.

These yearbooks are historical treasures that provide an insightful view of the problems, issues, and progress of the African-American population from 1912 through 1952. In addition, the earlier volumes provide a rare profile of African-American businesses and institutions through advertisements, such as those of Madame C. J. Walker (millionairess and inventor of hair-care products for African Americans); Fisk University; and *Southern Workman,* one of the early African-American magazines. These yearbooks should be required reading for any serious history student at the college level, and can be studied as works produced by African-American publishers. High school teachers of honors or advanced courses in history or social studies will also find many creative uses for these volumes.

Biographical Dictionaries and Directories

Biographical directories of current and deceased African Americans are profiled in this last section of chapter 1. The earliest publication annotated here is Clement Richardson's *The National Cyclopedia of the Colored Race* (1919), which provides biographical sketches and essays on the status of the black population. Three separately produced *Who's Who* publications cover the years from 1927 to 1940; the source, published by Gale Research Co., is an annual and provides biographical information on living African Americans.

In-depth and more comprehensive coverage of African Americans living before 1976 is provided by Rayford W. Logan and Michael R. Winston in *The Dictionary of American Negro Biography.* Although older, a comparable source for junior high students is Wilhelmena S. Robinson's *Historical Afro-American Biographies.* Sketches of more than one hundred men and women are given in two older but reliable books by Edgar A. Toppin and Russell L. Adams. Jessie Smith's *Notable Black American Women* is the only source included here that provides sketches of many black women.

1.23   Adams, Russell L. *Great Negroes, Past and Present.* 3d ed. Chicago: Afro-Am Publishing, 1969.

The third edition of this biographical dictionary is intended to serve as a supplementary text needed for teaching multiethnic history at the primary and secondary levels. The editor also mentions a guide that was written to correlate this text with standard U.S. history textbooks.

The 178 biographical sketches, which average about one page in length, unfortunately include only nine women. The range of personalities represented is wide—living and deceased, famous and obscure, from all occupations and professions. Arranged chronologically and topically, the twelve chapters are titled "African Heritage," "Early History," "From the Civil War Forward," "Science and Industry," "Business Pioneers," "Religion," "Leaders and Spokesmen," "Education," "Literature," "Theatre," "Music," and "Visual Arts."

Lesser-known figures included in this volume are Gustavus Vassa, seafarer and colonizer; Paul Cuffe, businessman; Robert Smalls, navigator and congressman; John Smythe, U.S. minister to Liberia; E. Simms Campbell, cartoonist; Elijah McCoy, inventor; William Leidesdorff, millionaire; Paul R. Williams, architect; William J. Simmons, biographer (see entry 2.55); Arthur Schomburg, bibliophile and collector (the world-renowned Schomburg Research Center in New York was named after him); and Gwendolyn Brooks, the first African-American woman to win the Pulitzer Prize for poetry. Information provided on each figure is presented in narrative style and consists of birth and death dates, birthplace, schools attended, early influences, training, background/experience, and most famous contributions.

A bibliography, an index, and illustrations of each personality are included. Providing greater depth and including more obscure figures than Robinson's *Historical Afro-American Biographies* (entry 1.29), this biographical dictionary gives comprehensive coverage of African-American figures for junior high and high school–level students.

1.24 *Bros, Joseph J., ed. *Who's Who in Colored America, 1927–1950: A Biographical Dictionary of Notable Living Persons of African Descent in America.* New York: Who's Who in Colored America, 1927–1940. 1941–1944 published by Thomas Yenser; 7th ed., 1950, published by Christian E. Burckel and Associates.

African Americans of achievement, more than half of whom represent the professions, are included in this significant biographical directory. According to the editors, African Americans of achievement are defined as "persons whose efforts show promise of future accomplishment."

---

*Not indexed in Spradling's *In Black and White.*

The biographers actually interviewed the individuals profiled here and selected "outstanding characters." People of both local and national prominence are represented, and the editors boast the inclusion of 169 women. Especially useful and noteworthy are the large number of photographs.

Arranged alphabetically, most entries are written in bullet format, although more lengthy narratives are provided for famous figures. The entries provide date and place of birth; name of spouse; background information on grandparents, if relevant; education; organizational affiliation; publications; awards and special achievements; and home and work addresses. An alphabetical list of all biographees, including occupation, address, and page number for location of each entry, is provided.

Jean Blackwell, one-time curator of the renowned Schomburg Collection [of Black Culture] at the New York Public Library, wrote an excellent essay, "Some Antecedents of *Who's Who in Colored America*," for the 1950 edition, which was published by Christian E. Burckel and Associates. Students and history instructors at the college level will want to consult this source for comparative biographical data on African-American men and women who lived during this period.

1.25 Lee, George L. *Interesting People: Black American History Makers.* Jefferson, N.C., and London: McFarland and Co., 1989.

All of the one-page biographical sketches included in this book appeared in leading African-American newspapers throughout the United States between 1945 and 1948 and from 1970 to 1986. Each short entry features an illustration of the biographee drawn by the author. Well suited for elementary and junior high students, the biographies focus on living and deceased men and women, both obscure and well-known.

These introductory sketches serve to entice the reader to investigate more fully the lives of these fascinating African Americans, including Elizabeth Forth Denison, Catherine Harris, Nat Love, Frank Yerby, Jane Edna Hunter, Faye Wattleton, Mary Hatwood Futrell, and Marva Collins.

No index or bibliography is provided. Elementary, high school, and junior high school teachers will want to steer students toward Adams's *Great Negroes, Past and Present* (see entry 1.23) or Robinson's *Historical Afro-American Biographies* (see entry 1.29) for further reading.

1.26 **Logan, Rayford W., and Michael R. Winston.** *Dictionary of American Negro Biography.* New York: W. W. Norton, 1982.

This comprehensive source bridges a vast gap in the reference literature by providing detailed, scholarly profiles of African Americans who died before 1970. The selection criteria, according to the editors, are not necessarily based on the national reputation of the subject; more emphasis is given to his or her status as a "first" in the profession or occupation he or she represents.

Dictionary of American Negro Biography contains extensive, well-written, interpretive narratives. Bibliographical essays containing primary and secondary sources are included at the end of each article. All professions, occupations, and historical periods are covered, as illustrated by the inclusion of figures such as Peter Hill (clockmaker), Esteban (pioneer and explorer), Charlie Glass (cowboy), Crawford Goldsby (Oklahoma bandit), Lorraine Hansberry (playwright), Mary McLeod Bethune (educator), Billie Holiday (jazz singer), and Zora Neale Hurston (writer and anthropologist). It is noteworthy that more women are included in this volume than in most of the other biographical source materials covered in this chapter. This is perhaps due to its currency.

This work contains a classified list of entries arranged by occupation. Senior high school through graduate-level students and their teachers will find this biographical dictionary an essential reference tool.

1.27 **Mather, Frank L.** *Who's Who of the Colored Race: A General Biographical Dictionary of Men and Women of African Descent.* Vol. 1, 1915. Detroit: Gale Research, 1976.

Mather's book records the "evidence of progress [of the Negro] in the 50th year of freedom," and thus is an important biographical source on deceased African Americans. Although the selection criteria are not explicitly provided, the author solicited personal data on hundreds of Negroes he considered eligible. It is the inclusion of fewer famous and more local persons that makes this a valuable source. Each entry is presented in a brief, bullet-type format and includes birth and death dates, occupation, education, career sketch, works published, accomplishments, personal data, and addresses. No index is provided. Additional features include the text of the Emancipation Proclamation (1863) and the Thirteenth Amendment (1865); statistics of the 1910 Negro population; and a partial list of public high schools for the Negro, arranged by state. High school and college students will want to use this source to locate biographical data on less famous African Americans who lived during the turn of the twentieth century.

1.28 ***Richardson, Clement.** *The National Cyclopedia of the Colored Race.* Vol. 1. Montgomery, Ala.: The National Publishing Co., 1919. Reprint, New York: Gordon Press, 1990.

According to the author, the purpose of this book is to "present the achievements of Negroes as a source for inspiration, self-respect, and pride." The focus is on people, organizations, and institutions of significance to the Negro community at the end of World War I. Perhaps due to the need to "inspire" young African-American men and women to achieve, the biographical narratives are written in a style that is informal and passionate, incorporating stories of each biographee that are illustrative of his or her character and personality.

Although no arrangement is discernible, persons of both national and local reputation are profiled. The narratives are one to two pages in length. Few women are included. Readers may be pleasantly surprised to see the lives of Alexander Pushkin, the great Russian poet of black ancestry, and Alexander Dumas, author of *The Three Musketeers* and *The Count of Monte Cristo,* as well as many businessmen, artists (e.g., Henry O. Tanner), and musicians (e.g., "Blind" Tom Bethune and Samuel Coleridge-Taylor) introduced in this book.

The second part of the volume is devoted to a brief history of the Negro race, and includes sections on the Negro in business, photographs of representative (middle-class) Negro homes, Negro inventors and explorers, Negro education, church among Negroes, national and fraternal organizations, the Negro in World War I, and a statistical review. An index by state, and then by each section covered, is provided. This reference book is a precursor to *The Negro Almanac* (entry 1.9) and presents a vital historical record of African-American life during the period. History and African-American studies students and faculty at the undergraduate level and museum curators will want to unearth this notable research tool.

1.29 **Robinson, Wilhelmena S.** *Historical Afro-American Biographies.* Vol. 4 of *International Library of Afro-American Life and History.* Washington, D.C.: Association for the Study of Afro-American Life and History, 1976.

---

*Not indexed in Spradling's *In Black and White.*

Biographical sketches of approximately four hundred living and deceased African Americans are introduced in this volume. The main selection criterion was not national reputation of personality; persons chosen for inclusion are intended to be "representative of the life of the Afro-American and his struggle for the attainment of freedom and equality." However, most famous African Americans are included in addition to the less well-known.

Each chronological section is preceded by an introductory statement; within each period, biographies appear in alphabetical order. Most of the narrative sketches are concise (one-half page long) and include birth and death dates, accomplishments, and career highlights. Almost all professions are represented, from antislavery leaders, engineers, government officials, and explorers to inventors, historians, and scholars. Illustrations are plentiful, and an extensive bibliography and index are provided. Information on living persons is dated; biographical sketches of deceased individuals are accurate. Junior high and high school students will find this an important and readable biographical tool.

1.30   *Smith, Jessie C., ed. *Notable Black American Women.*
         Detroit: Gale Research, 1992.

This invaluable biographical dictionary features five hundred African-American women who were born between 1750 and 1956. The editor, university librarian and professor of library science at Fisk University for more than a quarter of a century, formed an advisory board of ten eminent African-American women historians, journalists, higher education administrators, librarians, and educators to select the obscure and well-known women represented in this volume. Each of the biographees included in this volume met at least one of the ten criteria established by the editorial board. The noted scholars; educators; entrepreneurs; performing, literary, and visual artists; government and organizational officials; and crusaders for human and women's rights represent milestones in their fields of endeavor.

The approximately 1,200-word entries are arranged alphabetically by surname. Each narrative entry includes birthplace; early life and influences; education; contributions to the given field; publications; and civic, professional, and organizational affiliations and accomplishments. Each signed entry concludes with a list of primary and secondary references. The list of contributors reads like a list of who's who among African-American women in academia. Since many of the contributors

---

*Not indexed in Spradling's *In Black and White.*

are personally acquainted with the biographees, the articles are not entirely objective but are nonetheless accurate and thorough.

Following the table of contents is a section entitled Contents by Area of Endeavor. Although many more women from the performing arts are represented than are, for example, scholars and educators, women from nontraditional fields are adequately represented. Photographs and a subject index are additional features of the book. Hine's encyclopedia of African-American women (entry 1.3) supplements rather than replaces this work. Because Smith's work includes detailed biographies of African-American women who are often omitted from other reference books, it should be required reading for high school and college students in any field; it can also be used as a career and motivational tool.

1.31   Toppin, Edgar A. *A Biographical History of Blacks in America since 1528.* New York: McKay Co., 1971.

More than a biographical dictionary, this book is based on a series of articles that appeared in the *Christian Science Monitor* in 1969. The first section documents African-American history from 1528 to 1971 and is arranged by chronological period, followed by bibliographical references for each chapter. The second section contains short biographical sketches of notable African Americans. Of the 145 biographies included, only ten are of women. Information detailed in each narrative sketch includes birth and death dates, occupation/profession, education and career profile, family background, and notable achievements. Sketches are short but accurate and include persons who were living and deceased at the time the book was published. An index of proper names is included. High school and lower-division college students will want to use this book as a quick-reference source for basic facts on famous African Americans.

1.32   *Who's Who Among Black Americans.* N.p.: Who's Who Among Black Americans, 1975/76–1988. Detroit, Mich.: Gale Research, 1991/92– .

Users of previous editions of *Who's Who Among Black Americans* will note that this edition, the first to be published by Gale Research, has undergone several improvements in the physical format, especially the print, which is now easier to read. Before compiling this comprehensive biographical directory of living African Americans, more than

---

*Not indexed in Spradling's *In Black and White.*

four hundred organizations, individuals, and businesses were contacted for recommendations. Information was secured directly from each of the 17,000 subjects included. Each concise entry profiles standard biographical data: name, occupation, birthdate, personal data, education, career information, organizational affiliation, honors and special achievements, military service, and home and business addresses.

An obituaries section, which lists deaths reported since the last edition, and occupational and geographical indexes (arranged by city, state, and county of residence) contribute to making this directory complete and easy to use. High school and college students as well as the general public will find this an indispensable tool for locating biographical data on contemporary, living African Americans.

CHAPTER TWO

Collective Biography
and Genealogy

ALMOST ALL THE AUTHORS OF THE BIOGRAPHIES PUBLISHED IN the nineteenth century and the first three decades of the twentieth century wrote the essays to inspire or educate Negro youth about their race. Their goal was to motivate Negro youth to look up to its leaders as a source of pride in a world that denied them their dignity and humanity. Bearing this in mind, it is not surprising that the authors were not wholly objective in their profiles of these early African-American pioneers, many of whom they knew or had met personally. Several authors—most of them women—wrote books exclusively devoted to biographical sketches of African-American women.

The biographical works published in the twentieth century are more analytical and critical, having benefited from the prodigious primary and secondary source materials available. These texts reveal the complexities and subtleties of nineteenth- and twentieth-century African-American leadership and encourage readers to reexamine leadership styles and effectiveness in the context of the times.

Although the majority of the personalities profiled in these books are famous, they are not atypical of countless unnamed individuals whose personal struggles and triumphs will go unrecorded. Whenever possible, works that include more obscure individuals, especially women, are highlighted. These works serve as valuable secondary sources for use in history courses, but they are also useful tools for curriculum development and reference and research in social studies, sociology, education, women's studies, and American studies. High school history and social studies teachers will find many creative uses for these biographies, especially when used with primary sources.

This second chapter has two parts. Part 1 focuses on biographies in collections (entries 33–56). Narrative biographical essays that profile or analyze the lives of at least three individuals are included in Part 1. Part 2 includes genealogical sources (entries 57–60).

Mary Mace Spradling's *In Black and White,* a biographical index also referred to in the introduction to chapter 1, indexes all the sources in this chapter with the *exception* of those marked with an asterisk (*).

Collective Biography

The twenty-two sources included in this first part of chapter 2 provide in-depth profiles of living and deceased African Americans. Three sources, written in the nineteenth century by William Wells Brown (1865), William J. Simmons (1887), and Monroe Majors (1893), attest to the determination of early Negro writers to collect and research information on the achievements and work of their race. Biographical books on black women include works written as early as 1893 (Majors). Other early works include texts by Hallie Q. Brown (1926) and Sadie Daniel (1931). Works by Sylvia Dannett (1964–1966) and Marianna Davis (1982) also are referenced here, as is Brian Lanker's volume of photographic essays (1989).

Additional sources written by Lerone Bennett, Benjamin Brawley, R. J. M. Blackett, Langston Hughes, Mary White Ovington, Charlemae Rollins, and John Bruce provide detailed biographies of renowned and obscure nineteenth- and twentieth-century black Americans. Two contemporary sources edited by John Hope Franklin and by Leon Litwack and August Meier contain excellent analytical and interpretive essays of renowned African Americans. Videotapes on the lives of Booker T. Washington, Sojourner Truth, and Ida B. Wells are included to actively involve young people in understanding the role and contributions of these famous men and women.

2.33   Bennett, Lerone, Jr. *Pioneers in Protest.* Chicago: Johnson Publishing, 1968.

Although no scope note or foreword is provided, Bennett profiles twenty nineteenth- and twentieth-century figures who led significant protests and rebellions. The focus is on nineteenth-century men with the exception of the two most-renowned women of the period, Sojourner Truth and Harriet Tubman. Four of the biographees are white: William Lloyd Garrison, John Brown, Charles Sumner, and Thaddeus Stevens.

Each profile ranges between fourteen and twenty pages in length. The arrangement is roughly chronological and the information on each figure is presented in the dramatic, engaging, narrative style of a story-teller. The author is a journalist and senior editor of *Ebony* magazine who unveils the remarkable lives of these famous figures by creating mental images of their characters and personalities. Included are excerpts from speeches, letters, and diaries, and details of specific pivotal characters and events that influenced the lives of those profiled. For example, Benjamin Banneker's letter to Thomas Jefferson and Jefferson's reply are reprinted, as are several excerpts from speeches by Frederick Douglass and from W. E. B. Du Bois's diary. A photograph or illustration of each figure is provided.

Unfortunately, no footnotes or bibliographical references were compiled for this highly readable book; however, an index is included. Due to the author's writing style and the inclusion of lesser-known figures such as Prince Hall, Samuel Cornish, John Russworm, David Walker, and William Monroe Trotter, this book is especially appealing to junior high school and high school students.

2.34   **Blackett, R. J. M.** *Beating Against the Barriers: Biographical Essays in Nineteenth Century Afro-American History.* Baton Rouge: Louisiana University Press, 1986.

Blackett was motivated to research and write this book to educate more people about the lives and work of neglected African-American figures in American history. In this important book, Blackett presents an in-depth analysis of the lives of six African Americans who were involved in the Anglo-American abolitionist movement "after their return home." The author chose to include the following figures in the study: James W. C. Pennington, Howard Day, William and Ellen Craft, Robert Campbell, and John Sella Martin—all eloquent antislavery spokespersons who traveled abroad to galvanize financial and political support for the movement. The questions posed by Blackett in investigating their lives include: How were these figures received in America? How did their time abroad affect their lives and actions?

Approximately fifty pages are devoted to each abolitionist, with the exceptions of John Sella Martin and Howard Day. About these two the author writes one hundred pages each. Persistence in fighting against slavery and a drive to exert pressure to fight for America's ideals are common themes in the abolitionists' lives. An extensive bibliography of primary documents, secondary materials, theses, and dissertations is included. An index is also provided. Upper-division and graduate history students and professors will find that this important work fills a gap in biographical essays on lesser-known abolitionists.

2.35   Brawley, Benjamin G. *Negro Builders and Heroes*. Chapel Hill: University of North Carolina Press, 1937.

Brawley's work contains twenty-two individual sketches of African-American figures from slavery to 1937. The author's intent was to introduce African-American biography to readers. Eighteen men and four women from diverse fields are represented here. The early chapters focus on individuals; later chapters are biographical essays consisting of multiple profiles.

The chapters are arranged in chronological order. Information on each personality is presented in an essay that includes the date and place of birth and details on the people and circumstances that inspired the person. Brawley uses some quotations from primary documents to personalize the stories. The titles of the essays reveal a specific focus: "Frederick Douglass as an Orator," "Harriet Tubman and Her Underground Railroad," and "Early Effort for Practical Training—Martin Delany." The lives of several lesser-known figures are portrayed, such as Blanche K. Bruce, U.S. senator from Mississippi; Colonel Charles Young, Spanish-American War officer; Matthew Henson, explorer; and John Merrick, entrepreneur. Although Brawley incorporates sketches of only four individual African-American women, there are chapters on "Negro Women in American Life" and "Women Who Have Led in Education." Extensive bibliographical notes are located at the end of each chapter and a detailed index is provided. This biographical work is appropriate for junior high and high school students.

2.36   Brown, Hallie Q., ed. *Homespun Heroines and Other Women of Distinction*. Xenia, Ohio: Aldine Publishing, 1926.

Unlike many early-twentieth-century African-American authors, Brown wrote this book to inspire youth to "endure and overcome obstacles by reading how other women have done so." Brown's work helps fill a gap in the literature of the period by focusing on the lives of African-American women.

While Brown taught for many years at Wilberforce University in Ohio, she met several notable women who are included in this work.

Consequently, some of the fifty-six women profiled here had local rather than national reputations. When possible, Brown interviewed the subject or people who knew the subject well.

Biographical data provided for each woman include date and place of birth, accomplishments, character, and sometimes names of husbands or sons. The famous women represented are Sojourner Truth, Phillis Wheatley, Harriet Tubman, Frances Ellen Watkins Harper, Amanda Smith, Elizabeth Keckley, and Josephine St. Pierre Ruffin. Each narrative sketch ranges from two to five pages in length. The sketches are not comprehensive and are introduced in a personalized style. Many wives of ministers and bishops of the A.M.E. church are profiled here.

No index, bibliography, or note on contributors is provided. A classic work that has been reprinted under the same title by Oxford University Press for the Schomburg Library of Nineteenth-Century Black Women Writers series, this book deserves attention and examination by students at both high school and college levels.

2.37   Brown, William Wells. *The Black Man, His Antecedents, His Genius and His Achievements.* Boston: R. F. Wallcut, 1865. Reprint, New York: Arno Press, 1969.

Perhaps the earliest collection of biographies on the Negro, this book was written to "refute misrepresentations of Negroes as naturally inferior by illuminating the lives of Negro men and women of achievement." The author researched the archives and libraries of Europe to uncover information on fifty-seven nineteenth-century individuals, living and deceased at the time, from all walks of life and from all countries.

Biographical data is based on printed sources and interviews with many figures. The author includes a physical description in addition to detailed personal accounts to reveal the character, accomplishments, and contributions of each person profiled. Prominent Negro personalities portrayed include Frederick Douglass, Benjamin Banneker, Denmark Vesey, Crispus Attucks, Cinque, Ira Aldridge, and Henry Highland Garnet; lesser-known figures include Placido (African poet), Alexander Pushkin (Russian poet of African descent), and J. J. Roberts (ex-president of the Republic of Liberia). When appropriate, passages from selected writings are included. Brown has added to his book an appendix entitled "Opinions of the Press," perhaps to verify its authoritativeness and promote its sale. Unfortunately, no bibliography or index is provided.

Brown, one of the first African-American novelists, author of *Clotel* (1853), includes his memoir as a privileged slave to provide background information on his own life. Brown also authored another biographical book, *The Rising Son* (1874), which includes many of the figures presented in *The Black Man*. High school and undergraduate history and literature students will find *The Black Man* an illuminating study of nineteenth-century African Americans.

2.38 *Bruce, John Edward, comp. *Short Biographical Sketches of Eminent Negro Men and Women in Europe and the United States, with Brief Extracts from Their Writings and Public Utterances.* Vol. 1. Yonkers, N.Y.: Gazette Press, 1910.

Perhaps written as a teachers' guide for use in the classroom or for self-study, this book includes sketches of living and deceased Negroes in North America and elsewhere. This book portrays the lives of only two women: poet Phillis Wheatley and journalist and antilynching crusader Ida B. Wells.

The twenty-one sketches vary in length from one-third to one-half page and focus mainly on lesser-known figures. Several sketches are reprinted here from Simmons's *Men of Mark* (entry 2.55). Like William Wells Brown (entry 2.37), Bruce provides excerpts from or selections by individual authors. Information on each person profiled includes birth and death dates, place of birth, early life, major milestones, and commentary on the quality and nature of his or her work. At the end of each sketch is a series of study and review questions. Although this source contains no table of contents, index, or bibliography, the format and scope make it particularly useful for junior high and high school history and social studies teachers.

2.39 Cromwell, John W. *The Negro in American History: Men and Women Eminent in the Evolution of the American of African Descent.* Washington, D.C.: The American Negro Academy, 1914. Reprint, New York: Johnson Reprint Corp., 1968.

Cromwell wrote this book to "give to teachers and secondary school pupils the salient points in the history of the American Negro, and to tell the story of their most eminent men and women and a bibliography to guide further study." The first seventeen of the thirty-five chapters compose a concise historical outline of important events in the history of the Negro, from discovery, colonization, and slavery to the Spanish-American War. These seventeen chapters are each only two or three pages in length. Slave insurrections, educational progress, the early con-

---

*Not indexed in Spradling's *In Black and White*.

vention movement, and the African-American church are among the subjects covered.

The remaining chapters are devoted to biographical sketches of individuals. The narratives are told with great detail in a style that is very appealing to children. Information provided on each individual includes birthplace and date, early family life and influences, and career accomplishments. Direct quotes from the biographee or from his or her works are included to provide insight into personality, motivations, aspirations, and ambitions. In an effort to personalize the stories and inspire the reader, the narratives are captivating, though they are not always objectively written. Cromwell chooses to profile the lives of primarily famous African Americans—using contemporary criteria—such as Paul Laurence Dunbar, Booker T. Washington, Frederick Douglass, John Mercer Langston, and Henry O. Tanner. Of the fifteen sketches, only three women are highlighted: Phillis Wheatley, Sojourner Truth, and Fannie Jackson Coppin.

Special features of this book include illustrations, footnotes, a bibliography, a chronology, appendixes, and an index. Although many of the other works in this chapter provide sketches of the same individuals highlighted here, high school teachers may use this text to gain some insight into the craft of biography, which can be used to involve and inspire their students to question the purpose of historical biography and experiment with writing personal and family biographies.

2.40   **Daniel, Sadie Iola.** *Women Builders.* Washington, D.C.: Associated Publishers, 1931. Rev. by Charles Wesley and Thelma Perry. Reprint, Washington, D.C.: Associated Publishers, 1970.

Daniel identifies seven Negro women pioneers who contributed to the development of Negro youth in America by building educational, social, and financial institutions in their communities. Although the institutions founded by these women eventually awarded them a modicum of national recognition, to the general public and students of history their lives remain obscure.

Included here are Lucy Craft Laney, educator; Maggie Lena Walker, bank founder and president; Janie Porter Barrett, educator; Mary McLeod Bethune, founder and president of Bethune-Cookman College; Nannie Helen Burroughs, founder of a national training school for women; Charlotte Hawkins Brown, educator; and Jane Edna Hunter, founder of the Phillis Wheatley Association, a training center for young women.

The narrative biographies outline early influences that served to motivate and shape the direction of each woman's life. The author describes how these exceptional women encountered and overcame obstacles to achieve their goals. For example, each woman devised ingenious methods of securing funds to support the institution she built. Photographs of each woman and the institutions' buildings are provided.

The reprint edition profiles five additional women: Harriet Tubman, Underground Railroad conductor; Fannie Jackson Coppin and Maria Louise Baldwin, educators; Ida B. Wells-Barnett, antilynching crusader; and Hallie Q. Brown, elocutionist. No bibliography or footnotes are provided, although further references are included for women profiled in the 1970 edition. This book is noteworthy for its sketches of obscure women not easily found in other biographical sources and is, therefore, worthwhile for high school history and business students, teachers, and curriculum specialists.

2.41 **Dannett, Sylvia, ed.** *Profiles of Negro Womanhood.* 2v. Yonkers, N.Y.: Educational Heritage, 1964–1966.

Dannett's two-volume work fills a long-ignored gap by providing substantive and authoritative biographical sketches of black women. The focus of these volumes is on women who made significant contributions to America. Sketches are brief (less than one page) and are supplemented by passages from primary documents. More-lengthy and detailed sketches are provided for nineteenth- and twentieth-century women.

Volume 1 is arranged chronologically, while volume 2 is arranged by field or occupation. Each chronological and occupational section is preceded by an introduction to the period, which includes major historical events and themes. Standard biographical data are presented in a narrative format: early family life; education; influential people and events; selections from newspapers; and speeches, sermons, or writings of each woman. Examples of women portrayed in the first volume include abolitionists Sarah Mapps Douglass, the Forten sisters, Sarah Remond, and Sojourner Truth; businesswomen Maggie Lena Walker and Madame C. J. Walker; poets Frances E. W. Harper, Lucy Terry, and Phillis Wheatley; singer Elizabeth Taylor Greenfield; sculptor Edmonia Lewis; and medical doctor Susan Maria Steward.

The second volume contains ten- to fifteen-page sketches of more contemporary women in the fine arts, education, medicine, the performing arts, social work, athletics, literature, the legal profession, civil rights, and government. Photographs or drawings of each subject, an index, footnotes, and a bibliography of primary and secondary materials contribute to the authoritativeness of this work. In addition, information on each woman was obtained through interviews, correspondence, autobiographical sources, and scrapbooks. Appropriate for high school and lower-division college students, these volumes come the closest to providing a solid biographical encyclopedia of Negro women prior to the publication of Jessie Smith's *Notable Black American Women* (entry 1.30).

2.42   Davis, Marianna W., ed. *Contributions of Black Women to America.* 2v. Columbia, S.C.: Kenday Press, 1982.

Originally conceived as a research project to develop and disseminate information on the significant contributions of African-American women, the editor was forced to rely more heavily on secondary materials. The selection criteria for this work were "pioneer" status in a particular field and important life and career achievements against the odds.

These volumes are arranged by topic (e.g., arts, media, business, law, sports, civil rights, politics, government, education, medicine, and sciences). Each section consists of an introductory historical essay. The essays include chronology, major genres, events, and prominent personalities and pioneers in the field. Sketches of individual women are not provided; instead, women's lives are profiled within the context of the historical essay. This format may assist readers to identify the major contributors in a field, although readers will probably have to consult other sources to obtain detailed biographical information.

The essays are generally well written by various experts in the field but, with the notable exceptions of Lerone Bennett Jr. and Eddie Williams, few are nationally recognized authorities. Footnotes are included; however, many of the bibliographical sources are cited from more-popular rather than professional books and journals. At the end of each chapter, an index to the African-American women included in the essay is provided. Since there is no general index at the end of each volume, the reader may find it awkward to locate particular individuals. In spite of its shortcomings, these volumes provide useful background information by introducing high school students to the achievements of African-American women.

2.43V   Disney Educational Productions. *Booker.* 16mm or videorecording, 40 min. Deerfield, Ill.: Distr. Coronet/MTI Film and Video, 1987.

The biography of formidable nineteenth-century educator and leader Booker T. Washington is dramatized in this film. Voted best film in the Black Filmmakers Hall of Fame, *Booker* also won the Birmingham International Film Festival. Intermediate through high school students will find this story both captivating and educational.

2.44 **Franklin, John Hope, and August Meier, eds.** *Black Leaders of the Twentieth Century.* Urbana and Chicago: University of Illinois Press, 1982.

More than biographical accounts, this source and its companion volume (see entry 2.49) analyze the careers of fifteen nationally known African-American leaders "who sought in diverse ways to advance the race and overcome the racial barriers and oppression that pervaded American society." The editors clearly define the criteria for inclusion in this volume. The individuals must (1) be deceased, (2) have had a major organizational affiliation, (3) have possessed strong personal charisma, and (4) have contributed to African-American advancement. The group selected represents a broad variety of leaders.

The leaders included are indeed persons of national reputation and far-reaching influence: Booker T. Washington, T. Thomas Fortune, Ida B. Wells-Barnett, W. E. B. Du Bois, James Weldon Johnson, Marcus Garvey, A. Phillip Randolph, Charles C. Spaulding, Mary McLeod Bethune, Mabel K. Staupers, Charles Hamilton Houston, Adam Clayton Powell, Martin Luther King Jr., Malcolm X, and Whitney Young.

Each chapter begins with a brief historical commentary by the editors and ends with a note on sources. The in-depth biographical essays are twenty to twenty-five pages long and are written by scholars who, in most cases, have authored full-length biographies or articles on the respective leaders. The essays, then, are not introductory; authors summarize and analyze the influences of the leaders within the context of the times; pose and respond to questions about leadership style, effectiveness, and goals; and draw comparisons between each person and his or her contemporaries as both partners and adversaries in the struggle. With the exception of the essay written by Joyce Ross on Mary McLeod Bethune and reprinted from the *Journal of Negro History*, all articles were researched and written exclusively for this volume. Notes on contributors and a detailed index are provided. This scholarly, analytical but highly readable study is best suited for undergraduate and graduate history, African-American studies, and American studies students and professors.

2.45 **Hawkins, Walter L.** *African American Biographies: Profiles of 558 Current Men and Women.* Jefferson, N.C., and London: McFarland, 1992.

According to the author, this volume includes the nation's "most notable African-Americans." Most of the people profiled are still living, but the work includes a few deceased persons as well. The criteria for inclusion is fairly broad: individuals had to be born or spend most of their childhood years in the United States; play an important role in the development of African-American children by functioning as role models; and demonstrate significant leadership at the national, state, or local level or in a career or business. Individuals who died before or during 1968 are excluded.

Because the criteria are so broad, a large number of obscure individuals are profiled here. Perhaps due to the author's own background—Hawkins is a retired law-enforcement official—a large percentage of the individuals included in this book have a military background or are athletes. More men than women are represented. The arrangement is alphabetical by surname. Recent photographs are provided for many individuals, and occupational and geographical indexes are included.

Each brief narrative entry provides birth date and birthplace, degrees received, names of spouses and children (where applicable), career/business accomplishments, honors and awards, professional affiliations, and offices held. Unfortunately, no bibliographical notes or biographical sources are listed; therefore, the reader will not know where or how the biographical data were obtained. It is also difficult to ascertain the field of expertise for which each profiled individual is known. Often this information is provided in the third or fourth paragraph rather than in the beginning of the entry.

This source is appropriate for secondary school students and lower-division college students but should be used in conjunction with other, better-documented biographical works.

2.46   **Hughes, Langston.** *Famous American Negroes.* New York: Dodd, Mead, 1954.

This text's seventeen sketches of African-American men and women, living and deceased at the time, represent people from diverse fields of endeavor. The guiding selection criterion was that each individual exemplify achievement in spite of adversity. The sketches range in length from eight to thirteen pages; the arrangement is chronological. The individuals profiled are primarily renowned, but a few lesser-known personalities are included: Daniel Hale Williams, Ira Aldridge, Henry O. Tanner, Robert Abbott, and Charles Spaulding.

Hughes reveals the engaging life stories of the biographees by providing examples of their resourcefulness, ambition, influences, and family life. A photograph of each individual is included. There is also an index. Although this book was written fifteen years after Brawley's *Negro Builders and Heroes* (entry 2.35), which included several chapters on women, Hughes provides only three sketches of women. Hughes, a prolific writer and poet, describes the lives of each person with the kind of personal detail that is appealing to junior high and high school students.

2.47P Lanker, Brian. *I Dream a World: Portraits of Black Women Who Changed America.* New York: Stewart, Tabori, and Chang, 1989.

This exquisite photographic portrait of seventy-five living African-American women represents a two-year project by the Pulitzer Prize-winning photojournalist. Lanker began by locating twenty-five diverse women by taking referrals from individuals and by searching the pages of *Life* magazine and the shelves of the Schomburg Center for Research in Black Culture. As Lanker interviewed these women, they in turn referred him to other women whom they felt qualified for inclusion. Consequently, the lives of dancers, singers, educators, journalists, librarians, athletes, judges, politicians, writers, poets, and social activists are represented here.

Lanker interviews each woman personally and asks about her childhood and family, earliest experiences with racism and sexism—including a question about which one was most prevalent—what she did to fight discrimination, and her successes and failures. The interviews are approximately one page long and are replete with biographical stories and lessons, quotes, and philosophical statements; the black-and-white photograph of each woman is on the facing page. Lanker captures the personality and soul of each woman in these powerful images. Each interview is accompanied by a brief biographical statement. The result is a series of portraits of courage, activism, dedication, and achievement against the odds.

Renowned and obscure women are represented: Rosa Parks, Katherine Dunham, Maya Angelou (who also wrote the preface), Cicely Tyson, Alice Walker, Maxine Waters, Althea Gibson, Johnnetta Betsch Cole, Gwendolyn Brooks, Lena Horne, Oprah Winfrey, Sonia Sanchez, Clara McBride Hale, Unita Blackwell, Anna Arnold Hedgeman, Betty Shabazz, Sherian Grace Cadoria, Jean Blackwell Hutson, Eleanor Holmes Norton, Faye Wattleton, Gloria Dean Randle Scott, and Toni Morrison. Following the portraits is an index.

In 1989, the Corcoran Gallery of Art in Washington, D.C., featured an exhibit of these photographs that was eventually displayed in selected cities in the United States. Junior high school students through adults will find the portraits inspirational, educational, and aesthetically appealing. The biographical sketches may motivate students to search for more detailed information on these extraordinary women.

2.48V   Learning Corporation of America. *The Life of Sojourner Truth: Ain't I a Woman?* Videorecording, 26 min. Deerfield, Ill.: Distr. Coronet/MTI Film and Video, 1989.

The life and times of Truth, a famous orator, abolitionist, and fighter for women's rights, is poignantly portrayed in this videotape. Featured are dramatized interviews with Frederick Douglass, Harriet Beecher Stowe, Abraham Lincoln, and Truth's diarist, Olive Gilbert. Winner of several awards including the National Educational Award, Catholic Audiovisual Award, and Columbus International Film and Video Festivals, this video is appropriate for junior high and high school students.

2.49   *Litwack, Leon, and August Meier, eds. *Black Leaders in the Nineteenth Century.* Urbana and Chicago: University of Illinois Press, 1982.

Black Leaders in the Nineteenth Century and its companion volume, *Black Leaders of the Twentieth Century* (see entry 2.44), are two of the more than thirty-five books written by eminent historians in the Blacks in the New World series.

According to the editors, inclusion in this volume depended upon the significance of the person, the availability of primary and secondary documents, availability of scholars, and space considerations. In addition to the fifteen individuals whose lives and work are analyzed here, an essay by Eric Foner on African-American politics at the grassroots level is included. The text also includes essays on three persons whose lives extended into the twentieth century: Isaiah T. Montgomery, William Steward, and Mary Church Terrell. The editors note that the disproportionate number of ministers and politicians represented here is due to the important role of the African-American church in the nineteenth century and the unique opportunities provided by the era of Congressional Reconstruction.

Critical and analytical essays profile the following leaders: Richard Allen, Nat Turner, Harriet Tubman, Frederick Douglass, Mary Ann Shadd, John Mercer Langston, Henry Highland Garnet, Martin R. Delany, Peter Humphries Clark, Blanche K. Bruce, Robert B. Elliott, Hol-

---

*Not indexed in Spradling's *In Black and White.*

land Thompson, Alexander Crummell, and Henry McNeal Turner. The twenty- to twenty-five-page essays provide historical analysis of each leader. Some general themes explored are the subjects' rise to leadership status, differences in philosophy and ideology among leaders, inconsistencies and contradictions of leaders, and the appeal and effect of their leadership on both middle-class African Americans and African Americans in general.

The book concludes with a bibliographical essay of general sources, followed by a bibliographical essay on each person profiled. Notes on contributors and a detailed index are provided. History, African-American studies, and American studies students and professors at the undergraduate and graduate levels should be required to read these thoughtful and profound essays.

2.50   Lowenberg, Bert James, and Ruth Bogin, eds. *Black Women in Nineteenth Century Life: Their Words, Their Thoughts, Their Feelings.* University Park and London: Pennsylvania State University Press, 1976.

The lives of twenty-four slave and free women, based on their written or recorded observations, are included in this collection. In addition to the biographical sketches of primarily obscure women, the editors incorporate excerpts from autobiographical, biographical, or primary sources that illustrate how each woman developed her unique strengths and qualities.

The writings and biographical profiles are preceded by an introductory chapter on African-American women's history to provide a conceptual framework for the book. The editors group the selected writings into four general areas: social reform, education, religion, and family life. Readers can compare the lives, influences, and aspirations of an eclectic group of women who, regardless of their status, struggled, suffered, or sacrificed to transform their own lives and those of their people.

Maria Stewart, Sarah Parker Remond, and Nancy Prince exemplify social reformers; Charlotte Forten Grimke, Lucy Craft Laney, and Anne Julia Cooper represent African-American women educators; obscure women such as Louisa Piquet, Elleanor Eldridge, and Susie King Taylor are represented in family life; and pioneers Jarena Lee, Amanda Berry Smith, and Ann Plato are the focus of the religious section.

The thirteen-page bibliography is thorough; it is divided into works cited, guides (reference works), general biographical sources, individual biographical sources, and other works consulted. An extensive index of proper names is included. Women's studies, African-

American studies, and history students and faculty at the undergraduate and graduate levels will find this an insightful and valuable study of the lives and work of African-American women. High school teachers will also find creative uses for this volume.

2.51   Majors, Monroe A. *Noted Negro Women: Their Triumphs and Activities.* Chicago: Donohue and Henneberry, 1893. Reprint, Salem, N.H.: Ayer, 1986.

The author's purpose in writing this book was to "give inspiration to the girls of present and future generations." The portraits of famous and obscure women, living and deceased, are one to two pages in length and include the following data: birth and death dates, place of birth, early life and education, accomplishments, personal quotes and conversations, personal influences, and major writings.

Following the main section of the book is an appendix containing condensed minibiographical sketches of women, written by other women. Women not given significant coverage in similar works are Edmonia Lewis, sculptor; Sissieretta Jones, concert singer; Amanda Smith, evangelist; and Gertrude E. H. Mossell, author of a biographical work on African-American women written in 1894. Excerpts of poetry by selected women writers are included.

The table of contents serves as an index to the volume, and no bibliography is provided. Although more substantive coverage is provided by Daniel's *Women Builders* (entry 2.40) and Dannett's *Profiles of Negro Womanhood* (entry 2.41), the three sources do not overlap in coverage and perspective, and therefore complement one another. This book should be included with Dannett's and Daniel's works in a reference bibliography for course syllabi in women's history, American history, and African-American studies courses.

2.52   Ovington, Mary White. *Portraits in Color.* New York: Harper, 1927. Reprint, Freeport, N.Y.: Books for Libraries Press, 1971.

Ovington, a social worker and one of the founders of the NAACP in 1909, profiles twenty personalities whom she personally interviewed or whose work she observed. The author, who makes no claim to writing an objective, dispassionate account of the sixteen men and four women included in the volume, selects individuals from a wide array of professions. Each narrative essay is ten to fifteen pages long and provides key details that shed light on the influences and experiences that shaped the subject's life. Due to the author's personal relationship with each biographee and the fact that all the individuals were still living at the time, the sketches read as journalistic accounts or stories told by an observer.

Many individuals who can't be found in other biographical sources are covered here: Max Yergan, missionary; educator Robert Moton; Walter White, NAACP president; Ernest Just, biologist; Janie P. Barrett, reformer; and Louis Wright, physician. No index or bibliography is included. The writing style of this book will make it especially appealing to high school students.

2.53V   PBS Video. *Ida B. Wells—A Passion for Justice.*
Videorecording, 60 min. Alexandria, Va.: Greaves
Production, 1989.

This documentary study of Ida B. Wells—an antilynching crusader, journalist, and schoolteacher whose work is highlighted in Giddings's book (entry 4.82)—follows the life and times of a national figure. Winner of the Silver Apple, 1990 National Educational Film and Video Festival, this inspiring videotape is appropriate for high school through college-level audiences.

2.54   Rollins, Charlemae Hill. *They Showed the Way: Forty American Negro Leaders.* New York: Thomas Crowell Co., 1964.

This highly readable collection of biographies was written by a renowned and respected children's librarian and bibliographer who also wrote *We Build Together: A Reader's Guide to Negro Life and Literature for Elementary and High School Use,* published by the National Council of Teachers of English in 1967. Eight of the forty profiles included are of famous women, while the remaining biographical sketches are of men.

The general biographical accounts represent African Americans from all professions and occupations. Career highlights and influences are provided for the following persons who are not covered by other sources listed in this chapter: James Beckwourth, frontiersman; Jean Baptiste Pointe DuSable, first settler of Chicago; inventors Jan Matzeliger and Norbert Rillieux; Hugh Mulzac, master seaman; Maurice Pompey, judge; Salem Poor, Revolutionary War soldier; Carter G. Woodson, historian; and Bert Williams, entertainer.

An index is provided; however, there is no bibliography. This book is highly recommended for all junior high school libraries.

2.55   Simmons, William J. *Men of Mark: Eminent, Progressive and Rising.* Cleveland, Ohio: George Rewell, 1887. Reprint, New York: Arno Press, 1968.

Heralded as perhaps the first and most comprehensive biographical source on African-American men, Simmons's book of eighty-seven sketches is the single most authoritative work on nineteenth-century African Americans. When he wrote this text, Simmons was president of the State University in Louisville, Kentucky, which was operated by African Americans. In introducing to his students "the great men of their own race," Simmons hoped to inspire students to achieve in spite of obstacles. The author indicates in the preface that he planned to publish a companion volume on African-American women; unfortunately, he never accomplished this task.

Utilizing excerpts from primary documents of speeches, sermons, and articles, Simmons's profiles of great and obscure men are written in traditional flowery and descriptive nineteenth-century prose. The articles vary in length from five to twenty-five pages and illuminate the early life and influences, training and education, accomplishments, and ideas of each man. Ministers, inventors, writers, journalists, educators, artists, musicians, politicians, lawyers, entrepreneurs, scientists, historians, and doctors are represented in this volume. All personalities, according to Simmons, had slave parents or were slaves themselves, and all suffered because of racial prejudice.

An index to the sketches is provided, but no bibliography is included. A precursor to future biographical sources on African Americans, this book serves as a valuable reference and research tool for high school, college, and university libraries.

2.56   *Sterling, Dorothy. *Black Foremothers: Three Lives.* Old Westbury, N.Y.: The Feminist Press, 1979.

Sterling's purpose in writing this book was to rescue from obscurity the lives and works of three African-American women who were fighters for freedom. The book features Ellen Craft, an outspoken abolitionist—whose life and work is usually revealed alongside that of her husband, William, as in Blackett's *Beating Against the Barriers* (see entry 2.34)—Ida B. Wells, antilynching crusader, and Mary Church Terrell, civil rights and women's rights organizer. All were born in the nineteenth century of different backgrounds "but similar spirits and drives," according to Margaret Walker's introduction.

---

*Not indexed in Spradling's *In Black and White.*

Each chapter portrays the lives and forces that led these three women to fight for the rights of their people. Each entry provides first a chronology, then the early life, family background and influences, education, hardships and struggles, and unique contributions each woman made to the quest for equality. Several illustrations and photographs are provided, as well as a bibliography and an index. High school students and teachers and lower-division college students will find the lives of these women stimulating reading.

Genealogical Sources

The four books included in this section of chapter 2 are geared toward assisting amateur and experienced genealogists to locate and use appropriate resources. Charles Blockson's *Black Genealogy*, although older than the other sources, is still one of the best guides to conducting genealogical research for beginning and intermediate genealogists. *Black Genesis* by James Rose and *Afro-American Genealogy Sourcebook* by Tommie Young (1987) are bibliographies of genealogical sources. Young's more recent publication also includes location information. Finally, Jessie Carney Smith's collection of essays, *Ethnic Genealogy*, is intended primarily for the professional researcher, historian, and genealogist. It focuses on the range of genealogical sources and procedures available on African Americans as well as Hispanic, Asian, and Native Americans.

2.57   Blockson, Charles L. *Black Genealogy.* Englewood Cliffs, N.J.: Prentice-Hall, 1977.

This step-by-step guide to conducting genealogical research on African Americans is not only easy to read but interesting and valuable for beginning or intermediate researchers. Blockson, curator of his own rare collection of African Americana at Temple University, is a seasoned genealogical researcher who provides examples from his own family history to illustrate the use of various records and genealogy procedures.

Blockson identifies and focuses on some of the special problems in African-American genealogy—lost records of churches and fraternal and literary organizations; illiteracy of slaves; frequent use of first names only and adoption of "free" names; and lack of access to the public libraries and genealogical collections of the Daughters of the American Revolution and the Mormon Church until thirty-five years ago.

Each of the seven chapters describes the value and use of specific types of records. Blockson's approach begins by constructing a family tree to identify gaps. Oral interviews with relatives and family Bibles are described as sources of family-history information. The usefulness of public records, including local directories, cemetery inscriptions, birth and death certificates, records in county and court clerk's offices, records of churches and benevolent societies, and national records (census, military, pension, etc.) is detailed and examples are given in chapter 3.

Chapter 4 explains the use and location of plantation, share-cropping, and breeding records. Manumission papers and records from the Freedman's Bureau are identified in chapter 5. Problems presented by miscegenation are addressed in chapter 6, as is a description of local historical societies and archives for lists of slaves sold at ports. Chapter 7 specifically addresses sources of information for tracing roots to Africa. A comprehensive index and several valuable appendixes are included. Although this book was published more than 15 years ago, the information is still relevant and practical. *Black Genealogy* should be used in high school history and social studies classes and in local history classes in community and undergraduate colleges. It is an invaluable resource for those interested in pursuing an African-American family-history project.

2.58   **Rose, James.** *Black Genesis*. Detroit, Mich.: Gale Research, 1978.

Rose's book focuses on the myriad sources that can be used in genealogical research. Unlike Blockson (entry 2.57), one of Rose's purposes is to propose areas in which records need to be published, and to suggest ways in which genealogical materials can be used to reexamine history. Chapter 1, then, is the only chapter that is completely narrative. It was written to assist the novice in beginning his or her search. This chapter also includes general references and resources for African-American genealogy. The remaining chapters are annotated lists or bibliographies of national and state resources for African-American genealogical research.

Each chapter is devoted to groups of specific records including oral history sources, national archives and federal records, war records, migratory patterns, and slavery records. Chapters 8 through 14 survey the types of state records available for African-American genealogical research. They are alphabetized by state. Within each of these chapters, federal, state, county, and miscellaneous records are described. The appendixes include one on library location symbols used within the book, a second on branch genealogical libraries, and a third on federal archives and records centers. Author, title, and subject indexes are provided.

Rose's extensive description of sources serves to supplement Blockson's primer for conducting genealogical research. For this reason, *Black Genesis* is a useful resource book for genealogists, local historians, librarians, archivists, and high school social studies teachers.

2.59 Smith, Jessie C., ed. *Ethnic Genealogy.* Westport, Conn.: Greenwood Press, 1983.

This group of ten well-written, comprehensive essays by noted genealogists, librarians, and historians was compiled to "identify sources, problems, and issues, in tracing the genealogy of blacks, Hispanics, Asians, and American Indians." Considered a reference volume for librarians, researchers, oral historians, and archivists, the book, according to Smith, will be more helpful to the less-experienced or novice genealogist and researcher.

Ethnic Genealogy is divided into three sections—general information on sources, procedures, and genealogical research; major repositories for genealogical research; and sources available to specific ethnic groups. Following an introductory essay by Russell Bidlack, a historian, genealogist, and former library school dean at the University of Michigan, the remaining essays in the first section discuss sources and practical techniques for conducting genealogical research. Especially helpful are examples of forms provided by Jean Elder Cazort for researching and recording family-history data. These forms include a family group sheet, individual history sheet, and research record. Casper Jordan describes the types of records held in academic and public libraries that support genealogical research. Bobby Lovett provides a detailed approach to researching family history using ethnic history as an example and outlining different types of primary sources and typical problems encountered in researching and writing ethnic family history.

In the second section of the book, James D. Walker draws on his vast experience with the National Archives and Records Service (NARS) to discuss specific genealogical records relating to ethnic history. Detailed data are provided on the following records at NARS: federal census, federal immigration, naturalization, passport, military service, veteran's benefits, civilian personnel, and a special series of federal records of ethnic family history. Roger Scanland's essay on the holdings of the Genealogical Society of Utah Library, the world's largest genealogical library, is illuminating for its description of records relating to the history of African Americans, Native Americans, and Hispanics.

The final section highlights and discusses genealogical records available on Native Americans, Asian Americans, African Americans, and Hispanic Americans, written by Jimmy Parker, Greg Gubler, Charles Blockson, and Lyman DePlatt, respectively. Bibliographies are included at the end of most of the essays in the book. A detailed index and biographical sketches of contributors are also provided. In addition, numerous figures and tables of representative family-history documents are included. Clearly, this volume is the most comprehensive reference work on ethnic genealogy written thus far. It should be of tremendous value to genealogists, local historians, and teachers at all levels who are involved in genealogy.

2.60   Young, Tommie Morton. *Afro-American Genealogy Sourcebook.* New York: Garland, 1987.

Young surveyed more than two hundred libraries, collections of genealogy materials, and historical organizations and societies to locate the specific types of records used in African-American genealogical research.

Divided into four parts, the first section of the book includes an introductory essay followed by a bibliography of basic reference sources in African Americana and of genealogy reference sources. The second part identifies private resources in church records, cemeteries, photographic and manuscript collections, records of societies and organizations, and educational institutions useful for African-American genealogical research. The third part surveys public records including federal, state, county, and city records. The fourth part serves as a directory of resources with addresses and phone numbers of sources for vital statistics, public libraries, historically black colleges and universities, major collections and libraries for genealogical research, and a selected list of genealogical and historical societies and organizations. Unfortunately, no index was compiled.

Similar in content to Rose's *Black Genesis* (entry 2.58), Young's sourcebook goes a step farther in providing location information and current resources. This is a useful reference book for local historians, beginning and advanced genealogists, and librarians. The beginning genealogist will also want to consult the how-to advice provided by Blockson in *Black Genealogy* (entry 2.57) and by Smith in *Ethnic Genealogy* (entry 2.59).

CHAPTER THREE

Historiography

*T*HE *DICTIONARY OF AMERICAN HISTORY* DEFINES HISTORI-
ography as simply "the writing of history." It further provides
a narrative chronology of the development of American historiography—from descriptions of Norse voyages in 1070 through Pu-
ritan views of history, colonial historical writings, activities of American
historical societies in the late eighteenth and early nineteenth centuries,
the surge of biographical and multivolume histories to the emergence
of specialized (e.g., church, economic, social, political, urban, and family) histories. However, perhaps the ultimate question regarding the
writing of history is What relationship do historical inquiry and documents have to our lives?

In reviewing the books in this chapter (entries 3.61–73), the factor
that distinguishes these African-American historians who study African-
American history from their white counterparts is their concern for the
purpose and uses of history. Their aim is to present an accurate and
comprehensive view of the role African Americans played in shaping
their own destiny and that of America. These historians hope to influence not only public policy issues but the ways in which people view
the meaning of history. (See Thomas Holt's article, "Whither Now and
Why?" in *The State of Afro-American History* [entry 3.65].)

Works annotated in this chapter were primarily published since
1980 in an attempt to incorporate more-recent historiographical
developments. However, a few sources published before this period
are included because the works are considered classics in African-American historiography.

This chapter is limited to comprehensive general works that span several centuries and are national in scope as opposed to those that focus on a particular historical period, personality, or region. The exception is Leonard Sweet's *Black Images of America*, a book that evaluates nineteenth-century Negro thought against George Bancroft's views of the image of white America.

Particularly noteworthy and of special interest to high school history and social studies teachers is a thoughtful, creative book, *Thinking Historically*, by Thomas Holt, published by the College Entrance Examination Board. Holt encourages high school teachers to reflect on their own teaching by sharing his process for engaging students in actively questioning and imagining history. High school teachers and interested members of the general public will find Holt's introductory but comprehensive booklet on African-American historiography indispensable reading, as is Robert Harris's concise, informative booklet *Teaching African-American History*.

A few historians, such as Vincent Harding, make an impassioned but eloquent plea for the way in which African-American history can be taught to students of all ages in order to fashion a more humane, peaceful, democratic society. Clarence Walker, in his book *Deromanticizing Black History*, criticizes this type of historiography as presenting an overly idealized and perhaps less-accurate view of African-American history. John Hope Franklin's essays in *Race and History* represent a traditional, objective, and useful approach to the interpretation of topics in African-American history.

Essays included in *The State of Afro-American History*, edited by Darlene Clark Hine, summarize the need for additional historiographical sources that focus on the uses of quantitative methods, material culture, the teaching of African-American history at the college and secondary school levels, and the contributions of African-American women historians. Indeed, only one book annotated in this chapter is devoted exclusively to the historiography of African-American women: Hine's *Black Women's History: Theory and Practice*. Hopefully, the next five years will usher in a flood of scholarship about African-American women's history in addition to works on the influences and uses of public history and more works written for high school history teachers and their students.

Historiography

3.61 **Franklin, John Hope.** *Race and History: Selected Essays, 1938–1988.* Baton Rouge and London: Louisiana University Press, 1989.

The twenty-seven previously published essays in this collection by preeminent African-American historian John Hope Franklin are arranged into five sections: "Profession of History," "Practice of History," "The Near Great and Not So Great," "In the Public Interest," and "Leadership Roles." Each section is preceded by a unifying background essay that provides the reader with the purpose and an overview of the essays.

Of particular interest in the first section is an essay on Franklin's rewarding professional and personal experience in taking his University of Chicago graduate students to North Carolina archival institutions to conduct historical research using rich collections of primary documents. The essay illustrates the value and importance of exposing students to the effective use of primary documents.

In another noteworthy essay, Franklin argues that, more than any other source, the popular but racist film *Birth of a Nation*, produced by David Griffith in 1915, had a pernicious influence on America's view of Reconstruction. Franklin includes an essay on the enforcement of the Civil Rights Act of 1875, which provided a federal guarantee of the rights of all citizens to use public theaters, accommodations, and transportation.

In part 3, Franklin introduces readers to six renowned and obscure African-American history makers, including a special short autobiography he wrote in 1988. History students will find the essays in part 5 very illuminating, especially Franklin's reflections on historical problems—drawn from many decades of research, writing, and teaching. The book also includes extensive notes and an index.

The essays included in this text are most beneficial to undergraduate history faculty and students.

3.62 **Harding, Vincent.** *Hope and History: Why We Must Share the Story of the Movement.* Maryknoll, N.Y.: Orbis Books, 1990.

Harding continuously strives to synthesize, analyze, and creatively interpret the significance of the Civil Rights movement to serve as a guidepost to a more humane, democratic, freedom-loving future. This collection of twelve essays grew out of Harding's work as a consultant for the highly acclaimed PBS series *Eyes on the Prize.* By his own admission, his focus is personal and reflects his philosophy about the meaning and uses of history.

Harding's central thesis is that the Civil Rights movement was a national phenomenon that spread to southern Africa and eastern Europe, influenced the women's and student movements, and ultimately served as the moral voice of America. The twelve chapters are arranged thematically and include essays on the uses of biography, the meaning of religion, alternatives to violence, and the role of African-American artists in transforming the nation.

In the first chapter, Harding suggests that biography can have a profound impact in helping young people solve many present-day problems. He makes a strong argument that the lives of Fannie Lou Hamer, Malcolm X, Martin Luther King, Ella Baker, Bayard Rustin, James Farmer, and others are powerful sources of inspiration for young blacks and whites. In the second chapter, subtitled "Rediscovering Humanity's Great Lessons at Home," Harding offers practical and creative ways in which the Civil Rights movement can be used as a primer for teaching democracy. Examples highlighted include *Brown* v. *Board of Education* as a case study on the limits and strength of the courts in establishing democratic goals, the Montgomery bus boycott for civil disobedience and grass-roots initiatives, and sit-ins and freedom rides to discuss the relationship between federal and state governments in the struggle for democratic change.

In the chapter on religion, Harding implores readers to ponder self-love as a religious calling and to study the relationship between religious faith and social responsibility. In a spiritually inspired chapter on nonviolence, Harding challenges readers to "explore convictions . . . and capacities of human beings to become much more than we realize . . . to live more deeply and grow more fully in humanizing work of mutual responsibility and respect."

Readers looking for a conventional historiography may be more comfortable with one of the more-traditional sources in this section. With a fervor that takes on almost spiritual undertones, Harding inspires teachers to reflect upon the uses and meaning of history as a moral imperative. Open-minded teachers of American, world, and African-American history at the high school and college levels will find innovative ways to incorporate Harding's inspiring ideas into the curriculum. Footnotes and an index are provided.

3.63 **Harris, Robert L., Jr.** *Teaching African-American History.*
Washington, D.C.: American Historical Association, 1992.

According to its author, this concise and thorough booklet was "part
of an effort to make recent interpretations of African-American history
accessible to a broad audience." Geared toward teachers and students
of American and African-American history, the booklet summarizes the
last twenty years of scholarship in African-American history in what
the writer describes as a narrative outline: ". . . to define major themes
and to provide a conceptual framework for exploration in greater
detail."

Harris delineates the four major thematic and chronological tran-
sitions in African-American history—from Africa to America, slavery
to freedom, countryside to city, and segregation to civil rights—which
offers a conventional but useful framework. Harris introduces several
recent historiographical developments, such as the differences between
chattel slavery as it developed in North America and slavery as it existed
in Africa. Harris also explores comparative slavery both within and
outside North America, the status of African-American women prior
to and immediately following emancipation, and the impact of the Civil
Rights movement on various classes of African Americans.

Harris writes substantive footnotes, arranged by chapter, that
serve as an excellent bibliography for further reading. A short guide to
references is also provided.

Due to its readability and conciseness, Harris's booklet is especially well-suited for junior high and high school history instructors
and provides an overview and review for lower-division undergraduate
history students.

3.64 **Hine, Darlene Clark, ed.** *Black Women's History: Theory
and Practice.* 2v. Brooklyn, N.Y.: Carlson Publishing, 1990.

These two volumes of forty essays are volumes 9 and 10 in the Black
Women in United States History series published by Carlson. All the
essays included have been published in other sources but are brought
together here in a convenient format.

The purpose of these essays is to enhance readers' understanding
of the theory and practice of black women's history. According to
Hine, contributing scholars were concerned with uncovering specifics
of black women's experiences and posing the right questions to influence the development of future studies in this area.

Topics explored include the social and economic status of African-American women, the relationship between African-American women and white women, African-American women in education, African-American women in health-care education, the treatment of African-American women in the women's liberation movement, African-American women and feminism, teaching the history of African-American women, and patriarchy and the exploitation of African-American women.

Contributors include primarily African-American women, but selection was not limited by race or gender. Unfortunately, the table of contents does not list the dates the essays were first published. This would have served as a guide to the currency of the article. It is, however, still useful to have easy access to a full range of materials on this subject by reputable scholars. Articles are alphabetically arranged by author's surname rather than by topic. No index is included in these volumes.

High school history and social studies instructors as well as instructors of undergraduate history, American studies, and women's studies courses will find these essays invaluable reading.

3.65   Hine, Darlene Clark, ed. *The State of Afro-American History: Past, Present, and Future.* Baton Rouge: Louisiana State University Press, 1986.

This collection of essays by African-American history scholars and practitioners was prepared for a conference sponsored by the American Historical Association in 1983. The purpose of the conference was to explore the state of the art on the study and teaching of African-American history and to evaluate the outpouring of historical literature in the field since the 1970s. In the introduction, Thomas Holt states, "the papers represent assessments of the ongoing process of researching, writing, and disseminating Afro-American history as viewed by the post-sixties fourth generation of historians."

Eminent scholars such as John Hope Franklin, Leslie Owens, Eugene Genovese, Jacqueline Jones, Eric Foner, Nell Painter, Lawrence Levine, and Vincent Harding have contributed cogent, thought-provoking papers and commentary on slavery, emancipation, and urban studies. Other timely topics discussed in the volume include the integration of African-American history into American history, African-American history courses, African-American history and community, African-American women, African-American history textbooks, and the African-American scholar. Equally as important, historians and directors of African-American museums contribute valuable perspectives on bridging the gap between scholarly research and the interpretation and uses of history in the community.

Included at the end of the book is a biographical note on the contributors and an extensive index.

This work is required reading for history teachers, students, and curriculum specialists at all educational levels.

3.66   Holt, Thomas C. *African-American History*. The New American History series. Washington, D.C.: American Historical Association, 1990.

Holt's work represents just one in a series of thirteen scholarly pamphlets that were designed to familiarize high school teachers of American history with recent historical scholarship.

Holt's overview of recent historical developments juxtaposes two dominant schools of thought in African-American history. The first view is of African Americans as victims of a racist, hostile America in which they were powerless to make any changes in their lives unless sanctioned by whites. The second view is of African Americans as actors, creators, and makers of history who established their own institutions and culture, contributed to their emancipation, and fought for self-determination. Holt discusses seminal works from the slavery period to the twentieth century, which represent, on a continuum, one of these two views of African-American history.

Slavery studies include a discussion of U. B. Phillips's *American Negro Slavery*, Kenneth Stampp's *The Peculiar Institution*, and Stanley Elkins's 1954 study of slavery, which are illustrative of the first school of thought. These studies use sources created by slaveholders to draw conclusions about how slaves reacted to their condition. Blassingame's *The Slave Community* (entry 5.100), as well as works by Eugene Genovese, Lawrence Levine, and Jacqueline Jones, attempt to describe the slave's world from the point of view of the slave rather than that of the slaveholder.

Holt's review of studies on emancipation encompasses Du Bois's classic work, *Black Reconstruction* (entry 5.123), which emphasized the active role of African-American war refugees in influencing Lincoln to "abandon a hands-off policy toward southern slavery." Other studies on Reconstruction examine the role of freed people and planters in creating the system of sharecropping. Studies of segregation in the nineteenth century explore protests against Jim Crow laws in the South and the role of African Americans in embracing voluntary separatism in some areas for strategic purposes. The classic debate between Booker T. Washington and W. E. B. Du Bois is reviewed in light of new work by Louis Harlan.

Finally, Holt's survey of twentieth-century urban studies examines the impact of the Great Migration on African-American northern urban life. Holt describes the work of St. Clair Drake and Horace Clayton, E. Franklin Frazer, Osofsky, Spear, Kusmer, and Grossman, who represent schools of thought that viewed African-American urban life as pathological and those who viewed urban communities as places in which African Americans were able to create their own institutions in spite of adversity. A bibliography of recent works in African-American history is provided.

This pamphlet should be required reading for high school history teachers and anyone interested in a concise, cogent introduction to African-American historiography.

3.67   **Holt, Thomas.** *Thinking Historically: Narrative, Imagination and Understanding.* Educational Equity Project. New York: College Entrance Examination Board, 1990.

Thinking Historically is one in a new series of publications initiated by the College Board's Educational Equity Project, "a ten-year effort to improve the quality of education and ensure equal access to college for all students." Holt describes the book as a personal narrative of how he thinks about history.

Through interviews with several high school students about what history is and how they feel about it, Holt challenges high school teachers to reexamine the way in which history is taught. The questions he raises could have a profound effect on the future teaching of history, the materials that are used, and the way in which the personal experiences of students and teachers can be used to analyze and "imagine" history. He poses questions such as the following: "Can we help students take on the work of history in ways that are imaginative and rigorous? What does being a historian involve? What documents can be used to study history? Who produced the documents—an eyewitness or a participant? What was left unsaid in the document? What does the document assume?"

Holt also addresses the issue of subjectivity in teaching history. He suggests that just as teachers must question the validity of the documents, they must openly discuss the subjective influences readers bring to the documents. Finally, Holt emphasizes that there is no one correct version of history; he looks at history as a series of different histories told from various points of view.

This book is an invaluable resource for high school and lower-division college-level history teachers in that it suggests creative approaches to engaging students in a personal yet critical historical journey. A recent bibliography is included for further reading.

3.68   Meier, August, and Elliott Rudwick. *Black History and the Historical Profession, 1915–1980.* Urbana and Chicago: University of Illinois Press, 1986.

The focus of this historiography is "on the intellectual careers of historians rather than the works themselves." Specifically, the authors examine the factors that motivated men and women to become historians, how their intellectual perspectives shaped their work, and ways in which the actions of professional organizations, book publishers, history departments, and philanthropists affected the field over time.

The tools used by the authors to collect information include secondary sources of monographs and articles on African-American historiography, interviews with more than 175 living historians who have done scholarly work, and archival and manuscript collections. The authors define *scholars* as professionally trained historians who matured by the beginning of the twentieth century, earned a Ph.D. with a "record of significant publication," and are students of the African-American experience and race relations in the United States. Both established and lesser-known African-American and white historians are included.

The chapters are arranged in thematic, chronological periods beginning with "Carter G. Woodson as Entrepreneur," and continuing with "Generational Change and the Shaping of a Scholarly Specialty, Parts I and II," "Historiography of Slavery: An Inquiry into Paradigm-Making and Scholarly Interaction," and "Dilemmas of Scholarship in Afro-American History." Like Franklin and Greene, Meier and Rudwick acknowledge the early pioneers of African-American history as George Washington Williams, Carter G. Woodson, and W. E. B. Du Bois.

In the second chapter, Meier and Rudwick focus on the emergence of specialties within African-American history through the examination of Woodson's contemporaries—Charles Wesley, Lorenzo Greene, Alritheus Taylor, W. Sherman Savage, and Rayford Logan.

The authors go on to discuss the lives and careers of a group of liberal Jewish historians who wrote on African-American history, including Harvey Wish, Herbert Aptheker, Eric Foner, and C. Vann Woodward. Few women historians are mentioned during this period, perhaps due to the small number of women who received doctoral degrees in history at this time. Several more women, such as Mary Frances Berry, Nell Painter, Sharon Harley, Rosalyn Terborg-Penn, and Darlene Clark Hine, as well as more-contemporary historians are discussed in the third chapter.

In the final chapter, the authors identify the range of dilemmas experienced by students of African-American history, including the tension between studying African-American history as a distinct, separate field and incorporating it into the larger context of American history. The book also takes a close look at the particular dilemma of the African-American historian who must balance the tension between scholarship and advocacy.

Within the context of the evolution of the historical profession, Meier and Rudwick reveal the personal and professional experiences of historians that influenced them to pursue or change their academic work—whether it was racial injustice, the influence of a formidable historian or mentor such as Carter G. Woodson or an activist liberal minister, or their own participation in the Civil Rights movement.

This text is replete with historical notes and references. Also included are an essay on sources, an explanatory essay on notes, approximately fifty pages of footnotes, and an index.

Teachers of high school juniors and seniors and undergraduate and graduate history faculty and students will find this book intriguing reading.

3.69 **Quarles, Benjamin.** *Black Mosaic: Essays in Afro-American History and Historiography.* Amherst: University of Massachusetts Press, 1988.

Like Franklin's book (entry 3.61), *Black Mosaic* is a collection of essays previously published as articles between 1945 and 1977. The first two chapters include eight essays on the Revolutionary War and Civil War periods, Quarles's area of specialization within African-American history. The third chapter encompasses two essays on blacks in the twentieth century; one is a biographical treatise on A. Phillip Randolph, organizer of the Brotherhood of Sleeping Car Porters.

The final chapter on historiography provides biographical information on Quarles and his interest in exploring the ways in which blacks maintained their identity, culture, and sense of community in a hostile, racist environment. Quarles offers a valuable essay on the problem of materials in African-American history by identifying, for example, the paucity of linguistic studies and oral tradition in materials prior to the Civil War.

In a second historiographical essay, entitled "Black History's Diversified Clientele," Quarles suggests that the contemporary uses of African-American history are for the African-American revolutionary, the African-American academician, and the white community in general. He contends that each group offers a different perspective on and purpose for African-American history, which enhances our understanding of the discipline.

No index or bibliography is included. Instead, Quarles provides footnotes at the bottom of each page.

Primarily useful reading for undergraduate history students and faculty, high school history instructors should also find this book valuable.

3.70   Sweet, Leonard J. *Black Images of America, 1784–1870.* New York: W. W. Norton, 1970.

The purpose of this book is to examine and evaluate the views of nineteenth-century African-American leaders on their identity, their relationship to America, and their involvement in American history. These views are examined against the white image of America depicted by George Bancroft, a representative white historian often referred to as the father of American history, who articulated a common vision of America and its mission.

Sweet first outlines Bancroft's view of America, which includes the premise that God is the prime mover of history and that America was "chosen" to complete God's final plan for humankind. For example, according to Sweet, Bancroft supported Lincoln's plan for compensated emancipation. Consistent with this view, to remove any blemishes in America's image, slaves should be emancipated and sent to Africa to lay the groundwork for Christianizing and civilizing the African continent.

In chapter 4, Sweet characterizes African-American responses to colonization, expressed in the writings of W. C. Pennington, James Forten, Samuel Cornish, David Ruggles, Frederick Douglass, David Walker, and others, as "in direct proportion to the widespread conviction that black Americans had earned and deserved the right to be included as American citizens"; therefore, they vehemently renounced colonization.

The fifth chapter presents and discusses the views of nineteenth-century African Americans and whites on the destiny of African Americans regarding God's mission of spreading Christianity and democracy to Africa and civilizing the world. Sweet defines the views of writers and historians such as George Washington Williams, Thomas Fortune,

Edward Blyden, and others who found common ground in racial pride. They believed African Americans were destined to a future as free Americans equal to whites.

Sweet indicates that the second quarter of the nineteenth century was characterized by a preoccupation with self-improvement by African Americans. He, like Clarence Walker in *Deromanticizing Black History* (entry 3.73), agrees that African-American leaders believed that prejudice was based on condition, not skin color; therefore, they sought power and wealth for respect. In one of the final chapters, Sweet outlines the goals of African-American separatism in the nineteenth century as a "provisional prerequisite for full citizenship . . . in order to achieve integration and break the color barrier." Its specific objectives included creating a pool of positive role models.

The book concludes with a valuable twenty-page bibliographical review divided into ten sections and an index.

Upper-division undergraduate history and American studies students and faculty should find this book important reading.

3.71 **Thorpe, Earl E.** *Black Historians: A Critique*. New York: William Morrow, 1971.

This revised classic work was originally published in 1958 under the title *Negro Historians in the United States*. Thorpe's book is one of the first to analyze African-American historians and their contributions to American historiography from 1800 to 1960.

Thorpe discusses each writer's works according to the following criteria: quantity of writings, literary merit of writings, training in historical methodology, thoroughness in use of sources and documentation, philosophy of history, breadth and soundness of interpretations of historical events and movements, objectivity, and impact of writings on people of the writer's and subsequent periods.

The first chapter describes the central theme of African-American history and the motivations of African-American historians in writing about African-American history. The remaining chapters review, compare, and contrast the works and views of African-American historians by chronological period. For example, the beginning school of African-American historians, according to Thorpe, wrote to justify the emancipation of slavery by showing distinctive acts by members of the black race. This school includes Paul Cuffee, Prince Saunders, James C. Pennington, William Nell, William Wells Brown, William Still, Joseph Wilson, George Washington Williams, Benjamin Brawley, and Booker T. Washington.

The middle group (1896–1930) witnessed the emergence of

African-American scholars with graduate degrees in the social sciences who wrote histories to counteract claims of a scientific basis for white supremacy. W. E. B. Du Bois's sociological studies on black life; Carter G. Woodson, Charles Wesley; Monroe Work; Arthur Schomburg; William Crogman; Kelly Miller; and one lone woman historian, Laura Eliza Wilkes, exemplified the work of the middle group. Thorpe also discusses the contributions and works of African-American church historians such as Daniel Payne, Benjamin Mays, and R. R. Wright.

The members of the new school of African-American historians (1930–1960) began their professional careers after 1930 and could afford to be less preoccupied with refuting the stereotypical views of African Americans by historians such as Ulrich Phillips. Their works were characterized by better documentation of sources and an improved grasp of the methods of social science research. Rayford Logan, Lorenzo Greene, Luther Jackson, Benjamin Quarles, John Hope Franklin, Laurence Reddick, Eric Williams, Lerone Bennett Jr., John Henrik Clarke, and Thorpe himself were the most prolific historians of this period. Several women historians—Lula Johnson, Helen Edmonds, Merze Tate, and Elsie Lewis—are mentioned in this section.

Footnotes to each chapter are provided at the end, as are a selected bibliography and an index.

Secondary school history teachers and lower-division undergraduate history students and faculty will appreciate Thorpe's straightforward, concise style and general overview of the works of both obscure and well-known African-American historians.

3.72   **Van Deburg, William L.** *Slavery and Race in American Popular Culture.* Madison and London: University of Wisconsin Press, 1984.

Van Deburg uses a group of writings to describe how novelists, historians, dramatists, poets, filmmakers, and songwriters perceived and interpreted the African-American slave experience from the seventeenth century to contemporary times. His purpose is to "reveal how these cultural historians record the cultural underpinnings of American opinion on matters of race and slavery and the extent to which they shaped, created, and strengthened American opinions and values." Like Leonard Sweet (entry 3.70), Van Deburg records how African-American cultural historians responded to and helped to correct negative images of African Americans.

The five chapters of this book are "From African to Slave, 1619–1830," "The Debate Begins, 1830–1861," "Black Americans Fight Back," "From Slave to Citizen, 1861–1965," and "The Debate Continues, 1965–1980." According to Van Deburg, early images of slaves as violently suicidal on slave ships and, later, their portrayal as buffoons in stage plays served to reinforce the view of slaves as outsiders and intellectual inferiors undeserving of full participation in society. In the second chapter, George Bancroft's view of slavery is compared and contrasted with the image of slaves portrayed in Harriet Beecher Stowe's *Uncle Tom's Cabin.*

In the third chapter, Van Deburg highlights minstrel songs and plays, which, he argues, emphasized the lighter side of slave life by portraying slaves as happy and content with their condition. The response of pre–Civil War African-American writers, such as W. C. Pennington, Jupiter Hammon (poet), Phillis Wheatley (poet), and William Wells Brown (novelist and historian), pointed to themes of resiliency, strength, and an unrelenting desire for freedom.

According to Van Deburg, *Underground Railroad* (1872) by William Still (see entry 5.114), an African-American historian, is one of the earliest portrayals of African Americans as heroes and coincides with late-nineteenth-century social and intellectual developments toward less-antagonistic views of slavery and a heavier reliance on primary documents. Yet Ulrich B. Phillips's *American Negro Slavery* (1918) used primary documents that reinforced negative stereotypes of slaves and painted a picture of social harmony on the plantation. This image was not repudiated until Herbert Aptheker's *American Negro Slave Revolts* was published in 1943.

The remaining chapters discuss African-American northern novelists and storytellers such as Paul Laurence Dunbar, Charles Chesnutt, Countee Cullen, and Sterling Brown. The impact of influential works such as Margaret Mitchell's *Gone with the Wind* (1936) and William Faulkner's *Absalom, Absalom!* (1936) as well as David Griffith's movie *Birth of a Nation* (1915) and twentieth-century portrayals of African Americans in Hollywood movies are analyzed and reviewed.

This book provides a significant framework for examining portrayals of African Americans in popular culture. Useful comparisons can be made with complementary works by Leonard Sweet and Clarence Walker as well as Houston Baker's *Long Black Song*, a collection of literary essays not totally consistent with the scope of this book but of some relevance. Extensive footnotes arranged by chapter; a selected bibliography of reference materials, secondary sources of books and articles, dissertations, and theses; and an index are all included.

Due to the interdisciplinary nature of Van Deburg's book, it is highly recommended for undergraduate American studies, American literature, and history classes, and for high school teachers in these areas.

3.73 **Walker, Clarence E.** *Deromanticizing Black History: Critical Essays and Reappraisals.* Knoxville: University of Tennessee Press, 1991.

This highly controversial book challenges recent trends in historiography on slave culture found in John Blassingame's book (entry 5.100), Herbert Gutman's *The Black Family in Slavery and Freedom* (entry 5.103), and Vincent Harding's *There Is a River* (entry 4.85), as well as challenging Marxist theories on the significance of class. Walker's thesis is that race, not class, was the primary division in American society under slavery before the Civil War and that it remained the primary division after the war in a segregated society.

In each of the five chapters of the book, Walker questions existing historiographical paradigms using numerous historical examples. For instance, in the first chapter, Walker criticizes neo-Marxist paradigms of history that emphasize class conflict. Walker insists that many black leaders in the pre–Civil War nineteenth century, such as Frederick Douglass, William Wells Brown, and Martin Delany, believed black folks' problems stemmed from their condition, not their race. Subsequently, their efforts to improve their condition were met with resentment by white laboring classes. These whites did not identify with the plight of even free northern blacks as exemplified by the treatment of blacks by Irish immigrants during this period.

In a scathing article on Marcus Garvey in the second chapter, Walker insists that Garvey's Back to Africa movement was racist and reactionary, not an expression of American black nationalism as historians have conventionally interpreted it. Walker further contends that the basis for Garvey's movement was "uplifting" blacks to a higher level, to a "standard of civilized approval," reminiscent of Booker T. Washington (who had a profound influence on Garvey's philosophy).

Walker's essay on W. E. B. Du Bois's challenge to the Marxist view of history applauds Du Bois for rejecting the notion that blacks during Reconstruction were politically incompetent and that Reconstruction was a failure because of this perceived incompetence. Instead Du Bois asserted in his book *Black Reconstruction* (entry 5.123) that freedmen were not extended help by white northern workers or southern yeomen because these people saw blacks as threatening their jobs and lifestyles.

In a final essay, entitled "The American Negro as Historical Outsider, 1836–1935," Walker examines the idealistic tradition of writings by African-American historians about African-American history in the United States. Extensive footnotes, a bibliographic essay, and an index are provided at the end of this volume.

Because it assumes readers have a background in Marxist theory and have read the works of many of the historians whose paradigms are being challenged, this book is appropriate, thoughtful reading for graduate students and upper-division undergraduate faculty in African-American and American history.

CHAPTER FOUR

General Historical Surveys and Documentary Histories

ENERAL COMPREHENSIVE NARRATIVE AND INTERPRETIVE surveys of African-American history are annotated in this fourth chapter (entries 4.74–98). This chapter also includes photographic books, videotapes, exhibits, and documentary histories that are comprehensive and surveylike in scope.

Every effort has been made to concentrate on works published since 1980. However, a few classic works by Lerone Bennett, Benjamin Brawley, Kenneth Goode, Rayford Logan, Meier and Rudwick, and Thomas Frazier, which are still timely and especially useful for secondary school teachers and students, are provided.

Historians such as John Hope Franklin, Mary Frances Berry and John Blassingame, and Vincent Harding—whose works are represented in this chapter—recognize and acknowledge the research conducted by their predecessors. These forerunners include George Washington Williams, Booker T. Washington, and Carter G. Woodson, whose early meticulous work and foresight paved the way for more in-depth and interpretive research. A cursory review of these sources provides a historical foundation for the contemporary works that are annotated in this chapter.

Williams, a self-taught historian, lawyer, minister, newspaper editor, and politician, wrote the ground-breaking two-volume *History of the Negro Race in America from 1619–1880* in 1883; it was the first work of history by a Negro to be given serious attention by white American scholars. The sixty chapters begin with life in Africa and conclude with the Reconstruction period. Williams spent seven years conducting research on this book in the Historical and Philosophical

Society of Ohio and other scholarly libraries. Although Booker T. Washington's *The Story of the Negro: The Rise of the Race from Slavery* (1909) is poorly documented, it provides social and economic coverage that was lacking from Williams's book. Three of the fifteen chapters are devoted to Negro women and their work; Negro communities and homes; and poetry, music, and art among Negroes.

Woodson's *The Negro in Our History* (1922), which was written especially for use by high school teachers, was the most popular and authoritative textbook on African-American history until John Hope Franklin's *From Slavery to Freedom* was first published in 1947. Woodson, often referred to as the "father of Negro history," devoted his life to disseminating important information about Negro history to the general reader and preparing materials for use in secondary and elementary schools. The focus, as in Williams's and Washington's books, was on documenting the contributions of Negroes to the making of America in order to correct historical distortions and omissions, gain respect, and foster racial pride.

In 1942, Woodson published *Story of the Negro Retold*, which was specifically written for high school students. More concise and less detailed than *The Negro in Our History*, this work focused more on the Negro in the international world. Each chapter included a section on projects and problems for students to supplement the curriculum (and separate sections of books for the instructor). There were also source books for the student. Arna Bontemps's *Story of the Negro* (1948), a book that is especially appealing to junior high students, tells Negro history through a series of interesting narrative stories.

The documentary histories included at the end of this chapter provide a rich selection of primary documents to draw upon to study the history of African Americans. In *Thinking Historically* (entry 3.67), Thomas Holt suggests that teachers can select and compare and contrast the documents produced by participants and lesser-known individuals with those produced by eyewitnesses and renowned personalities.

Thanks to the efforts of these trailblazers to educate Negroes about their history, present-day historians have been able to transcend this early focus on "contributionist history" and use primary documents, census records, statistics, photographs, and other sources to tell African-American history from the point of view of African Americans.

General Historical Surveys

4.74   **Bennett, Lerone, Jr.** *Before the Mayflower: A History of the Negro in America, 1619–1964.* Chicago: Johnson Publishing, 1964.

This history of the black experience grew out of a series of articles published in *Ebony* magazine; therefore, the book's intended audience is the average reader. The author, a senior editor at *Ebony* since 1960, devoted fourteen months to researching and writing this popular history book.

The thirteen chapters are arranged chronologically and cover African-American history to 1964. The writing style is journalistic and narrative. Bennett personalizes history for readers by retelling stories about individual captives, common folks, and famous personalities through excerpts from actual documents they produced. The middle passage, slave resistance, slave revolts, black participation in the battle against slavery, and other forms of protest used by blacks through the centuries are highlighted by Bennett to demonstrate the role they played in their own emancipation and the quest for equality.

A chronology of major events and milestones in black history; a bibliography of books, unpublished studies, newspaper and magazine articles, and pamphlets; and an extensive index are provided.

High school teachers and students will want to include Bennett's book as one of several texts to study African-American history.

4.75   **Bennett, Lerone, Jr.** *The Shaping of Black America.* Chicago: Johnson Publishing, 1975.

Bennett writes in a passionate, journalistic style that engages the reader in a personal exploration of black history. Although an abridged version of the ten chapters was previously published in *Ebony*, all of the chapters were rewritten for this book. Bennett acknowledges that it was his intention to write a developmental rather than a chronological general history on the forces that made black America what it is today.

In Bennett's dramatic and poetic first chapter, he vividly describes how America was forever transformed by the arrival of the first black captives on its shores:

> . . . No one knows the hour or the day of the black landing. But there is not the slightest doubt about the month. John Rolfe, who

betrayed Pocahontas and experimented with tobacco leaves, was there; and he said in a letter to his superiors, that the ship arrived "About the latter end of August" in 1619. Rolfe had a nose for nicotine, but he was obviously deficient in historical matters, for he added gratuitously that the ship "brought not anything but 20 and odd Negroes." Concerning which the most charitable thing to say is that Rolfe was probably pulling his superior's leg. For in the context of the meaning of America, it can be said without exaggeration that no ship ever called at an American port with a more important cargo. In the hold of that ship, in a manner of speaking, was the whole gorgeous panorama of black America, was jazz and the spirituals and the Funky Broadway. [Charlie Parker] Bird was there and Bigger [Bigger Thomas, the main character in Richard Wright's *Native Son*] and Malcolm and millions of other X's and crosses, along with Mahalia [Jackson] singing, Gwendolyn Brooks rhyming, Duke Ellington composing, James Brown grunting, Paul Robeson emoting, and Sidney Poitier walking. It was all there in embryo in the 160-ton ship.

The book is organized into two separate thematic sections. The first section, entitled "Foundations," focuses on the first generation of black founding fathers (and a few mothers) and explores the relationship between blacks and Indians. It also introduces black pioneers. The second section, "Directions," analyzes the history of black labor and black capital. In a chapter entitled "The World of the Slave," which appears in the first section, Bennett paints a picture of the physical, emotional, cultural, and psychological world of the slave community and the specific ways in which values, traditions, family life, love relationships, division of labor, religion, and relationships with "house" slaves were shaped, adapted, and developed in the midst of a brutal, oppressive system of slavery.

The final chapter, "Money, Merchants, and Markets," is a rare, comprehensive overview of the historical development of black businesses including a discussion of the connections between the financial workings of the black church, black fraternal orders, black banks and insurance companies, pioneer black entrepreneurs and inventors, and the influence of a rising black middle class on the development of a black political economy.

Complementing Bennett's spiritually inspired writing are the powerfully striking images of the renowned, deceased artist Charles White, whose ten illustrations adorn the book and tell a story of their own. An appendix of charts on black-owned firms (now outdated, but updated by the *Negro Almanac*), a bibliography of books and periodicals, and an index are provided.

High school history teachers will want to assign specific chapters of this book to their students to stimulate discussion of key themes. This book can also be used to compare and contrast the effectiveness and purposes of different historical writing styles.

4.76   Berry, Mary Frances, and John Blassingame. *Long Memory: The Black Experience in America.* New York and Oxford: Oxford University Press, 1982.

Unlike the more general narrative surveys of black history, Berry and Blassingame chose instead to write an interpretive history focusing on "themes and subjects most revealing of the complexities of the black experience in America." Drawing upon rich documentary sources of autobiographies, poetry, songs, folklore, novels, cartoons, plays, and speeches, the authors attempt to restore a human element and spirit to the dry facts of history, illustrative of Thomas Holt's suggestions in *Thinking Historically* (entry 3.67).

The eleven chapters are arranged thematically and emphasize struggle, survival, strength, and support through the traditional institutions of church, family, and schools. Each chapter is further divided by subtopics and is written in an informal, readable style. Chapter titles are reflective of the thematic and interpretive approach taken by the authors and include "Africa, Slavery, and the Shaping of Black Culture," "Family and Church: Enduring Institutions," "Sex and Racism," "Blacks and the Politics of Redemption," "The Economics of Hope and Despair," "American Archipelago: Blacks and Criminal Justice," and "Military Service and the Paradox of Loyalty." In the chapter on slavery, the authors underscore the role slaves played in transforming African cultural elements into a unique black American culture; highlight the differences between the religious beliefs of slaves and those of the slaveholders; and analyze the social structure of the slave community.

In the poignant chapter on sex and racism—subjects seldom addressed in more conventional general surveys—the authors emphasize how sexual exploitation and myth were used to justify the subordination of blacks. The final chapters draw from plays, poetry, and novels to demonstrate the role of black creative artists in encouraging protest.

A useful bibliography, arranged by chapter, a chronology of important dates, and an index are included.

Due to its interdisciplinary approach and highly readable and authoritative style, this important book should be used as a supplementary textbook in high school and college history and American studies courses.

4.77 Brawley, Benjamin G. *A Social History of the American Negro, Being a History of the Negro Problem in the United States Including a Study of the Republic of Liberia.* New York: Collier Books, 1970.

Brawley's classic text, originally published in 1920, was one of the first social histories on blacks. According to C. Eric Lincoln, who wrote the preface to the 1970 edition, the strength of this book comes from Brawley's viewing the "Negro problem" from an independent point of view at a time when independent thinking about black Americans was rare.

The chronological arrangement of the seventeen chapters begins with the arrival of black captives to America and concludes with "The Negro Problem." Brawley's independent thinking is demonstrated in the chapters on Negro response to colonization and organized agitation against colonization as well as a chapter on social progress from 1820 to 1860. Most useful as a study of black history from a 1920s perspective, this book can be compared and contrasted with contemporary perspectives on black history. A select bibliography and an index are included.

History instructors at the college level may wish to consult this classic text for comparative approaches to the study of black history.

4.78V Capital Cities ABC Video Entertainment. *In Search of the American Dream: A Story of the African-American Experience.* Videorecording, 6 parts, 312 min. Princeton, N.J.: Distr. Films for the Humanities and Sciences, 1991.

This series, hosted by the late Arthur Ashe, explores the social, political, cultural, and economic history of African Americans from 1619 to the present. By combining historical footage with contemporary interviews, the series documents a living history in six one-hour video cassettes.

The first tape, entitled *Resurrection*, follows the life of a black man from his hometown in Griffin, Georgia, to portray life in a southern town between 1900 and 1950. The second tape, *Stirrings*, focuses on the Civil Rights movement, while the third videotape, entitled *Origins*, takes the audience to Jamestown, Virginia, in 1619, when the first African captives arrived in America. *Saviors* provides a perspective on the role of Congress, the presidency, and the Supreme Court in legislating rights for blacks. The fifth video in the series, *Inspirations*, profiles neighborhood leaders and community activists and documents their work in addressing the problems that plague inner cities. In the final tape, *Liberty*, participants in the previous five programs discuss race relations in the 1990s.

This timely and comprehensive series is especially well suited for high school through adult audiences.

4.79P   Coar, Valencia Hollins. *A Century of Black Photographers, 1840–1960.* Providence, R.I.: Rhode Island School of Design, Museum of Art, 1983.

This exhibit catalog documents the work of twenty-nine black photographers whose historical images were rescued from obscurity. The curator indicates that it was impossible for the catalog and the exhibit to be all inclusive; instead, she highlights a limited number of photographers whose works are representative of the type of work produced by black photographers as a group. Unfortunately, the works of many of the nineteenth- and early-twentieth-century photographers have gone undocumented and may be lost forever.

Three eloquent essays and an introduction by the curator describe the technical, aesthetic, cultural, documentary, and historical value of and context for the photographers and their works. Deborah Johnson (now Deborah Willis), then photography curator at the Schomburg Center for Research in Black Culture, wrote an essay entitled "Black Photography: Contexts for Evolution"; and Michael Winston, a Howard University historian and administrator, wrote "Historical Consciousness and the Photographic Moment." The final essay, "Photography and Afro-American History," was written by Angela Davis. Ironically, none of the twenty-nine photographers represented in the exhibit is a woman.

The catalog is arranged chronologically by date of the image. Each image, which takes less than a full page, is accompanied by a detailed description of the photograph, including technical, aesthetic, and historical commentary. Most of the 150 images are of black families, events, or scenes, like those included in Willis-Thomas's (entry 4.93) book; but several photographs are of white families or individuals. Of significant historical interest are the images of Tuskegee University classes—printing, electronics, masonry, and chemistry—and portraits of famous black figures such as Booker T. Washington, W. E. B. Du Bois, Paul Laurence Dunbar, Dr. Charles Drew, and others.

The powerful images of Addison Scurlock, Prentice H. Polk, Moneta Sleet Jr., Gordon Parks, Roy DeCarava, Arthur Bedou, and many others are represented here. Willis-Thomas includes several of these photographers in her source book, but since Coar's book is an exhibit catalog, the images are more vivid, the contrast is better, and the photographs are printed on high-quality paper. Following the catalog portion is a biographical sketch of each photographer represented in the exhibit. Coar also includes a list of black photographers whose works are not represented in the catalog and a bibliography. In this list are several black women photographers whom Jeanne Moutoussamy-Ashe includes in her book on black women photographers, *Viewfinders* (see entry 4.91).

Junior high and high school history and art students would benefit greatly from studying the aesthetic and historical value of these photographs. Creative history, social studies, and art teachers can collaborate to design lesson plans on family and community history using the photographs as examples and students' own family pictures (collected and to be taken) as a laboratory.

4.80   **Foner, Philip.** *History of Black Americans.* 3v. Westport, Conn.: Greenwood Press, 1975–1983.

Foner, professor emeritus of history at Lincoln University, plans to write a six-volume series on the history of black Americans. Thus far, three of the six volumes have been published: vol. 1, *From Africa to the Emergence of the Cotton Kingdom*; vol. 2, *From the Emergence of the Cotton Kingdom to the Eve of the Compromise of 1850*; and vol. 3, *From the Compromise of 1850 to the End of the Civil War.* Foner was interested in writing a multivolume history of black Americans that would incorporate both his own research and the prodigious body of primary and secondary sources published between 1954 and 1975. Foner insists that single-volume histories neglect the black experience in the seventeenth and eighteenth centuries and instead focus on the nineteenth and twentieth centuries.

Volume 1 consists of twenty-five chapters that cover from the early African past to about 1849. The major themes explored in this volume include African cultural survivals in America; slave resistance during the middle passage through the 1820s; black and white protest against slavery; black participation in the American Revolution and in the War of 1812; black revolutions in the West Indies, Santo Domingo and North America; the status of free blacks in the North and South; and the emergence of separate black institutions including mutual-aid societies, black masons, churches, and schools.

The second volume covers free blacks during the Cotton Kingdom and the struggle against slavery, and analyzes the nature of the anti-slavery movement and the role of black abolitionists. In the first chapter, Foner provides an excellent, comprehensive historiographic essay on American historians and antebellum slavery and analyzes major slavery studies. The twenty-five chapters in this book cover the status of cotton as a crop and the impact of technology on the production of cotton, the nature of the slave community, urban and industrial slavery compared with rural slavery, the structure of plantation slavery including techniques of control and the role of religion, forms of slave resistance, free blacks in the South and North, the colonization controversy, the convention movement, the split in the antislavery movement, black abolitionists, the Underground Railroad, and blacks and antislavery political parties.

Volume 3 focuses on four major themes: black resistance to the pernicious Fugitive Slave Act of 1850; black emigration during the 1850s, which was, in part, a reaction to the effects of the Fugitive Slave Act; black participation in political struggles over slavery; and the role of blacks in the Civil War. Foner analyzes the history through the words and lives of blacks during this period.

This volume includes twenty-seven chapters that portray in vivid detail the drama behind the events and people who were responsible for shaping the passage of the Compromise of 1850 and the Fugitive Slave Act. Black reaction to the law in the form of protests, escapes to Canada, and emigration to Liberia and other countries is explored. A chapter is also devoted to the impact of the Fugitive Slave Act as a motivating factor for Harriet Beecher Stowe's *Uncle Tom's Cabin*. The remaining themes are meticulously investigated in the last ten chapters. Using slave testimony, journals, diaries, and many secondary sources, Foner provides detailed accounts of black protest against the Dred Scott decision, the relationship between blacks and white revolutionary abolitionist John Brown, blacks and the election of 1860, and the Civil War.

Due to the fact that this is to be a six-volume series, it is more detailed and comprehensive in its coverage than the single-volume general histories annotated in this chapter. Each volume includes an extensive bibliography of books and articles that is arranged by chapter and subtopic within each chapter. An index for each volume is also provided.

Although most useful for undergraduate history and American studies students and faculty, senior high school teachers also should use this book as a curriculum development resource, especially for seventeenth- and eighteenth-century black history.

4.81 **Franklin, John Hope, and Alfred A. Moss Jr.** *From Slavery to Freedom: A History of Black Americans.* 6th ed. New York: Alfred A. Knopf, 1988.

Franklin's renowned, comprehensive work was the first general survey of black history since Woodson's *The Negro in Our History* (1922), and perhaps the most widely used general survey of African-American history published thus far. Originally written in 1947, this scholarly source, now in its sixth edition, outlines the history of African Americans from the African beginnings to the present. Franklin's purpose is to "interpret the critical forces and personalities that have shaped the history of Negroes in an objective way." In the preface to the fifth edition, Franklin respectfully acknowledges the work of Carter G. Woodson, Charles Wesley, W. E. B. Du Bois, and others whose research he has drawn upon.

The sixth edition is the first edition coauthored by historian Alfred Moss "to assist in giving the new edition the freshness that it requires and deserves." Changes in this edition include the omission of chapters on African, Caribbean, and Latin American history due to the increase in new, quality works in these areas, and the addition of a chapter taking the reader through the Reagan years.

Included among the twenty-four chronologically arranged chapters are seven chapters devoted to the slave trade and slavery. Chapters on philanthropy and self-help, race and the nation, the Harlem Renaissance, and two worlds of race illustrate that the scope of the text extends beyond traditional history surveys. Throughout the book, Franklin and Moss attempt to give proper consideration to the work of outstanding persons and the masses. More attention is given, for example, to women and women's organizations than in comparable survey texts. An extensive section of bibliographical notes arranged by chapter and an index are included.

This book is an important text for high school history teachers and students and teachers at the undergraduate level, especially if used with other interpretive texts such as Berry and Blassingame's *Long Memory* (entry 4.76).

4.82 **Giddings, Paula.** *When and Where I Enter: The Impact of Black Women on Race and Sex in America.* New York: William Morrow, 1984.

Giddings's narrative history of black women from the seventeenth century to the present is both illuminating and rich in revealing their values and concerns and roles as women and African Americans. Drawing upon primary sources and interviews with black women, Giddings describes the nature and meaning of the experiences of black women through their ideas and thoughts.

Themes explored in the book include the relationship between sexism and racism, the relationship between the progress of the race and feminism, and the ways in which black women transcended double discrimination through education and training.

The twenty chapters are arranged chronologically by chapter, then thematically within each chapter. In the first chapter, Giddings dramatically reveals the life and work of Ida B. Wells-Barnett, antilynching crusader and journalist, and highlights how Wells-Barnett's life intersected with that of another black woman of achievement, Mary Church Terrell. Themes of morality, slavery, and resistance are investigated in the second chapter entitled "Casting of the Die." (These themes are more fully developed in books by Jacqueline Jones [entry 4.88] and Deborah Gray White [entry 5.106].)

In the chapter on black women during Reconstruction, the roles of black men and women are explored within the context of work and family. Giddings also discusses the debate over the support of the Fifteenth Amendment by black women leaders Sojourner Truth and Frances Ellen Watkins Harper. The remaining three chapters in part 1 discuss (1) the sexual exploitation of black women by white men and black mothers' desperate attempts to protect their young daughters from the licentiousness of white men; (2) the black women's club movement, the struggle of their female leaders to pursue a professional career, political and personal life, and the conflicts between black male and female leaders over women's roles and rights; and (3) the contributions of black women to the suffrage movement.

Part 2 of the book documents the achievements of black women in education, health, politics, and social welfare, and provides a chronical of their struggles against racial and sexual oppression. This part takes a look at the role organizations such as the National Association of Colored Women and the YWCA played in assisting black women and families to adjust to harsh city life. The suffrage campaign and the relationships and tensions between black and white women suffragettes are also explored.

Subsequent chapters in part 2 include a discussion of the image of black women in the years following World War I as revealed through the lives of Madame C. J. Walker, who developed products for the treatment of black hair, and as portrayed in the works of black women novelists Zora Neale Hurston, Nella Larsen, and Jessie Fauset. The activism of black women in Garvey's Universal Negro Improvement Association is also examined. Two chapters are devoted to the remarkable life and work of Mary McLeod Bethune, educator and founder of Bethune-Cookman College and a member of Franklin Delano Roosevelt's "Black Cabinet."

The final chapters of part 3 examine the often-overlooked role and involvement of black foremothers and black women such as Rosa Parks, Ella Baker, Fannie Lou Hamer, Angela Davis, and Jean Smith in the Civil Rights movement, as well as investigate the forces that bred discontent of black women in the women's movement.

As the only general book on the history of black women in the United States, Giddings's work fills a gap in African-American historiography. Its highly readable, personable style will capture the attention of the general reader as well as high school teachers and students of history and social studies, and undergraduate students of history and women's studies.

4.83   Goode, Kenneth G. *From Africa to the United States and Then: A Concise Afro-American History.* Glenview, Ill.: Scott, Foresman, 1976.

Intended as a core text for high school African-American or American history teachers and for undergraduate survey courses, Goode's book is both highly readable and succinct. Each of the chronologically arranged chapters is approximately five or six pages in length. West African origins through the Civil Rights movement and the Nixon years are given coverage. High school students will appreciate the chapter subtopics that summarize the main facts and points covered.

References are provided at the end of each chapter; a section of general references is included at the end of the book. There are also a chronological table of events and an index. Although Robert Harris's *Teaching African-American History* (entry 3.63) updates Goode's book by using recent scholarship in the field and provides an excellent historical framework for purposes of interpretation, it lacks Goode's detail. When the two books are used in concert with, for example, Katz's book of primary documents (entry 4.96), high school teachers will find them most useful as background reading.

4.84   Harding, Vincent. *The Other American Revolution.* Los Angeles and Atlanta: Center for Afro-American Studies and Institute of the Black World, 1980.

Harding's interpretive survey of black Americans traces the themes of struggle, protest, resistance, and transformation from African roots to the Civil Rights movement. In summarizing the purpose of the struggle for freedom, Harding eloquently presents his case: "to fulfill broken promises of the Declaration of Independence . . . in order to create a new human nation by transforming society."

Instead of a chronological, narrative general survey of events and personalities in black history, Harding structures the thirty chapters around these common themes of struggle, transformation, and hope. Each chapter is written in a subjective, journalistic style and is imbued with spiritual undertones, suggesting that Harding's passion for the subject emanates, in part, from his personal involvement in and commitment to the Civil Rights movement.

Events, institutions, organizations, and individuals that demonstrated protest and resistance are highlighted in the chapters; therefore, great significance is given to the meaning of the slave rebellions promoted by Nat Turner, Gabriel Prosser, and Cinque; [David] *Walker's Appeal*; Ida B. Wells-Barnett's antilynching crusade; Henry McNeil Turner; and the more contemporary struggles of Paul Robeson, W. E. B. Du Bois, Malcolm X, and others. In the final chapter, Harding suggests that the larger meaning of the struggle for freedom is to create a new economic ordering of society's priorities—to provide jobs, housing, and health care for all.

Although no footnotes or index is provided, Harding includes an extensive bibliography. This book is perhaps most valuable when used as a supplementary text to provide high school and college-level history students with a different perspective on the meaning of black history.

4.85   **Harding, Vincent.** *There Is a River: the Black Struggle for Freedom in America.* New York and London: Harcourt, Brace, Jovanovich, 1981.

In this second interpretive history, Harding expands upon the themes of protest and transformation presented in *The Other American Revolution* (entry 4.84) by using the metaphor of the river to illustrate the powerful movement of black history—from bondage, despair, pain, and inequality toward justice, equity, and self-determination. Harding unapologetically describes this book as an "experiment in history, solidarity, and hope . . . an attempt to discover and develop sources of creative tension among my responsibilities as a historian, my commitment to human liberation, and my urgent determination to keep faith. . . ." To Harding, history is purposeful in that it provides readers with a version of black people coming together to create a new future, much like the freedom fighters in the Civil Rights movement.

Again, Harding acknowledges that this book is both objective and subjective in its approach to redefining the history of the black struggle for freedom and justice. Unlike a general survey history text, Harding emphasizes the development of creative black initiative and seeks to answer these questions: Beyond protest, what was the freedom sought by black Americans? What were the sources of their vision and hope?

The sixteen chronologically arranged chapters begin with the struggle of the African captives and take the reader through Reconstruction. Harding provides readers with a detailed panorama of the events, forces, people, and institutions that represented the move toward freedom, including the abolitionist movement, the Fugitive Slave Act, the Dred Scott decision, Black Codes, civil disobedience, and illegal schools. Oral histories, journals, periodicals, and monographs are some of the primary and secondary sources Harding draws upon to resurrect this history. Illustrations, detailed endnotes arranged by chapter, a bibliography, and an index add to the authoritativeness of the book.

High school history teachers and undergraduate students will find this text both inspiring and eloquent, especially when used to stimulate discussion about the contemporary values and uses of history and to raise questions about the experiences the historian brings to the writing of history.

4.86 Hine, Darlene Clark, ed. *Black Women in United States History: From Colonial Times through the Twentieth Century.* Vols. 1–8. Brooklyn, N.Y.: Carlson Publishing, 1990.

These eight volumes of a sixteen-volume set represents the most comprehensive range of scholarship on black women yet compiled within one source. All the articles have been published previously in journals, but this source brings them together in a loose thematic format. The first four volumes include articles on black women's history in the nineteenth century; volumes 5 through 8 cover black women's history in the twentieth century.

Articles in the first four volumes can be categorized as biography and specific themes. Biographical articles on prominent black women abolitionists, medical doctors, educators, and others include Harriet Tubman, Sojourner Truth, Phillis Wheatley, Sarah Parker Remond, Susan McKinney Steward, Mary Ann Shadd, Pauline Hopkins, Fannie Jackson Coppin, Charlotte Forten, Edmonia Lewis, Harriet Powers, and Ida B. Wells-Barnett.

Themes explored in these eighty-five essays include the slave experiences of black women, structure of the family, sex roles, the nature of the women's slave resistance, the mortality of slave women and children, entry into professions, religion and the role of women in the development of churches and benevolent societies, the lives and work of black women in community organizations, and black women in literature. The authors of the eighty-five essays included in volumes 1 through 4 are scholars in their respective fields: Jacqueline Jones (entry 4.88), Deborah Gray White (entry 5.106), Elizabeth Fox-Genovese, James O. Horton, Bettina Aptheker, Darlene Clark Hine, Dorothy Porter, and Ruth Bogin.

Among the themes explored in volumes 5 through 8 are black women workers, voting rights, black women's organizations and clubs, community work, and black women in the professions. There are profiles of individual women, such as nursing pioneer Mabel Staupers; poets Alice Dunbar-Nelson and Gwendolyn Brooks; civil rights activists Fannie Lou Hamer, Rosa Parks, and Ella Baker; educators Mary McLeod Bethune, Nannie Helen Burroughs, Anna Julia Cooper, and Mary Louise Baldwin; Dorothy Bolden, organizer of domestic workers; and author Era Bell Thompson.

The essays in each volume are arranged alphabetically by the author's last name; unfortunately, the date each article was published is not included in the table of contents. Footnotes are provided at the end of each article, although there is no general index or note on contributors at the end of each volume. These volumes are highly recommended for high school and undergraduate teachers of history and women's studies, who will find the articles a convenient and easily accessible way to enhance their knowledge of black women's history.

4.87   Hughes, Langston, Milton Meltzer, and C. Eric Lincoln. *A Pictorial History of Blackamericans.* 5th ed. New York: Crown Publishers, 1983.

First published by Hughes and Meltzer in 1956 under the title *A Pictorial History of Negro Americans*, this book combines text with photographs, reproductions of drawings, cartoons, playbills, title pages of books by African-American authors, and primary documents to portray the history of African Americans. Updated from the 1973 edition by all three authors, the book covers African-American history from 1619 to 1983. The graphic representation of salient events, personalities, locations, and significant organizations in African-American history is an effective tool for helping students bridge the gap between historical (and often "cold") facts and dates and the real people who created and participated in the given historical moment.

The nine chapters are arranged chronologically; within chapters, sections are arranged thematically. The book is arranged in such a way that it can be used as a reference tool by consulting the index for the appropriate subjects or topics. Biographies of renowned African-American and white abolitionists, African-American inventors, educators, politicians, artists, writers, and military personnel are interwoven throughout the book. The final chapters on the Civil Rights movement include bone-chilling photographs of the heinous violence perpetrated against African-American and white freedom fighters and demonstrators. The last section highlights contemporary topics including the black Muslims, historically black colleges, African-American studies, the black church, and African-Americans and television.

An index and picture credits are provided. Hughes's work is especially appealing to the general reader and high school history and social studies students.

A revised, updated version of this book is scheduled for publication in February 1995. It will be written by Meltzer and Lincoln plus Jon Michael Spencer.

4.88   **Jones, Jacqueline.** *Labor of Love, Labor of Sorrow: Black Women, Work, and the Family from Slavery to Freedom.* New York: Basic Books, 1985.

Jones's study of black women and work focuses on slaves and on postslavery rural and working-class women and agricultural workers in the South. Excluded from this book are free black women in the antebellum South and nineteenth-century northern women. According to Jones, recent scholarship on women's history has tended to focus almost exclusively on northeastern urban black women; therefore, her study fills in some important historical gaps in the literature. Jones intends for her study to open a wider discussion on the interrelationships of race, sex, and class.

In the most comprehensive study on black women and work written thus far, Jones explores their contributions in the area of home and public welfare and in the labor force as domestics and manual laborers. She sets out to destroy the myth of the black matriarchy by establishing the fact that by any conventional standards of power—wealth, autonomy, control over workers, votes, inheritances—black women had only informal authority as spiritual counselors and healers.

The first two chapters of the book cover the slavery period; Jones describes the work of black women in both the field and the house, and the sexual division of labor in the slave quarters. For example, Jones concludes that black bondswomen were assigned to work in the field without consideration for their gender, yet these women fulfilled the duties of motherhood as a way of controlling and defining their lives. Black women, then, worked alongside their husbands and fathers, although, unlike the male slaves, they were rarely trained to serve as artisans or mechanics. Moreover, there appears to have been little difference in the punishment of male and female slaves. The relationship between the slaveholder and the female slave was complicated by sexual exploitation.

Household labor of bondswomen, however, was not less strenuous than field labor. House slaves were under closer scrutiny than were field laborers, and female slaves who worked in the fields were less likely to be subjected to the sexual advances of white planters. Divorce petitions examined by Jones revealed that wives of slaveholders were jealous over their husbands' sexual exploitation of bondswomen; thus the female house slave often felt the brunt of the wife's wrath.

Within the slave quarters, the forces that were most disruptive to black family life were the separation of families and the sexual violation of black women. Unfortunately, fathers, sons, or husbands of bondswomen usually were powerless to protect families from both of these devastating forces. Jones also discusses the attitudes of bondsmen toward the work of the bondswomen.

During the Civil War, approximately 14 percent of the black male population fought in the Union Army. The welfare of their families was a major concern of black male troops, especially since, in the absence of their men, bondswomen sometimes were subjected to even more cruel treatment at the hands of the slaveholders, according to Jones's study. Some women even followed their husbands to the front lines.

The remaining six chapters of Jones's book concentrate on black women during and after Reconstruction (through 1980). Common themes include the attempt by black working women to subordinate the demands of their employers to the needs of their own families; the struggle to define their lives in their own terms and to "live their lives apart from racism without being oblivious or untouched by it"; and the special gratification black women gained from raising and caring for children, a part of their lives over which they exercised some degree of control.

Jones discusses black women's work as domestics and in urban southern factories from 1850 to 1915. In southern tobacco factories, for example, black women performed racially segregated tasks; both gender and race discrimination limited their opportunities. Once black families had migrated to northern cities, even though black women worked primarily as domestics, they contributed as much financially to the household as their men, who were shut out of factory work due to white employers' preference for hiring white immigrants. Black women, too, were excluded from clerical and sales work even though their education was, in many cases, better than or equal to that of their white immigrant counterparts.

During World War II, factory jobs offered higher wages and shorter working hours, which allowed black women to spend more time with their families. Jones explains that higher factory wages affected wages in domestic work. In the chapter on the Civil Rights movement and the women's movement, Jones contrasts racism and sexism experienced by black women with the interests of white women who were just beginning to enter the labor force in large numbers. In the final chapter, Jones explores black women's involvement and participation in the Civil Rights movement and the roots of black feminism.

An epilogue, appendixes, notes, a ten-page selected bibliography, and an index are provided, as are numerous photographs of black women laborers and slaves.

This work should be required reading for history instructors at high school and undergraduate levels.

4.89 Logan, Rayford W. *The Negro in the United States.* Vol. 1, *A History to 1945.* New York: Van Nostrand Reinhold, 1970.

————, and Michael R. Winston. *The Ordeal of Democracy.* Vol. 2. New York: Van Nostrand Reinhold, 1970.

Logan and Winston were history professors at Howard University when they coauthored this concise two-volume introductory general history of the Negro. Volume 1 includes seven chapters that cover from slavery and emancipation to World War II. The seven chapters in volume 2 cover the era from post–World War II through the Civil Rights movement. Significant primary documents are provided as supplementary material in both volumes.

Each chapter is further divided by subtopics to aid the reader in following the text. Sample primary documents contained in volume 1 are the Emancipation Proclamation and the Thirteenth, Fourteenth, and Fifteenth Amendments. According to the authors, the purpose of volume 2 is to analyze the struggle of Negroes to overcome economic and social obstacles through legal and political means. The second volume begins with a historical overview of the period covered, including a discussion of the status and influence of foreign affairs on domestic issues. Primary documents from this period include the text of the Civil Rights Acts of 1964 and 1965, the Voting Rights Act of 1965, and the Kerner Commission Report; speeches by A. Phillip Randolph, Martin

Luther King Jr., and Malcolm X; and occupational and economic statistics of Negro and white workers, 1964 and 1965.

A selected bibliography and an index are provided in both volumes. High school teachers will find these volumes useful due to their authoritativeness and length, but they will need to supplement them with more contemporary and interpretive works.

4.90 Meier, August, and Elliott Rudwick. *From Plantation to Ghetto.* New York: Hill and Wang, 1970.

In this analytical, interpretive, and interdisciplinary history of African Americans, Meier and Rudwick assume readers have a basic knowledge of the facts of American history. According to the authors, this book emphasizes the role of African Americans as creators: how they contributed to developing institutions in their community to meet their needs, patterns of interracial violence, and protest movements in the black community.

Major themes are discussed broadly in the seven chronologically arranged chapters. For example, in the first chapter on West African heritage and African-American history, the authors analyze ways African Americans perceived and thought about Africa, investigate the degree to which African culture and traditions survived in America, explore the differences in the way slavery was practiced in West Africa and the United States, and describe the resistance of captives during the middle passage.

Especially interesting is the discussion on the reaction of the free black community to legal restrictions on voting rights and the courts during the late eighteenth and early nineteenth centuries. The role of the church, fraternal and mutual benefit organizations, the black self-help movement in education, and the work of skilled craftspersons and unskilled laborers in addition to the racial ideologies of free African Americans are analyzed.

A selected bibliography and an index are provided. This book is geared toward the college student and the general reader but is also appropriate for high school teachers.

4.91P Moutoussamy-Ashe, Jeanne. *Viewfinders: Black Women Photographers.* New York: Dodd, Mead, 1968.

This unique historical book rescues from obscurity the contributions and works of African-American women photographers. The author, herself an accomplished photographer, is the widow of Arthur Ashe, the tennis star, author, and social activist who died of AIDS in 1993.

Moutoussamy-Ashe focuses on pioneer rather than contemporary black women photographers. She explains in her introduction that the criteria used in selecting "accomplished" photographers refers to "their ability to document their community and personal lives."

The book is divided into five parts that are arranged chronologically. The narration includes biographical data on each photographer; particular attention is given to the professional career of each woman. A photo of the photographer, if available, and several pages of her photographic images are provided.

As in DeborahWillis-Thomas's work (entry 4.93), a full range of images is represented in Moutoussamy-Ashe's book. The photographers documented African-American life in their own communities, including church choirs, special events and occasions, black families, individual women in the community, black-owned businesses, musicians, and social clubs.

Unlike their male counterparts, few black women had opportunities to serve as photographers for famous black leaders, so many of their images are of African Americans in their immediate communities, and many of the portraits are of women. The exceptions to this are Valeria "Mikki" Ferrill, whose credits include published work in magazines such as *Ebony, Jet,* and *Time*; Louise Martin, who was one of the national press cadre to cover the funeral of Dr. Martin Luther King; and Michelle Agins, the official photographer of the late Chicago mayor, Harold Washington.

Following the profiles of individual photographers and their works is a bio-bibliography of all the photographers included in the book. Also included are general listings of black women photographers from 1860 to 1960 and from 1960 to 1980. A geographical index, footnotes, a selected bibliography, and a general index are provided.

Largely due to the quality of the paper used, the photographic images reproduced in Moutoussamy-Ashe's book are of a higher quality than those included in Willis-Thomas's work. Junior high through high school students and teachers will find the biographical data and photographs in this book to be a powerful visual history of black America. Hopefully, this book will inspire them to pursue further information on the pioneering African-American women documented here.

4.92 Quarles, Benjamin. *The Negro in the Making of America.* New York and London: Collier Books, 1987.

Quarles's book was first published in 1964 and was intended to provide the general reader with an up-to-date survey of black history in the United States. This best-selling classic covers major historical periods, events, personalities, and forces that shaped the African-American experience. Like Berry and Blassingame's *Long Memory* (entry 4.76) and Meier and Rudwick's book (entry 4.90), Quarles's book is interdisciplinary and focuses on how blacks responded to their condition and struggled toward emancipation and equality.

The twelve chapters are arranged chronologically and span the years 1619 through 1986. Considerable coverage is given to W. E. B. Du Bois, Frederick Douglass—Quarles's dissertation was devoted to the life of Douglass—black participation in the Civil War and world wars, slave revolts, and the Harlem Renaissance. The portrayal of blacks in the media, the emergence of all-black plays during the 1940s and 1950s, and the influence of the music of black Americans are examples of topics not usually covered in general surveys.

Coverage of black women in this survey is reserved for the last chapter, which is entitled "Widening Horizons" and covers the period from 1970 to 1986. Black-owned businesses, the effects of Nixon and Reagan Supreme Court appointees, black laborers and blacks in the professions, educational reforms and progress, and black achievements in the arts comprise other nonconventional topics covered in the last chapter. A selected bibliography and an index are supplied.

This text will provide new perspectives on curriculum development. History and American studies students and teachers at the high school and college levels will want to use this book for its exhaustiveness and highly readable style.

4.93P **Willis-Thomas, Deborah.** *Black Photographers, 1840–1940: An Illustrated Bio-Bibliography.* New York: Garland Publishing, 1985.

This valuable source book by the former chief curator of photography at the Schomburg Center for Research in Black Culture is broader in scope than its title might indicate. The first third of the book is arranged chronologically by the name of the photographer. This portion identifies books and articles in which the photographers' images appear. It also cites other works about them. The remaining two-thirds of the book is devoted to reproductions of some of the photographers' works. These reproductions dramatically document a range of scenes from black American life from 1840 to 1940.

Among the images that breathe life into history for junior high students and adults are portraits of famous black writers, musicians, entertainers, and leaders; Tuskegee Institute students in carpentry and dressmaking classes; recreational scenes in Mississippi; vaudeville stars; black women's organizations; black families in the North and South;

the famous Schomburg reading room in the New York Public Library; a 1924 portrait of black women basketball players; and members of the Alpha Phi Alpha black fraternity in 1909.

The renowned and obscure photographers of these exquisite works include James Van DerZee, P. H. Polk, Richard Samuel Roberts, Austin Hansen, Gordon Parks, Roy DeCarava, Frank Cloud, Morgan and Marvin Smith, James Latimer Allen, E. Elcha, Walter Baker, R. E. Mercer, Addison Scurlock, Arthur Bedou, and C. M. Battey. Unfortunately, the works of black women photographers are not included among these images; however, information on a few of them is provided in the first part of the book. Of course, Moutoussamy-Ashe's book fills in this gap (see entry 4.91P). The photographic images are then followed by name and geographical indexes and an index of photographic collections. A group of twenty-three of the most striking images collected in this book have been reproduced in a postcard collection that is now available for purchase in many museum shops.

In addition to the obvious uses for these images as supplementary, creative teaching aids in history classes, curriculum specialists, social studies teachers, and art instructors may find ways to use photography books such as this one to introduce junior high and high school students to careers and hobbies in photography.

Documentary Histories

4.94 **Aptheker, Herbert, ed.** *A Documentary History of the Negro People in the United States.* 3v. Secaucus, N.J.: Citadel Press, 1973.

Aptheker's comprehensive collection of primary documents on black history was originally published in 1951 and was one of the first sources of its kind. The documents were selected from the archives, libraries, and museums of the Schomburg Center for Research in Black Culture; the New York Public Library; the Library of Congress; and Atlanta, Fisk, Howard, Tulane, and Columbia Universities. The source and significance of individual documents are described in the editor's comments preceding each section.

The documents represent a wide array of materials produced by blacks. Volume 1 includes 257 documents, spanning the colonial period through the Civil War. It contains such varied sources as petitions for freedom, protests against kidnapping and the slave trade, the Negro's response to colonization, an early Negro educational society (1818), a Negro woman on women's rights, two militant pamphlets by Negroes, proceedings from the first annual National Negro Convention, a slave auction described by a slave, and the minutes from an African Methodist Episcopal Church conference.

The 154 documents in volume 2 encompass the years 1910 through 1932. Documents by and about Booker T. Washington, W. E. B. Du Bois, Marcus Garvey, and the Scottsboro Boys; minutes from the National Association of Colored Women's Clubs and the NAACP; protests against the film *Birth of a Nation*; antilynching speeches; editorials and newspaper articles; and writings by Walter White on racist textbooks are but a few of the eclectic sources included in this volume. These documents raise many questions and discussions about the conditions, motivations, and aspirations of the creators of the documents, both individually and collectively.

The third and final volume begins with 1933 and concludes with the end of World War II. The documents selected for this volume cover segregation, education, the role of black writers and artists, the black family, black workers, civil rights, riots in Harlem, race relations in Puerto Rico and the Virgin Islands, and black participation and segregation in World War II. As in volumes 1 and 2, Aptheker provides a small, representative sample of documents by and about black women, including an article written by a black female doctor on birth control in Harlem and an article by a black domestic. An index is provided in each volume.

High school and college-level history teachers should consult this major work to supplement and complement the textbooks they use.

4.95   Frazier, Thomas. *Afro-American History: Primary Sources.* New York: Harcourt, Brace, and World, 1970.

Frazier describes this collection of primary documents as history through documents. There are far fewer documents represented here than in Aptheker's three volumes (entry 4.94): fifty-five compared with more than five hundred. With a few exceptions, Frazier presents the documents in their entirety.

The documents are divided into fourteen chronological periods, with each section preceded by a brief historical introduction that gives its specific historical context. Descriptions of black life, speeches and writings by black leaders, and position papers of black organizations are provided. To illustrate different forms of activism and protest, selected spirituals, poetry by Harlem Renaissance writers, and freedom songs are included.

The works of only three women are represented here: Mary Reynolds, a slave; Charlotte Forten, an educator; and Ella Baker, a civil rights activist. Writings by more renowned blacks such as Nat Turner, David Walker, Frederick Douglass, Booker T. Washington, W. E. B. Du Bois, Whitney Young, and Stokely Carmichael are featured.

Each section concludes with an extensive annotated bibliography. A general bibliographic essay is provided at the end of the book. Although the scope of the documents selected is narrower than that of Aptheker's book, high school teachers may find this source more useful for reading, analyzing, and examining documents of greater length.

4.96   Katz, William Loren. *Eyewitness: The Negro in American History.* New York: Pitman, 1974.

Katz's highly readable and still timely documentary history was designed for use in high school history classes. Motivated by inadequate and distorted coverage of black history in American history textbooks and in high school courses in general, Katz began searching for supplementary material with eyewitness accounts. In the 1960s, he received grants to conduct research at the Schomburg Library, the Library of Congress, the Moorland-Spingarn Research Center, and the National Archives to choose a wide range of documents for inclusion in a textbook for high school teachers. High school history students assisted Katz in selecting many of the documents included in *Eyewitness*.

The twenty chapters of text, documents, and pictures cover the period from the African background to the Civil Rights movement. Each chapter begins with a ten- to fifteen-page introduction that is presented in an appealing and informative style. Excerpts of several primary documents follow the narrative introductions as do numerous illustrations and photographs of individuals and events in Negro history. Most of the documents included were created by slaves and freed people in search of emancipation and equality. Slave codes, antislavery protests, documents by and about famous personalities, slave inventors, colonization, education, civil rights, segregation, the Underground Railroad, women's rights, the Civil War from the perspectives of Negro troops, voting rights, the Freedmen's Bureau, the Great Migration, lynching and riots, the Harlem Renaissance, and World War II to the contemporary Civil Rights movement represent the wide range of topics covered. A selected bibliography and an index are provided.

High school teachers may choose to use Katz's text for the thoughtful narrative introductions and the range of documents included but should supplement its use with either Aptheker's or Frazier's book (entries 4.94 and 4.95, respectively), either of which provides complete documents or longer excerpts.

4.97 **Lerner, Gerda, ed.** *Black Women in White America: A Documentary History.* New York: Random House, 1963.

No discussion of primary documents on black American history is complete without a documentary history of black women. Although Lerner's book is thirty years old, it is one of the first general documentary histories of black women, and therefore it is a classic. Many documents included in this text were previously unpublished, and include works created by many renowned and distinguished but neglected black women.

Particularly noteworthy is Lerner's lengthy preface detailing the problems that confront the study of black women's history—for example, the double "invisibility" of black women due to racism and sexism. The documents of black women are often buried in manuscript collections with no indexes or references and, thus, are seldom edited or published. Few biographies or scholarly interpretive works have been researched or written about black women. Of course, since 1963, works on black women's history have grown dramatically, although several critical gaps exist in the scholarly literature. (See Darlene Clark Hine's *Black Women in United States History,* entry 4.86.)

Lerner provides excerpts from letters, diaries, speeches, journals, autobiographies, and newspaper and magazine articles to personalize the experiences, perspectives, and contributions of black women from slavery to 1970. Each of the ten chapters is subdivided into several topics; each chapter and subtopic is preceded by a valuable introductory essay or historical commentary. Topics include slavery, family, slave resistance, lynching, domestic and factory work, sexual exploitation by white men, discrimination, racism, sexism, racial pride, community and organizational service, education, and womanhood.

Through the voices of Fannie J. Coppin, Maria Steward, Septima Clark, Ida B. Wells-Barnett, Susan Mapps Douglass, Charlotte Forten, Susie King Taylor, Mary McLeod Bethune, Mary Church Terrell, Harriet Tubman, Ella Baker, Shirley Chisholm, Sojourner Truth, Daisy Bates, Anna Arnold Hedgeman, Anne Moody, and Pauli Murray, readers learn of the struggles and triumphs experienced by black women in America.

Also included are an essay on sources, an introduction by Mary McLeod Bethune, and bibliographical notes. Unfortunately, no index is provided.

No history curriculum at the high school or college level would be complete without a documentary history of black women by either Lerner or Dorothy Sterling (entry 5.135).

4.98   **Meltzer, Milton, ed.** *In Their Own Words: A History of the American Negro.* Vol. 1: 1619–1865. Vol. 2: 1865–1916. Vol. 3: 1916–1965. New York: Thomas Y. Crowell, 1965.

Specifically designed for use by high school students, Meltzer's book contains easy-to-read, concise excerpts from letters, speeches, diaries, autobiographies, newspapers, and pamphlets of famous and lesser-known black voices. A blend of narrative introduction, documents, and photographs provides an effective way to introduce students to Negro history. The author explains that the purpose of the book is to help readers understand what American Negroes felt, thought, did, suffered, and enjoyed.

The three volumes contain information on the lives of slave and free Negroes, slave narratives, documents about protest and the struggle to gain freedom, lynching reports by Ida B. Wells-Barnett, and documents on education by Daniel Payne and others. They also include articles written about the Harlem Renaissance, and works by W. E. B. Du Bois, Richard Wright, Langston Hughes, A. Phillip Randolph, Martin Luther King Jr., and Fannie Lou Hamer. Each volume concludes with an annotated reading list and an index.

CHAPTER FIVE

Sources by Chronological Period, from Slavery to Reconstruction

A S THEY ENDEAVORED TO RESEARCH AND INTERPRET THE African-American experience from a new perspective, it is perhaps no small coincidence that several prominent contemporary scholars of African-American history found in Ralph Ellison's eloquent language a voice for their own historical quest:

Can a people live and develop for over three hundred years simply by reacting? Are American Negroes simply the creation of white men, or have they at least helped to create themselves out of what they found around them?

. . . People are more than the sum of [their] brutalization.

—Ellison, *Shadow and Act*, New York: Random House, 1964; and "A Very Stern Discipline," *Harper's Magazine* 234 (Mar. 1967): 84.

In this chapter, recent sources that reflect African Americans as "more than the sum of their brutalization" are presented. Chapter 5 provides an overview of general sources by chronological period and is divided into two major parts: (1) sources on slavery and slave resistance and the participation of African-Americans in the American Revolution, and (2) sources on the Civil War, emancipation, and Reconstruction.

Books published prior to 1975 generally are excluded; exceptions are a few historical and classic works. Sources that are limited to a specific state or city are also omitted except in cases where the book has implications for national trends. Books by and about black women

91

are appropriately integrated into the various chronological sections rather than placed in a separate area. Finally, primary documents are included at the end of the appropriate chronological period in a separately alphabetized list.

Slavery and Slave Resistance

The literature is replete with works on the study of slavery—the institution, its origins, and its causes. The focus of African-American history, according to Thomas Holt, "is more likely concerned with explaining how slavery affected the slave. . . . There can be no adequate history of the master that neglects the slave and vice-versa" (see entry 3.66).

Books included in this first section of chapter 5 center around slavery as the formative experience of African-American life and culture to provide readers with a general, critical, theoretical but practical framework for understanding the lives, culture, and ethos of the people behind the institution. Therefore, specific narratives of individual slaves are omitted, but general slave narratives or anthologies are provided as examples of primary source materials. Sources on slave revolts and escape through the Underground Railroad—two common forms of slave resistance—are included, as are works on the involvement of African Americans in the American Revolution and the Civil War.

A brief historiography of slavery provides a context for a discussion of the books in this first section. As noted in the introduction to chapter 3, slavery studies began with Ulrich B. Phillips's *American Negro Slavery* (1918), a work that contemporary historians now acknowledge portrayed a racist and inaccurate view of slavery as a benign institution in which slaves suffered little and rebellions and resistance were infrequent. In fact, Phillips went so far as to claim among slavery's redeeming characteristics the "civilization" of the "barbarians" who were afforded an opportunity for redemption. Although Phillips's research into plantation records written primarily by slaveholders was meticulous, his racism superseded his objectivity and scholarship.

Not until 1955 were Phillips's views repudiated by Kenneth Stampp in *The Peculiar Institution: Slavery in the Antebellum South*, a work that demonstrated that slavery was a labor system that employed any means necessary to make a profit. He successfully dispelled Phillips's myths about the conditions of slavery and the reaction of slaves—in the form of resistance and rebellions—to the brutalities of the system. Stampp posited in his preface that "Negroes are only white men with black skins, nothing more, nothing less," a perspective that denied the presence of a distinctive black culture and ethos created by blacks, in part from their unique experiences as slaves in the United States.

In his book *Slavery: A Study of American Institutional and Intellectual Life* (1959), Stanley Elkins insists that slaves did indeed possess a personality that was shaped by the slave experience. By drawing upon existing research using comparative studies of slavery in the United States and Latin America, Elkins characterizes the slave "personality" as "Sambo"—a shiftless, lazy, obsequious individual. Indeed, according to Elkins, the only person of significance in the slave's life was the master.

Subsequent slavery studies began to articulate and portray a slave culture that assisted slaves to adapt to the system but also to shape positive and sustaining kinship and family bonds and to create a slave culture that thrived and contributed to the making of American culture.

Each of the studies discussed in the first subsection (entries 5.99–106) builds upon and enhances readers' understanding of the other yet makes a distinctive contribution to the literature on the period of slavery. These studies include works by John Blassingame, Eugene Genovese, Herbert Gutman, Lawrence Levine, Leslie Owens, and Deborah Gray White.

The second subsection (entries 5.107–115) of this chapter focuses on slave resistance in the form of revolts, rebellions, and escapes via the Underground Railroad and is discussed in six seminal books: Herbert Aptheker's *American Negro Slave Revolts* (1974), Eugene Genovese's *From Rebellion to Revolution* (1979), Benjamin Quarles's *Black Abolitionists* (1969), William Still's *Underground Railroad* (1872) and Charles Blockson's 1987 book of the same title, and Shirley Yee's *Black Women Abolitionists* (1992).

Black contributions to the American Revolution are explored in the third subsection (entries 5.116–117), and include William Nell's *The Colored Patriots of the American Revolution* (1855) and Benjamin Quarles's *The Negro in the American Revolution* (1973).

The fourth subsection (entries 5.118–119) contains collections of primary documents on slavery, including Blassingame's *Slave Testimony* (1977) and George Rawick's *The American Slave: A Composite Autobiography*, a monumental compilation of 20,000 narratives from the Federal Writers' Project.

Slave Society

5.99E   *Before Freedom Came: African American Life in the Antebellum South.* Rice, Kym, Curator. Washington, D.C.: Smithsonian Institution Traveling Exhibition Service, 1993–1994.

This exhibition explores African-American lifestyles and methods of adapting to change during slavery. Personal remembrances of slavery are told through manuscripts, dramatizations, three-dimensional objects, engravings, and photographs to create a living history of the period. The exhibition is accompanied by a teachers' resource binder, young people's gallery guide, and interactive activities. A book of the same title was featured as one of the twelve notable books of 1992 by the American Library Association.

Two versions of this exhibit are available for loan: an extensive, but expensive, version and a scaled-down, but affordable, version. This exhibition was curated by Kym Rice of the Museum of the Confederacy in Richmond, Virginia. Students from junior high through lower-division college levels will find this exhibit a valuable supplement to their texts.

5.100   Blassingame, John. *The Slave Community: Plantation Life in the Antebellum South.* New York: Oxford University Press, 1972.

Determined to dispel Stanley Elkins's characterization of slaves as "Sambos" and demonstrate the existence of a slave culture that enabled slaves to survive the brutalities of the system, Blassingame used Freedmen's Bureau statistics from the 1860s to show that the majority of slaves lived in two-parent families. He also reviewed autobiographies of slaves and studied several hundred autobiographies by whites, plantation records, agricultural journals, and travel accounts to gain an understanding of the nature of the interaction between masters and slaves.

By examining religious and family life in particular, Blassingame concluded that a distinctive slave culture developed within the relative autonomy of the slave quarters. Slaves adapted the Christian religion to their belief system. Through the study of creative expression of African dance, music, folktales, and magic, Blassingame concludes that slaves survived the traumatic experiences of slavery without becoming docile and submissive and were able to establish a sense of self-worth within the slave quarters.

The Slave Community is arranged into seven topical chapters: enslavement, acculturation, and African survivals; culture; the slave family; rebels and runaways; plantation stereotypes and roles; plantation realities; and slave personality types. An appendix on a comparative examination of total institutions, a critical essay on sources, and a select bibliography are included.

High school teachers, junior and senior high school students, and lower-division undergraduates will find this clearly written and succinct work fundamental reading for African-American, American history, and American studies courses.

5.101E   *Climbing Jacob's Ladder: The Rise of Black Churches in Eastern American Cities, 1740–1877.* Washington, D.C.: Smithsonian Institution Traveling Exhibition Service, 1992– 1993.

The historic and pivotal role the black church played in the black community is explored in this exhibition. The church as a religious and spiritual house of worship and an educational and abolitionist institution is revealed through photographs and primary documents. The exhibit is accompanied by an extensive resource guide with suggestions for enhancing the exhibit with local artifacts. A brochure, two video programs, and a soundtrack accompany the exhibition. A catalog is also available from the Smithsonian Institution Press.

5.102   **Genovese, Eugene D.** *Roll, Jordan, Roll: The World the Slaves Made.* New York: Pantheon Books, 1974.

In this classic work, Genovese defines the relationship between master and slave as a paternalistic one in which the master accepted responsibility for the slave's welfare in return for the slave's work. However, Genovese insists that this paternalism created a tendency for slaves to see the world as their masters viewed it, which minimized their identification with each other as a class of people, and undermined their sense of self-worth.

Genovese uses letters and diaries to examine the ways in which slaves modified the system of paternalism, primarily through the practice of religion. Yet, unlike Blassingame, who saw religion as a humanizing experience that provided a sense of self-esteem, Genovese views religion as merely compensation for slavery's moral and psychological aggression.

Holt, Foner, and other historians have applauded Genovese's efforts to understand the relationship between master and slave within the same system but criticized his thesis that the slaves' world view was shaped only or primarily by the master's value system. They contend that the slaveholders' papers and publications and Works Progress Administration (WPA) narratives collected in the 1930s reveal more about the views of masters than slaves and the slaves' world as it was remembered rather than lived. Herbert Gutman (entry 5.103) insisted that studies by Genovese and Blassingame began their work too late in the period to accurately record slave behavior and attitudes.

Genovese's work covers 825 pages and is topically arranged in four sections, which the author calls *books*. Book 1 is entitled *God Is Not Mocked* and includes two parts: part 1 focuses on the system of slavery and the master, and part 2 focuses on the slave. Included in part 2 are topics such as "De Good Massa," and "Our White Folks." Book 2, entitled *The Rock and the Church*, is also divided into two parts. Part 1 analyzes slave religion in nine chapters, including "Black Conversion and White Sensibility," "Let the Dead Bury the Dead," "The White Preachers," "Origins of Folk Religion," and "The Gospel in the Quarters." Part 2 of the second book examines the work ethic of slaves in three chapters. Book 3, *The Valley of the Shadow*, describes life in the plantation household, miscegenation, and language of slaves. Part 1, "Of the Sons of Jacob," includes seven chapters. Part 2 reviews the complexity of relationships in the slave quarters in fourteen chapters. Book 4, entitled *Whom God Hath Hedged In*, discusses forms of slave resistance and revolts.

Special indexes and notes are numerous. Included are information on manuscript collections cited in notes, a note on sources arranged by chapters, and separate subject and name indexes.

Due to its complexity and detail, this source is recommended for upper-division undergraduate history students.

5.103 Gutman, Herbert. *The Black Family in Slavery and Freedom: 1750–1925.* New York: Pantheon Books, 1976

Gutman's meticulous and painstaking research on black family life was written in direct response to Patrick Moynihan's report, *The Negro Family in America: The Case for National Action* (1965), which was based, in part, on black sociologist E. Franklin Frazier's book, *The Negro Family in the United States* (1939). Moynihan and Frazier concluded that contemporary black family life was disorganized and dysfunctional and embedded in a "tangle of pathology" originating from the destruction of black family life during slavery.

Gutman hypothesizes that this "tangle of pathology" should have been as severe, if not more severe, in 1830 and 1860 as it was in 1959 and 1960 if indeed this was the cause of the "destruction of contemporary black family life." To test this hypothesis, Gutman first studied the Buffalo, New York, black community by examining New York State manuscript census schedules for 1855 and 1875, and then 1905 and 1925. The census records showed that between 82 percent and 92 percent of African-American families in Buffalo were double-headed, kin-related households.

When critics questioned how these findings related to other African-American communities, Gutman enlarged the study to include occupational and household status of all members of 13,924 New York City black households in 1905 and 1925. The findings were consistent with the Buffalo study: 85 percent of kin-related households were double-headed, and five out of six children under the age of six lived with both parents.

The purpose of Gutman's book, which includes the 1925 New York City findings, is to study the black family prior to and after emancipation, the cultural beliefs and behavior of a distinctive lower-class population, and to examine its adaptive capacities. Gutman's study using Freedmen's Bureau records reveals that most slave families were two-parent families, and slave marriages, regardless of status of spouses, were long-lasting.

Gutman then poses additional questions about why most slave families consisted of two parents and why the marriages were long-lasting. He hypothesizes that slave beliefs originated within a *cumulative* slave experience that enabled slaves to adapt their lifestyles over time, beginning with the external changes associated with initial enslavement and the spread of plantation slavery, to the Civil War and emancipation.

Gutman's chapter 2 study of slaves on the Good Hope plantation in South Carolina describes how the slaves' common sexual, marital, familial, and social beliefs were shaped by a cumulative slave experience that was passed on to subsequent generations. The birth register for Good Hope plantation was unusual in that it recorded the first slave birth in 1760 and the last birth almost one hundred years later. This active model, absent from earlier slave studies, shows slaves adapting to changing external circumstances in light of earlier experiences. The document reveals marriage taboos against blood-cousin marriage, the belief that prenuptial pregnancy should be followed by marriage, the expectation of spousal fidelity, and the naming of slave children for blood kin.

Chapters 3 and 4 reconstruct family life and kin networks in settings very different from Good Hope: Virginia, North Carolina, Alabama, and southern and northern Louisiana. Records show that patterns similar to those in South Carolina are found everywhere.

Chapters 5 and 6 explore the cultural significance of slave-naming practices (e.g., slaves' children were often named after kin groups) and the retention of owners' surnames. Chapter 7 relates the book's findings to some other aspects of slave life and behavior, to the inaccurate perception of slave "family" by contemporary northern and southern whites, and, finally, to explicit models in studies by Frazier, Stampp, Elkins, and Genovese.

Chapter 8 focuses on important but neglected eighteenth-century processes affecting Africans and black Americans. Chapters 9 and 10 shift to the ex-slaves and their descendants in late nineteenth and early twentieth centuries. The afterword brings the reader up to date by suggesting some of the larger historical issues affecting the financial conditions of poor rural southern blacks who migrated to northern cities after 1930.

Gutman's groundbreaking, classic study of black family life should be required reading for all high school and college instructors of American history, black history, and American studies. Advanced junior and senior high school students and undergraduate students should also be required to read portions of this work.

5.104   **Levine, Lawrence.** *Black Culture and Black Consciousness: Afro-American Folk Thought from Slavery to Freedom.* New York: Oxford University Press, 1977.

Using documents and oral expressions of slaves, Levine seeks to demonstrate that black history was not an "unending round of degradation and pathology. . . . Black folks were able to sustain a greater degree of self-pride and group cohesion than the system ever intended for them to be able to do." The sources Levine examines include songs, folktales, proverbs, aphorisms, jokes, verbal games, and oral poems. He readily acknowledges the problems presented by studying these sources: unknown identity of authors/creators, alteration of stories and songs through the years, lack of dates, and unclear geographical distribution.

Levine defines culture as a style of life that is a process rather than a condition; therefore, he describes African cultural transformations instead of cultural survival. One of the most salient cultural transformations used daily by slaves was song, which Levine traces to their African origins, where songs served to mock rulers and recite the injustices the people suffered. In America, songs functioned as a psychological release from tedious, arduous work on the plantation. Songs often were used as social commentary on the slaves' condition and to insult whites, but the words were disguised so they could not be understood by slaveholders. Levine classifies the types of songs as out-group satire; songs of nostalgia; nonsense songs; children's songs; lullabies; and songs of play, work, and love.

Spirituals, in particular, permeated all aspects of slave culture and reflected deeply held beliefs, values, and feelings. Levine describes spirituals' call-and-response patterns as a testament to a strong sense of community. The most consistent theme of spirituals was that of a chosen people.

A second type of cultural expression was dance. Unlike the stiff staid movement of whites, according to Levine, dance by slaves was reminiscent of African dance, with its gliding, dragging, shuffling, flexible, improvisational, and pelvis-oriented movement.

Several other examples of slave cultural expressions can be seen in the use of magic and folktales. Levine summarizes the function of magic as a way for slaves to reinforce the notion that whites could not control everything in their lives; there was indeed a way to neutralize the whites' "powers." Folktales, including slave and trickster tales, were brought directly from Africa. Levine concludes that didactic folktales taught elements of proper conduct and righteous living and provided strategies for survival. Animal trickster tales provided an outlet through which slaves could express repressed feelings about certain types of behavior or people while also bringing about a psychological release from the inhibitiveness of society. These tales served to encourage trickery, stimulated a search for ways out of the system, and empowered a sense of perseverance and a contempt for the powerful.

Although Blassingame, Genovese, and Gutman also incorporate some elements of culture in assisting readers to understand the slave community, Levine's work is the first major study to interpret slave folk culture. He contends that oral culture reveals a multidimensional complexity of the black American past that assists us to progress beyond uncritical assumptions. Levine concludes that songs, tales, music, and dance are the enduring areas of culture. Whites tended not to interfere with the cultural forms largely because they did not understand them and viewed them as innocuous and meaningless.

The six chapters in this book are divided as follows: "The Sacred World of Black Slaves," "The Meaning of Slave Tales," "Freedom, Culture, and Religion," "The Rise of Secular Song," "Black Laughter," and "A Pantheon of Heroes." The first chapter provides an overview of slave songs and their origin, and a discussion of slave spirituals and folk beliefs. Chapter 2 analyzes specific types of slave tales and their meaning, while chapter 3 reviews the development of gospel song and the language of freedom. Chapter 4 explores black secular music, including work songs, the blues, and protest songs, within the context of the black community, both in slavery and freedom. The meaning and uses of laughter and insult are discussed in chapter 5; chapter 6 explores the concept of black heroes.

Levine concludes with an insightful epilogue followed by extensive footnotes to each chapter and an index. Secondary school teachers and undergraduates should find this work invaluable for its approach to understanding the mind of blacks and its effect on the development of black culture.

5.105   Owens, Leslie Howard. *This Species of Property: Slave Life and Culture in the Old South.* New York: Oxford University Press, 1976.

Owens, like Levine, Gutman, and Blassingame, emphasizes a common slave culture that was different from the slaveholder's culture; however, he focuses on the personality and behavior of the slave within the context of what it meant to be "property." In particular, Owens's investigation into the effects of illness, diet, and nutrition on slave behavior enhances readers' understanding of the world of both slave and master.

For example, Owens's research on the problem of slave illness reveals that planters' complaints of lost days were usually misinterpreted as "laziness" on the part of the slaves instead of the effects of disease. Overseers and slaveholders often ignored the first signs of disease, and when illness was noticed, slaves were usually treated by the planters themselves or by other slaves. Often slaveholders would merely break even due to their unwillingness to pay attention to the health of slaves. According to Owens, slaveholders often responded to the death of slave children in a cavalier manner, as if these deaths were an expected phenomenon. This attitude sometimes extended to the slaveholder's own children as well.

A second example of the way in which health affected slave behavior is explored in chapter 3, entitled "Blackstrap Molasses and Cornbread—Diet and Its Impact on Behavior." Owens convincingly argues that the staple slave diet of cornmeal and fat pork was inadequate to provide the nutrition needed to perform strenuous labor. Planters, too, were largely ignorant about the importance of a well-balanced diet and, therefore, did not understand the need to introduce a steady portion of protein and vegetables into the slave diet. Due to the lack of nutrition, many slaves suffered from pellagra and beriberi, among other diseases. The lack of healthy and plentiful food led to stealing. It also brought about the necessity of slaves supplementing their diet through hunting, fishing, and collecting wild fruits and berries. The effects of the poor diet of most slaves led to a lack of energy and fueled the perception by slaveholders that slaves were docile and lazy.

In chapter 4, Owens discusses the logic of slave resistance by investigating two questions: Why did slaves conduct themselves as they did when resisting laws of slavery, and what roles did they play in shaping the nature of their own enslavement? Owens contends that slaves analyzed the character, personality, and idiosyncrasies of the slaveholder to "manage whites." Since it was virtually impossible for slaves to be restrained at all times in all places, whites tried to use an informal patrol system to control and contain slaves. However, through the use of bribery and other forms of resistance—such as slowing the work pace, breaking and misplacing tools, overworking animals, improperly planting crops, giving food to runaways, and assisting fellow slaves to escape—bondsmen and bondswomen were constantly challenging the hierarchy. These acts, according to Owens, "prompted slaveholders to recognize the needs considered important to slaves."

In the remaining six chapters, Owens discusses the nature of the work of household slaves, the role of black slave drivers, the importance of religious and spiritual beliefs of slaves in shaping their self-esteem, the use and meaning of music (which he explains is inseparable from slave identity), and the role of family in strengthening slave resolve.

The book concludes with a section on manuscript sources consulted, an extensive section of footnotes arranged by chapter, and an index. High school history instructors, professors of undergraduate history, and American studies majors will need this important work to comprehend the complexities of slave behavior and the range of factors that influenced that behavior.

5.106 **White, Deborah Gray.** *Ar'n't I a Woman: Female*
Slaves in the Plantation South. New York and London:
W. W. Norton, 1985.

Deborah Gray White, like Jacqueline Jones (entry 4.88), draws upon WPA interviews with female ex-slaves in studying slave women. Unlike Jones, White devotes this entire study to the role of slave women; therefore, the book provides greater insight into this period. White readily acknowledges the dearth of original source materials on female slaves that helps explain their "invisibility" in traditional slavery studies. Therefore, it is necessary to make inferences based on the interview material examined.

The purpose of this study is to examine the complex role of slave women and to argue that they held a position similar to that of their African foremothers as complementary to men. Furthermore, White contends that the relationship between black bondswomen and bondsmen was one of mutual respect. A third point made by the author is that black slave girls and women were highly dependent upon one another due to the nature of the slavery system.

In the first chapter, entitled "Jezebel and Mammy," White describes the origin of the dominant myths about black women and dispels them through material presented in the documents. For example, she traces the myth of Jezebel, a stereotype of seductiveness and promiscuity, to the way in which slave women were presented for sale at public auctions—an image developed as the antithesis of the Victorian ideal. White concludes that this and other stereotypes of black women were created to soothe the consciences of whites and to explain miscegenation and sexual exploitation.

In an enlightening second chapter, White compares and contrasts the two systems of slavery—one for women and one for men. The differences between the two systems were considerable and included the ways in which women were treated on the slave ships, the forms of resistance and rebellion by slave women as opposed to slave men, the role of slave women in childbearing and childraising responsibilities that affected their ability to work in the field and shaped the nature of work in the slave quarters, and the impact of fertility or barrenness on the lives of slave women. For example, slave women seldom attempted to run away due to either fear of losing their children or the difficulty of traveling with children. Slave resistance for black women, then, included inventing schemes and excuses or feigning illness to get out of work, and using poison in the preparation of food for the slaveholder.

In chapter 3, "Life Cycle of the Female Slave," White provides an overview of a series of passages for female slaves. Of all the passages, motherhood was the most important one; slaveholders were less likely to sell parents who were part of a nuclear family. Although motherhood enhanced the status of slave women, it also made their days even more exhausting. Often elderly women cared for and nurtured children whose mothers were working in the fields.

In chapter 4, "Female Slave Networks," White explores the relationship among slave women that she characterizes as more stable, in many ways, than those between men and women. Marital and sexual relationships were often broken up through purchase by different planters. Kinship, as defined in the slave community, extended beyond the bounds of blood kin and included a network of women who cooperated to work and play in an effort to ameliorate their condition.

Chapter 5, "Men, Women, and Families," is a discussion of the complex ways women affected, and were affected by, men. Issues explored include love and affection between slave men and women, slave marriages and separations, and "abroad" marriages (between slaves living on different plantations). In spite of the fact that the separation of slave families through sale was not universal, the precarious nature of slavery contributed to the independence of women from men and strengthened the bonds between mother and child.

An epilogue, footnotes to each chapter, a selected bibliography, and an index are provided. One of only three books on black women in slavery—the others are Jacqueline Jones's book (entry 4.88) and Fox-Genovese's *Within the Plantation Household,* a complex study more appropriate for graduate history students—it is also a highly readable and succinct study. High school history instructors and students will want to use this text as supplemental reading; undergraduate students and professors should use it as a required text for this period.

Slave Resistance

5.107   **Aptheker, Herbert.** *American Negro Slave Revolts.* New York: International Publishers, 1983.

In this book, originally published in 1943 and based on his dissertation, Aptheker documents the extent and types of slave insurrections and revolts. The author describes rebellions or the conspiracy to rebel as the highest form of protest. His reasoning is that the price of the failure of such acts was death.

The first eight of the sixteen chapters of the book are arranged topically; seven chapters are divided into chronological periods in which a concentration of rebellions occurred. The conclusion composes the final chapter. In the introduction, the author classifies two forms of protest: individual and collective action. Individual action included laziness; thievery; feigned illness; poison; arson; sabotage of tools, animals, or crops; self-injury; and escape. Examples of collective forms of protest are group flights, arson, conspiracy, and uprisings.

Generalizations about slave insurrections and conspiracies include: they came in waves (1710–1722, 1730–1740, 1790–1802, 1819–1823, 1829–1832, 1850–1860); free Negro participation was generally uncommon and white participation was rare; and external factors such as reports of unrest in the West Indies, political campaigns in the United States, and war influenced slave revolts. Aptheker concludes that slave insurrections dispelled the stereotype of the happy-go-lucky, satisfied, servile slave and produced several heroes.

In the second and third chapters, Aptheker discusses white fear of rebellion, especially when the American Revolution and the Civil War awakened and engendered a widespread spirit of independence, liberty, and equality among slaves. White reaction to this fear included attempts to institutionalize a "machinery of control" that included religious instruction in meekness and docility, the brainwashing of slaves to believe they were innately inferior to whites, the enactment of laws to restrict mobility and communication among slaves, and enforcement of the strategy of "divide and rule."

In chapter 5, Aptheker describes events and circumstances that served to fuel the fires of rebellion: antislavery activities; increase in the ratio of Negroes to whites in several states; industrialization and urbanization; economic depression; and the systematic, dehumanizing, oppressive brutality of slavery itself. Aptheker then documents slave insurrections from 1663 to 1831, including the most famous revolts and the men who masterminded them: Cato in 1739, Gabriel Prosser in 1800, Denmark Vesey in 1822, and Nat Turner in 1831. He concludes that discontent and rebellion were characteristic of American Negro slaves.

The final chapter includes a bibliography of primary sources divided by type of material and an index.

High school history teachers, lower-division undergraduate students, and general readers will find this book insightful reading on slave resistance.

5.108   Blockson, Charles L. *The Underground Railroad.* New York: Prentice-Hall, 1987.

Blockson's book is an extension of an article on the Underground Railroad that was commissioned by Wilber Garrett for the *National Geographic* in 1984. Blockson conducted research and traveled extensively for three years in the American South and Midwest and in Canada; he interviewed descendants of slaves and their helpers on the Underground Railroad.

Based upon his research, Blockson concludes that the role and work of white abolitionists and Quakers on the Underground Railroad was exaggerated. The involvement and participation of other religious groups including the Roman Catholics, Jews, Wesleyans, Methodists, and Unitarians as well as those of free blacks and Free Soil Party members in this effort has been neglected. It is Blockson's thesis that the most assiduous organizers were black free men and women and that slaves played a pivotal role in their own escape.

The forty-seven narratives of famous and obscure black men and of eleven women are eloquently told in seventeen chapters that are arranged by state and geographical region including Canada. Each chapter is preceded by a lengthy introduction and description of Underground Railroad activities and personalities in the state or region, and includes a source note for the narrative. Most of the narratives were drawn from other published works such as William Still's book (see entry 5.114), Harriet Beecher Stowe's *Key to Uncle Tom's Cabin:*

Reminiscences of Levi Coffin, and Benjamin Drew's *North Side View of Slavery*, as well as newspaper accounts.

Narratives of famous slaves who escaped on the Underground Railroad are revealed. There are also narratives of black and white abolitionists, which detail their experiences in meeting potential escapees, and black conductors. Dramatic escapes achieved through the help of a dog, aboard ships or across half-frozen rivers attest to the courage and resolve of blacks and some whites to sacrifice their lives and families for freedom or to aid the freedom movement.

Blockson is able to draw from a broader range of narratives than Still and thus includes more narratives documenting the black involvement in the Underground Railroad. Blockson's bibliographical essay and suggested readings assist the reader to identify other sources of narratives. He also includes an index of proper names.

High school and lower-division undergraduate teachers and professors will want to use both Blockson's and Still's texts to help students understand the perils of those arduous journeys north.

5.109   **Genovese, Eugene D.** *From Rebellion to Revolution: Afro-American Slave Revolts in the Making of the Modern World.* Baton Rouge and London: Louisiana University Press, 1979.

In this book, Genovese contends that slave revolts sought escape and autonomy and did not challenge the world capitalist system or attempt to overthrow white power. Genovese concludes that slave revolts were infrequent and of low intensity in the Old South compared with the Caribbean or Brazil. The book explores the conditions that contributed to this infrequency and discusses the role of slave revolts and guerrilla warfare in the international political movements that were occurring during the Age of Revolution.

In the chapter on paternalism, Genovese concludes that resistance to slavery represents a conscious effort on the part of slaves to develop an alternative strategy for survival and settling of personal and local scores. The factors that affected the probability of slave rebellion include planter absenteeism, cultural distance between masters and slaves, economic depression, famine, plantation size, a larger percentage of blacks than whites, and a preponderance of African-born compared to Creole slaves. Since these circumstances existed less frequently in North America, especially after the eighteenth century, revolts in the South were less common.

In the chapter entitled "Turning Point," Genovese discusses the impact of slave revolts on the slaveholders and slaves. He notes that slave revolts provided the first major impetus to the abolition of the African slave trade; however, white fears of slave rebellion contributed to the suppression of civil liberties (such as free speech and assembly) and contempt for home rule (Fugitive Slave Act) for whites as well as blacks throughout the United States. Although Aptheker (entry 5.107) did not compare slave revolts in North America to international revolts, both authors conclude that revolts were shaped by struggles for national liberation and social change.

In the afterword Genovese decribes slaveholders' attempts to isolate and insulate slaves from revolutionary orations that would fuel unrest, such as Frederick Douglass's speech, "The Meaning of the Fourth of July to the Negro." A bibliographical essay and an index follow the chapters.

Genovese's book serves to complement Aptheker's more comprehensive study by placing slave revolts in an international context. For this reason, Genovese's book may be more useful in undergraduate history courses and should be reviewed by high school history teachers.

5.110V   Learning Corporation of America. *A Slave's Story: Running a Thousand Miles to Freedom.* Videorecording, 29 min. Deerfield, Ill.: Distr. Coronet/MTI Film and Video, 1972.

This dramatization of the escape of William and Ellen Craft is based upon a slave narrative they wrote. The great-granddaughter of the Crafts introduces the videotape, which depicts their perilous escape from the South to Philadelphia in 1848. Winner of the American Library Association Selected Films for Young Adults, this videotape is appropriate for junior high through college-level students.

5.111V   Maryland Instructional Technology. *The Freedom Station.* Videorecording, 30 min. Alexandria, Va., 1988.

The dramatic escape of a young slave girl and her subsequent meeting with a farm girl from an abolitionist family provide the story for this video about the Underground Railroad, the hardships of slavery, and the complexities of freedom.

Junior high school students will find this videotape interesting and revealing.

5.112   Quarles, Benjamin. *Black Abolitionists.* New York: Oxford University Press, 1969.

Quarles sets out to document the prominent and pioneering black presence and activism in the abolitionist movement. He explains that the primary reason for the neglect of the Negro abolitionist was the contemporary white media that followed the lead of the southern press in ignoring the role of blacks in the movement. According to Quarles, the southern white press seemed almost obsessed with perpetuating the myth of the contented, docile and passive slave, which contradicted the true image of the black reformer abolitionist. Quarles's work illustrates that black abolitionists were eloquent spokespersons and activists for their own freedom rather than passive recipients of good deeds.

Broad topics explored by Quarles include the participation of blacks, and to a lesser degree, women auxiliaries in the American Antislavery Society; formulation of Negro antislavery societies and women's auxiliaries; the split in the antislavery movement; the role of black clergy and the press in abolitionism; Negro self-help initiatives; international efforts to promote abolitionism; black participation in the Underground Railroad; the politics of freedom; the rights of women; and the colonization question.

Quarles contrasts the early antislavery movements—which reflected a Calvinistic, southern belief in the gradual abolition of slavery communicated in an unemotional, temperate, low-key language and style—with the American Antislavery Society's (AAS) philosophy. The latter organization deplored gradualism, and its leaders included blacks such as David Ruggles, David Walker, Robert Purvis, James Barbadoes, and James McCrummell, many of whom were college trained. The AAS was characterized by the organization of Negro societies and women's auxiliaries. Lucretia Mott, Sarah and Margaretta Forten, Sarah Douglass, and the Grimké sisters were active in establishing organizations such as the Female Antislavery Society of Philadelphia.

Quarles notes that the Negro societies viewed their role as supportive, supplemental, and subsidiary in that they provided financial and moral support to Negro antislavery journals such as *Freedom's Journal* and *The Colored American*. Negro auxiliary societies also initially supported the efforts of the American Antislavery Society's most outspoken and radical leader, William Lloyd Garrison.

Quarles attributes the split of the AAS to a range of philosophical differences between many of the white and black abolitionists. Garrison espoused religious reforms that were not related to abolitionism (for example, he scorned the Bible as divine inspiration), and was deeply skeptical and cynical of electoral politics to the point of urging Negroes not to vote. Negro abolitionists criticized their white brethren for failing to commit to and implement the society's second goal—to elevate the free Negro. They also charged white abolitionists with ignoring the common man and preferring abstraction to common sense. Black abolitionists, on the whole, were also more receptive to women voting in their sessions. The black activists in this separatist movement included Charles Lenox Remond, Frederick Douglass, Henry Highland Garnet, Henry Bibb, and William Wells Brown.

Self-help initiatives, a third important topic discussed by Quarles, was linked to abolitionism by black activists who believed that the elevation of the free Negro and the liberation of the slave were interrelated. Since most of the resources in antislavery societies concentrated on abolition, Negroes assumed elevation efforts by establishing mutual-aid societies to follow relevant intellectual and cultural pursuits such as public lectures and literary societies. Quarles also provides an overview of Negro self-help efforts in establishing their own schools, especially in the northeast.

Quarles credits black abolitionists' oratorical engagements in England with influencing international diplomacy and the outcome of the Civil War. The successful reception of black abolitionists Charles Remond, Paul Cuffe, James W. C. Pennington, Henry Highland Garnet, Josiah Henson, Frederick Douglass, William Wells Brown, Ellen and William Craft, Alexander Crummell, and Sarah Remond (sister of Charles) are chronicled in chapter 6.

Negro abolitionists held the view that the struggle for human rights must include the rights of women—a view that Giddings espouses in a chapter on women's suffrage in *When and Where I Enter* (entry 4.82). Quarles underscores that women took an active role in the fundraising functions of the abolitionist movement. Negro women abolitionists such as Sojourner Truth, Frances Ellen Watkins Harper, and Charlotte Forten believed in equal suffrage among races and sexes.

The book concludes with a bibliographic essay, footnotes arranged by chapter, and an index. Quarles's book remains a classic on the work and influence of black abolitionists and should be required reading for high school history teachers and academic historians.

5.113V   Roja Productions. *Roots of Resistance: A Story of the Underground Railroad.* Videorecording, 60 min. Alexandria, Va., 1989.

This videotape captures the intrigue, drama, and danger of escape via the Underground Railroad. The story is told through narratives of escaped slaves.

Appropriate for high school through college-level students, this video is also a winner of the Red Ribbon American Film and Video

Festival and the Silver Apple National Educational Film and Video Festival.

5.114 **Still, William.** *Underground Railroad.* Philadephia: Porter and Cooke, 1872.

This classic study of the experiences of men, women, and children who were passengers on the Underground Railroad was written by the corresponding secretary of the Underground Railroad at the request of the Pennsylvania Antislavery Society. These dramatic accounts of escape were confined to Still's own personal knowledge and to records of "his own preserving." Indeed, Still took no notes in order to maintain the secrecy upon which the entire operation depended. The names of the individuals who supported the Underground Railroad's activities were never disclosed to escapees.

The purpose of writing the book, according to Still, was to facilitate the reunions of relatives, to show efforts made and successes gained, and to give hope to all by fueling the fires of freedom. He attempts to record only the factual stories of escapees without exaggeration or embellishment; however, he can't hide his joy and enthusiasm over successful escapes and reunions.

Each narrative includes excerpts from actual letters and quotes from passengers in order to re-create the intensity of both the emotions and the danger. The stories vary in length from one quarter of a page to ten or twelve pages, and describe the great lengths to which slaves would go to escape, including disguises, "passing" as white, having themselves "boxed" up for more than sixteen hours, or stowing away on steamers. One woman, Clarissa Davis, dressed in male attire and fled with her two brothers from Portsmouth, Virginia. Poignant, painful, suspenseful narratives discussing directions for passenger pickup and delivery, letters from fugitives notifying conductors of safe arrival, and letters expressing desire for reunion with wives and children are but a sampling of the stories told in this book. There are also several narratives of escapes by women with their children. Most letters refer to escapees as "packages," "goods," and "bundles," terms used to preserve the atmosphere of secrecy. Also included are advertisements for runaway slaves and letters from former owners asking slaves to return.

The last chapters of this 780-page book are devoted to portraits and sketches of twenty-three men and four women who were active abolitionists. Included in this group are Lewis Tappan; William Lloyd Garrison; Samuel Burris; Lucretia Mott; and Frances Ellen Watkins Harper, the famous teacher and poet. No index is provided. Illustrations are plentiful.

No high school American history course would be complete without reading and discussing these real-life stories to highlight for students the significance of the Underground Railroad.

5.115 Yee, Shirley J. *Black Women Abolitionists: A Study in Activism, 1828–1860.* Knoxville: University of Tennessee Press, 1992.

Yee explores free black women's participation in the struggle to end slavery in the United States. She limits her study to the activities of women who were either born into freedom or who acquired their freedom through manumission or escape. She further limits her study to centers of antislavery agitation: Cincinnati, Philadelphia, New York, and Boston. This significant work fills in the historical information about the role black women played in the abolition of slavery and in the struggle for women's rights.

Yee focuses on several experiences of women abolitionists: community-building, political organizing, and establishing networks of personal and professional friendships with other activists. She also examines the responses and reactions of black men and white women to black women's involvement in abolitionist and feminist activities during this period.

The six chapters are arranged thematically. In chapter 5, entitled "Breaking Customs," Yee reveals that as long as black women's abolitionist activities were confined to traditional women's domestic responsibilities (for example, in education, social services, moral reform, or temperance), their work was supported. However, when black women such as Mary Ann Shadd and Harriet Tubman ventured into delivering antislavery speeches, organizing antislavery societies, and writing antislavery poetry and essays, they overstepped the boundaries of respectable "ladylike" behavior and deference to whites. Therefore, they were often criticized by whites and by black men. Frederick Douglass and Charles L. Remond, active abolitionists, proved the exceptions to this rule; these men supported the work of black women on the grounds that their activities instilled racial pride in all black citizens. However, according to Yee, women activists were still expected to defer to men of their race.

In the final chapter, entitled "Sowing the Seeds of Black Feminism," Yee concludes that racial equality was an integral part of the black feminist agenda from the beginning and that "the struggles against racism and sexism precluded the possibility for black and white women to work together on an all-inclusive feminist agenda."

Following the six chapters are a conclusion, footnotes, a bibliography, and an index. High school history and social studies teachers and college faculty should incorporate this highly readable book into the curriculum; it provides an important analysis of the activities of black women abolitionists.

Negro Participation in the Revolutionary War

5.116 Nell, William. *The Colored Patriots of the American Revolution.* Boston: Robert F. Wallcut, 1855. Reprint, New York: Arno Press and the New York Times, 1968.

The reprint of this classic book (originally published in 1855) is described by historian Benjamin Quarles (see entry 5.117) as "the first serious attempt by a Negro American to write scholarly history."

The book is divided into two parts. The first part contains concise sketches of outstanding blacks from twenty states, and the second part is a general overview of the status of the Negro at that time. Although most of the biographical sketches are of military men, other prominent blacks of the period, such as David Walker and George Horton, are included. Quarles also states that although this book does not contain substantive data, the information is accurate (with the exception of Nell's belief that Deborah Gannett, who impersonated a male soldier, was a Negro). The source of most of Nell's information was personal interviews and visits to graveyards.

The book is arranged by state, beginning with Massachusetts. Each section contains excerpts from speeches and newspaper articles in addition to the biographical data. The second part of the book is divided into three chapters. The first chapter focuses on citizenship and includes information on naturalization; passports of black men; and speeches of John Mercer Langston, Hosea Easton, and others. The second chapter is entitled "Elevation" and provides information on such abolitionists as Frederick Douglass, James W. C. Pennington, William Whipper, and others. The third chapter is a conclusion and is followed by an appendix.

Although little new information is provided here, this classic work was far ahead of its time in rescuing from obscurity the black men who served in the American Revolution. This work is of great interest to historiographers.

5.117 Quarles, Benjamin. *The Negro in the American Revolution.* New York: W. W. Norton, 1973.

According to Quarles, the purpose of his study is to investigate the role of Negroes in the American Revolution and the extent to which changes occurred in their status. Quarles does not provide great detail on individual battles—especially since the Revolutionary War had no all-Negro units—nor does he focus on the study of individual participation in the war. This is a study of the involvement and participation of Negroes as a group. Quarles readily identifies two problems in studying this topic: the limitations of source material and the inability to determine the race of soldiers since most participants were racially anonymous.

Several themes emerge in this book: (1) the major loyalty of Negroes who participated in the American Revolution was to the principle of unalienable rights, rather than to a place or people; (2) Negroes saw limited service in the war until manpower needs became so acute that Negro enlistment was mandatory; (3) Negroes served on land and sea, but it was difficult to determine the precise count; and (4) the revolutionary spirit that engulfed the nation inspired many slaves to petition for manumission.

The ten chapters are arranged chronologically. In the introduction and first two chapters, Quarles notes that white fears of slaves with guns, especially in states with a heavy concentration of Negroes, such as Maryland and South Carolina, prevented Negroes from bearing arms in the early stages of war. Yet, although Congress refused to sanction Negro enlistment, Massachusetts and Rhode Island proceeded to include blacks among draftees. Once Lord Dunmore invited slaves to leave their masters and join the British royal forces, colonists panicked and waged psychological warfare to discourage slaves from joining Dunmore. No more than eight hundred slaves succeeded in reaching the British, who used them to steal food and supplies.

In the third chapter, entitled "The Negro and the Rights of Man," Quarles traces the origins of the revolutionary movement to the Declaration of Independence, which emphasized that all men were created equal. Black reaction to this cry for freedom prompted a group of slaves in Connecticut to petition for their liberty in 1779. In chapter 4, Quarles discusses the change in policy regarding the enlistment of Negroes once the Continental Army developed the need for reinforcements. Although Negro recruitment became prevalent in the New England states after 1779, among the southern states, only Maryland authorized slave enlistments. South Carolina and Georgia never sent slaves to war.

According to chapter 5, once enlisted, most slave soldiers received certificates of manumission, although some received only verbal promises. Most slaves enlisted for up to three years and were in the infantry where they served as orderlies, cooks, waiters, and drummers. Unlike the slaves who were motivated to attain their liberty, free Negroes joined for a variety of reasons. Some joined to pursue adventure, some for the prospect of receiving land bounty. Some fought because of their strong belief in the principles of the American Revolution. In chapter 6, Quarles discusses the many ways in which Negroes served in the war—as laborers, spies, messengers, and guides.

In the next three chapters, Quarles contends that the reason more blacks did not flee to the British was that many of them knew that the Tories were slaveholders. Naturally, this did nothing to inspire their confidence in the British. It appears that their fears were well founded; the British used slaves as property to make restitution to loyalists. Quarles also documents the evacuation of slaves from the United States to Canada—especially Nova Scotia, the British West Indies, and Jamaica—once the British surrendered. Quarles concludes the book by evaluating the attitudes of George Washington, Thomas Jefferson, Benjamin Franklin, and the Quakers toward slavery. Quarles contends that, "although the conditions of slaves on plantations were unchanged, the seeds and spirit of the principles of liberty and equality were forever planted."

Following the last chapter is a bibliography listed by the type of source and an index. The footnotes are listed within the text. This valuable, concise book provides a thorough overview of black participation in the Revolutionary War and the spirit and hope the war brought to slaves.

Documentary Histories

5.118   Blassingame, John, ed. *Slave Testimony: Two Centuries of Letters, Speeches, Interviews, and Autobiographies.* Baton Rouge: Louisiana State University Press, 1977.

Blassingame's carefully edited book of primary source material by slaves is the first systematic attempt to compile in one volume several different types of slave sources. This work also provides the reader with a rich compendium of slave testimony and insightful commentary on the problem of using these eyewitness accounts.

First, there is the problem of analyzing interviews conducted with former slaves in the twentieth century. Second, it is difficult to determine how many stories were written by blacks themselves. Third, verifying autobiographies published by independent sources remains an arduous task. Finally, there is the question of how to determine who edited published narratives. On the latter point, Blassingame notes that the editor's education, religious beliefs, values, literary skill, attitude toward slavery, and occupation affected how he or she recorded the account of the slave's life.

The purpose of the book is to analyze complex black responses to bondage, compare and contrast the sources used, and determine the reliability of each source. Themes documented in the sources include thoughts and feelings of the slaves, survival, culture, and family life. The stories of domestic servants, field hands, rebels, and docile slaves (those with both kind and inhumane masters) are represented here. The documents weigh heavily toward individual perceptions of people and events.

The sources included in this volume are 111 letters written by slaves between 1736 and 1864; 8 speeches; 129 interviews conducted by journalists, scholars, and government officials between 1827 and 1938; and 13 autobiographies that appeared in periodicals and rare books between 1828 and 1878. Each of the seven sections is arranged by type of source and is preceded by a short introduction.

Especially noteworthy are the American Freedmen's Inquiry Commission interviews conducted with former slaves in 1855 and 1863. The Commission was established in 1863 to collect slave testimony and make a report to Secretary of War Edwin Stanton about what was to be done with former slaves after the Civil War ended. These reports helped form one of the earliest blueprints for Reconstruction.

The average age of the forty-eight slaves interviewed was 49.8 years. Most of them had been free for ten to thirty years. Areas of inquiry posed by the interviewers included treatment of slaves by masters, instances of cruel punishment, slave family relations, degree of miscegenation, slaves' feelings about freedom, and the extent and form of slave resistance and rebellion.

The seven parts conclude with a name index and a subject index. Footnotes included within the documents indicate sources and additional information. High school teachers and undergraduate students will find this book a valuable and powerful tool to use in teaching and learning about slavery from the people who experienced it.

5.119 **Rawick, George P., ed.** *The American Slave: A Composite Autobiography.* 19v. 1977. Westport, Conn.: Greenwood Press, 1972. Supplement, series 1, 12v. 1977. Supplement, series 2, 10v. 1979.

This vast collection of slave narratives was part of a major project inaugurated and carried out under the auspices of the Federal Writers'

Project of the Works Projects Administration during 1936 through 1938. The project produced more than 10,000 pages of typescript containing more than 2,000 interviews with ex-slaves. These interviews compose the first nineteen volumes in the collection.

From Sundown to Sunup: The Making of the Black Community, the introductory volume, is also written by Rawick. Rather than concentrating on the treatment of slaves and their relationship with slave-owners, it focuses on how slaves lived within the slave community (after sundown) and how they created a culture that prevented them from becoming merely victims. According to Rawick, the value of the narratives is not in the historical facts they reveal, but in the stories they tell about slave beliefs, customs, values, hopes, aspirations, and fears.

Volumes 2 through 19 contain personal accounts of two thousand ex-slaves from seventeen states: South Carolina, Texas, Alabama, Indiana, Oklahoma, Mississippi, Arkansas, Missouri, Georgia, North Carolina, and Florida. Volume 16 includes narratives from the states of Kansas, Kentucky, Maryland, Ohio, Virginia, and Tennessee. Narratives for the states of South Carolina, Texas, Arkansas, Georgia, and North Carolina are so extensive that they span several volumes each.

Volumes 1 through 12 in the first supplement include narratives from Alabama, Arkansas, Colorado, Minnesota, Missouri, Oregon, Washington, Georgia, Indiana, Ohio, Mississippi, and North and South Carolina. The first volume of the second supplement contains narratives from Alabama, Arizona, Arkansas, District of Columbia, Florida, Indiana, Kansas, Maryland, Nebraska, New York, North Carolina, Oklahoma, Rhode Island, South Carolina, and Washington. Volumes 2 through 10 all include narratives from Texas.

The narratives within each volume are arranged alphabetically by the name of the informant. Each slave narrative includes the date the interview was edited, the name of the editor, the name of the informant and interviewer, and the date and location of the interview. Many interviews are introduced by a short biographical note on the informant, if available. Each interview is approximately five to eight pages long.

Although many of the narratives are difficult to read due to the editor's desire to retain the original style and language of the interviewee, this comprehensive collection should be examined and studied by history instructors who are presenting the slavery period.

Civil War, Emancipation, and Reconstruction

The second part of chapter 5 includes resources on the Civil War, emancipation, and Reconstruction. African-American contributions to the Civil War, annotated in the first subsection (entries 5.120–121), include the PBS documentary on the Civil War and Benjamin Quarles's *The Negro in the Civil War* (1968).

Authors of books on emancipation and Reconstruction, much like those on slavery, place black life and thought at the center of their studies. They emphasize that African Americans played a primary role in creating and defining their freedom. The next subsection (entries 5.122–130) of works on emancipation and Reconstruction include John Hope Franklin's *The Emancipation Proclamation*; Leon Litwack's prizewinning *Been in the Storm So Long*—a book that examines the variety of ways freed people attempted to define freedom on their own terms; Joel Williamson's *After Slavery*; George Bentley's *A History of the Freedmen's Bureau*; Eric Foner's *Nothing but Freedom*; W. E. B. Du Bois's classic 1935 work, *Black Reconstruction in America*; Kenneth Stampp's excellent collection of essays on the Reconstruction era; and Lawrence Powell's more-recent book on northern planters during Reconstruction.

There is also a section on primary documents of this era. These include (entries 5.131–135) *Free at Last: A Documentary History of Slavery, Freedom, and the Civil War* (1992); *Black Abolitionist Papers* (1985); *Witness for Freedom* (1993); *The Negro's Civil War* (1965); and *We Are Your Sisters* (1984).

Negro Participation in the Civil War

5.120V   **PBS Video.** *The Civil War.* Videorecording, nine parts, 14 hr. Alexandria, Va., 1992.

This highly acclaimed documentary series has aired several times on PBS. Utilizing original source documents and oral histories, it presents a comprehensive history of the war—from battlefields, home fronts, politicians, and generals to enlisted men and their families, including the participation of African Americans in the Civil War.

An invaluable resource for teachers, the series includes a four-color, thirty-six-page teacher's manual containing more than forty individual student handouts; an oversized time-line poster; a copy of *National Geographic*'s two-sided map of the battlefields; and an index of people, places, and events. The home video version includes nine sixty-minute tapes for about half of the regular purchase price.

Winner of five video awards, including the George Foster Peabody Award and the Angel Award for the best TV miniseries of the year, this series is appropriate for high school and college students and the general public.

5.121   **Quarles, Benjamin.** *The Negro in the Civil War.* New York: Russell and Russell, 1968.

In this classic survey of Negro participation in the Civil War, first published in 1953, Quarles describes the role of slaves in the war effort and in the service, as well as the effects of war on slaves' pursuit of freedom. Instead of focusing on battle narratives and on the individual actions of blacks, Quarles concentrates on the experiences of blacks as a group, and provides details for only two battles involving all-black regiments: Fort Wagner (South Carolina) and Port Hudson (Louisiana).

The fifteen chapters of the book are arranged chronologically and topically. Themes emphasized in these chapters include slaves' eagerness to participate as soldiers and laborers to secure their freedom, gain respect, and earn better wages; slaves' demonstration of courage and soldiership through brave and honorable service during the war and especially during the battle of Fort Wagner; and the reluctance of whites, including President Lincoln, to authorize Negroes to bear arms.

Quarles explains that Negroes made excellent soldiers and laborers in war because their personal freedom was at stake. Slaveholders attempted to discourage black participation in the Union army for fear that the taste of freedom would mean uprisings and mass migrations to the North. Their fears were well founded; blacks often ran away to the North or joined the Union army by forging passes. The Union found that the slaves were valuable laborers who were knowledgeable about the South's terrain and waterways; therefore, fugitive slaves often served as skillful scouts, spies, and guides.

Quarles describes the significance of the Emancipation Proclamation—Lincoln's last resort to restore the Union by weakening the Confederacy—in lifting the hopes and spirits of slaves and allowing them to serve in the armed services of the United States. The Emancipation Proclamation freed nearly four million bondspeople. In the final chapters of the book, Quarles describes the aftermath of the war and its effects on the freed slaves.

Following the chapters are a bibliography and an index.

This concise, highly readable, well-documented source is one of the best books available on Negro participation in the Civil War. High school history teachers and undergraduate students should use this book for an accurate and cogent presentation on black participation in the war and its significance in American history.

Emancipation and Reconstruction

5.122   Bentley, George R. *A History of the Freedmen's Bureau.*
New York: Octagon Books, 1970.

Bentley's comprehensive, classic history of the Freedmen's Bureau, first published in 1944, discusses the forerunners of the Freedmen's Bureau; the forces that led to the establishment of the bureau; the obstacles facing the bureau, once established; and the shortcomings and successes of the bureau.

Bentley describes the use of contraband during the war and temporary efforts by Union officers to respond to the needs of freedmen by putting them to work or locating jobs for them, establishing labor contracts, distributing food and clothing, and providing shelter for them. The American Freedmen's Inquiry Commission was established to investigate conditions of Negroes within Union lines and recommend measures for their protection and improvement. The commissioners reported great abuses of land leases and the use of Negroes as laborers. These efforts constituted the first steps toward centralized national attempts to deal with the freedmen.

It was the freedmen's aid societies in the North that lobbied Lincoln to create a bureau of emancipation. As a result, the Freedmen's Bureau Bill was introduced in Congress in 1863 to protect freedmen from exploitation by northerners and from reenslavement by former southern masters. It was not until 1865 that the Bureau of Refugees, Freedmen, and Abandoned Lands was established in the War Department. The purpose of this bureau was to assist freed people to make the transition from slavery to freedom. Most important, the bill provided that every male freedman "shall be assigned not more than 40 acres of abandoned and confiscated lands to rent with the option to purchase land in 3 years at not more than 6% of their value as appraised in 1860."

Bentley enumerates the problems that plagued the bureau from the beginning. There were no funds appropriated by Congress until a year after the bureau was established. In addition, President Andrew Johnson's policy of restoring abandoned lands to pardoned southerners depleted the bureau's funds, and the lack of enforcement power to direct the activities of freedmen's aid societies and civil governments in the southern states limited its ability to administer justice to Negroes.

In spite of these obstacles, the bureau contributed to assisting freed people by providing medical assistance, feeding the hungry, and urging Negroes and whites to enter into formal, bureau-approved labor contracts that would provide a minimum wage for freed people and fair treatment to Negroes. In practice, however, the activities of the bureau agents were not unfavorable to landowners. Bureau agents attempted to enforce a system of compensatory work upon freed people who were demoralized about not receiving their forty acres and therefore reluctant to work for former masters.

The Freedmen's Bureau was also responsible for helping freed people locate missing relatives, educating freedmen, and adjudicating many cases. The major challenge of the Freedmen's Bureau, according to Bentley, was in the area of land reform. Andrew Johnson's amnesty proclamation restored abandoned lands to white owners, which undermined the economic base of freedmen and the Freedmen's Bureau. It was Johnson, then, not the Freedmen's Bureau, that prevented Negroes from receiving a full opportunity for independence and citizenship in the form of land promised by the freedmen's bill.

Bentley also describes the work undertaken by the bureau once monies were appropriated in 1866. Half of the money was allocated to clothing and rations for freedmen and the remaining half provided schoolhouses and support for teachers. The bureau nurtured Negro education and built and repaired school buildings but did not provide funds for teachers' salaries. The bureau courts were established to provide protection for freed people, although they did not protect Negroes from white violence.

An appendix, bibliographical notes, a bibliography, and an index follow the fourteen chapters. High school teachers and students and lower-division college students should refer to this basic primer to better understand the significant role the Freedmen's Bureau played in preparing freed people for life after slavery, and the forces, events, and personalities that affected the work of this critical agency.

5.123   **Du Bois, W. E. B.** *Black Reconstruction in America: An Essay Toward a History of the Part Which Black Folk Played in the Attempt to Reconstruct Democracy in America, 1860–1880.* New York: Atheneum, 1973.

In this groundbreaking work, originally published in 1935, Du Bois shifted the historiography of this period toward an analysis of the role blacks played in their own emancipation and in Reconstruction. In the final chapter of the book, "The Propaganda of History," Du Bois, like Stampp (entry 5.129), criticizes the works of white historians, such as John Burgess and William A. Dunning, whose views of this period were tainted by racist attitudes. He also refers to contemporary elementary and secondary school textbooks, which provide a distorted history of blacks and the emancipation and Reconstruction eras.

Black Reconstruction is a radical departure from these earlier studies. According to historian Thomas Holt, because of the meticulous work of Du Bois, "now most historians accept the view that together with military and diplomatic pressures, it was black war refugees who forced Lincoln to abandon his hands-off policy toward southern slavery." In the final chapter, Du Bois notes that if he were afforded an opportunity, in time and money, to use original sources in all cases, the work would have been stronger and more convincing. However, he had to rely largely upon secondary material such as state histories of Reconstruction that frequently ignored or concealed the facts.

The book begins with an overview of the black worker in the eighteenth and nineteenth centuries to illustrate how blacks historically challenged U.S. democracy. The chapters most often cited in other works on this era are perhaps chapter 4, "The General Strike," and chapter 5, "The Coming of the Lord." In these chapters, Du Bois argues that during the Civil War, slaves staged a general strike in which they left southern plantations to work in the Union army, thereby leaving only women, the elderly, and children to work on the plantations. This deliberate act of defiance helped convince Lincoln to issue the Emancipation Proclamation, which legally allowed blacks to join the Union forces and fight for their freedom.

Subsequent chapters focus on the collective and individual efforts of former slaves to challenge the authority of their former masters and shape Reconstruction policy. A bibliography and index follow the chapters; however, the bibliography is far from conventional. Du Bois lists the books on his own racist-to-fair continuum. A few of these categories are titled "Standard Anti-Negro Propaganda," "Historians (fair to indifferent on the Negro)," "Historians (who have studied the history of Negroes and write sympathetically about them)," "Monographs (these authors seek the facts in certain narrow definite fields and in most cases do not ignore the truth as to Negroes)," and "Negro Historians (these are the standard works of Negro historians, some judicial, some eager and even bitter in defense)."

All serious history students and teachers should read this work for historical context on the period. Current history books at the elementary and secondary levels should incorporate the work of Du Bois with that of modern-day historians on this era.

5.124 Foner, Eric. *Nothing But Freedom: Emancipation and Its Legacy.* Baton Rouge: Louisiana State University Press, 1983.

Foner analyzes the consequences of emancipation at the international, regional, and local levels by focusing on Haiti, the British Caribbean, and America. According to Foner, his purpose in writing a comparative analysis of emancipation is "to illuminate a series of interrelated historical processes and conflicts involving land, labor, and the postemancipation state that shed new light on the experience of the United States."

The first chapter, entitled "The Anatomy of Emancipation," examines slavery in Haiti and the British Caribbean and early twentieth-century racial and economic relations in southern and eastern Africa. In chapter 2, "The Politics of Freedom," Foner describes how Caribbean emancipation influenced American perceptions of slavery and abolition, and discusses how issues common in the Caribbean and Africa were duplicated in the postemancipation United States.

The final chapter looks at a specific set of events during American Reconstruction—strikes of rice workers in South Carolina—to show how many of these same issues involving relations between planter and laborer were resolved at the local level. It is Foner's belief that the strikes and the general fate of the postemancipation rice economy demonstrate how the existence of liberal local and state governments during Reconstruction allowed American freed people a form of political and economic power unmatched by their counterparts in other societies.

In examining the consequences of emancipation in Haiti and the Caribbean, Foner concludes that Caribbean freed people, like their American counterparts, strived to define and determine the conditions and compensation of the work for themselves and their families.

The American postemancipation experience, Foner explains, although strikingly similar in outcome to that in the Caribbean and South Africa, was profoundly affected by radical Reconstruction. The economic dominance of the planter class was offset by a comprehensive legal and judicial system including the Fourteenth and Fifteenth Amendments. Freed people "stubbornly clung" to some measure of autonomy in day-to-day labor relations, and for a while blacks were provided an unparalleled opportunity to shape their own destiny. Although these legal rights were grossly violated in practice, Foner contends they "planted the seeds of future struggle and left intact a vehicle for future federal intervention in southern affairs."

Following the three chapters, detailed footnotes and an index are included.

Due to its comparative focus, Foner's well-written book is appropriate for undergraduate American and black history students and faculty. Combined with Du Bois's and Stampp's works on Reconstruction (entries 5.123 and 5.129, respectively), this book provides a thoughtful, comprehensive overview and analysis of a most provocative yet paradoxical period in American history.

5.125   Franklin, John Hope. *The Emancipation Proclamation.*
Garden City, N.Y.: Doubleday, 1963.

In an engaging and captivating style, Franklin recounts the history of the Emancipation Proclamation and its significance to contemporary and later generations. By providing insight into internal and external pressures to free the slave, U.S. and foreign developments, the writing of the preliminary document, the hundred days leading up to the signing of the final document, and the victories and initial effects of the document, Franklin allows the reader to develop a fuller understanding of Lincoln and his contemporaries, the Civil War, and U.S. history between 1860 and 1865.

The revolutionary spirit inspired by the Revolutionary War; the Haitian revolution; the emancipation of slaves in Mexico, Bolivia, and the British empire; and the emancipation of Russian serfs all greatly contributed to creating an international environment of freedom. In addition, the influence of abolitionists in Congress and the use of slaves by the Confederate army necessitated that Lincoln reexamine his intention to exclude Negro troops from serving in the Union army.

Franklin asserts that even though Lincoln continued to struggle over the legality of the effect of emancipation on the course of the war, after the Confederacy captured Frederick, Maryland, he decided to issue an emancipation proclamation and read it to his cabinet members in the summer of 1863. Franklin discusses Lincoln's interest in the colonization of Negroes, which never gained much support in the United States or abroad but which Lincoln hoped would eventually come to pass. He even conducted a colonization experiment with the Republic of Haiti to permit a group of Negroes to settle there. Unfortunately, the Negro settlers were reduced to a life of bondage and brutality. An embarrassed Lincoln secretly had the survivors—half of the original group—brought back to the United States.

The provisions of what came to be referred to as the preliminary emancipation proclamation, completed on July 22, 1863, included reference to the Confiscation Act of July 17, 1862. This act gave freedom to fugitive, captured, and abandoned slaves or rebels, and called for the emancipation of slaves on January 1, 1863, in those states or parts of states that were in rebellion against the United States.

Franklin documents the range of public, editorial, military, and abolitionist opinion generated by the appearance of this preliminary emancipation proclamation in the newspapers. Predictably, abolitionist leaders congratulated Lincoln on his commitment to equality, while southerners and southern newspapers were bitterly opposed to the proclamation, which they regarded as undermining their institutions and authority.

The final document was clearly issued as a military move "for suppressing said rebellion." The proclamation stated that "such persons of suitable condition will be received into the armed services of the United States." The intention of this document was to defeat efforts of the Confederacy at home, to erode its support abroad, and to strengthen the Union forces.

Franklin contends that Lincoln's first position was to save the Union without freeing a single slave; therefore, the issuance of the final Emancipation Proclamation was an act of final desperation. Lincoln knew that slaves would work doubly hard to save the Union and free themselves. Lincoln also personally believed that blacks and whites could never be equal, which explained his struggle over issuing the Emancipation Proclamation. However, due to the heroic efforts of black Union troops, Lincoln eventually applauded their contributions. Franklin concludes that the proclamation not only affected the course of the war but also may have influenced Lincoln's way of thinking about the problem of Negroes in the United States.

The six chapters are followed by a bibliographic essay on sources, extensively documented footnotes arranged by chapter, and an index.

High school teachers and students as well as undergraduate history instructors will find many creative uses for this text. Indeed, anyone who has an interest and curiosity about this period and who seeks a fuller, more accurate understanding of the Emancipation Proclamation and the man who wrote and signed it will benefit from reading this book.

5.126   Litwack, Leon. *Been in the Storm So Long: The Aftermath of Slavery.* New York: Alfred A. Knopf, 1979.

The purpose of Litwack's eloquent, prizewinning book is to explore "the countless ways in which freedom was perceived and experienced by the black men and women and how they acted on every level to shape their condition and future as freedmen and freedwomen."

Litwack uses sources created by the slaves themselves to articulate and interpret these perceptions. He draws on interviews with more than two thousand ex-slaves and testimony relayed to Union soldiers, Freedmen's Bureau officers, visitors, clergy, reporters, missionaries, teachers, and to a much lesser degree, slaveholders.

Each of the ten thematically arranged chapters begins and ends with the testimony of real slaves to illustrate the ways in which they perceived and were affected by freedom.

All aspects of slaves' lives were profoundly affected by emancipation: personal, familial, and political. For example, Litwack discusses slaves' reactions to the tragedies experienced by their owners during the Civil War, which he describes as a complex mixture of empathy and a sense of satisfaction. The dangerous and often fatal physical and symbolic act of escaping to Union lines was a risk many slaves were willing to take in order to be free. And blacks serving as Union soldiers in some ways facilitated the emotional transformation from slave to freedman.

Litwack cautions, however, that the death of slavery was very slow, even though there were significant moments that helped slaves perceive themselves as in a state of transition to freedom. The two most important measures of freedom were the ability to work for themselves and to reunite with their families. In chapter 5, entitled "How Free Is Free?" Litwack insists that freedom in the most meaningful sense could be understood in terms of the limitations it would place on white behavior: the freedom from the most oppressive aspects of bondage, freedom from whippings and harassment, and the freedom of action—to secure their families from involuntary separation. The practical and symbolic manifestations of freedom could be found in the choices that were now available to former slaves: the ability to marry legally and take a new surname and the opportunity to become literate and work for a salary.

The freedom to move about was exercised by many former slaves during the first year of emancipation. During this time, there was an exodus of former slaves from plantations to "prove to themselves it was real and to demonstrate to former owners that they no longer were controlled by them." However, the letters from freedmen during this period illustrate that they were experiencing contradictory feelings and emotions about freedom and their relationship with former slaveholders.

Unfortunately, slaves experienced little significant change in labor arrangements and compensation. Litwack explains that the real difference between slavery and freedom in this arena was not in the amount of compensation received but in the way blacks perceived themselves and their relationship to whites. They refused to obey orders and be obsequious. They also tended to work less, set their own pace, and take time off on Sundays to rest.

In spite of the newfound feelings of freedom experienced by blacks, whites still looked upon them as property without any rights. According to Litwack, former slaveholders were convinced that blacks still needed strict forms of control, without which they would become idle and lazy. The result of these attitudes was the passage of a series of black codes that were designed to reduce blacks to property. Blacks resisted these controls but Freedmen's Bureau officials often identified with planters.

Litwack argues that while many southern planters questioned the willingness of freed people to work, the real question was for whom they would work and at what rates. In "Back to Work: The New Dependency," Litwack agrees with Du Bois that freed people bargained for labor conditions during and after the Civil War. He identifies the unsettled labor issues as a form of compensation—when and how often it was to be paid, the arbitrary nature of employer's deductions, the kind of crops to be grown, the quality of the provisions received, the availability of schools for children, the right to unrestricted travel, and the freedom from verbal and physical abuse.

The labor contracts forced on blacks by southern legislatures after the war defined freed people's return to a state of dependency. Disputes arose over the terms of unfair labor contracts in which whites frequently took advantage of the illiteracy of freed people. Planters' exploitation of blacks was so great that they feared black uprising due to unfair pay and inhumane treatment. Some former slaves moved to towns or cities for greater security and opportunities. Others took advantage of contract talks at the end of the year to express their dissatisfaction with their conditions and to suggest how these conditions might be improved. Still other freed people organized plantation strikes.

In the chapter, "Gospel and the Primer," Litwack discusses the role of missionary teachers in assisting freed people in the transition from slavery to freedom. Litwack suggests that blacks first taught themselves to read and write or were taught by free blacks. He discusses the role of the American Missionary Association in, on the one hand, providing leaders of the black education movement in the South and, on the other hand, assuming that blacks would require the direction of white allies before they were able to take control over their lives.

In the political arena, Litwack highlights the radical role of the Reconstruction Acts in allowing blacks to vote for delegates to the southern state conventions. As a result, blacks voted in overwhelming numbers in their first exercise of political clout.

At the end of the text are a section of footnotes arranged by chapter; a selected bibliography of books, articles, government documents, and manuscript sources; and an index.

High school through graduate-level history instructors should read this book to gain a rich perspective on the myriad, complex ways in which freedom affected the lives of the former slaves.

5.127E   *The Long Road Up the Hill: African Americans in Congress.* Grandy, Lilian, Curator. Washington, D.C.: Smithsonian Institution Traveling Exhibition Service, 1993–1994.

Between 1870 and 1897, twenty-two blacks from southern states were elected to Congress; their road was anything but an easy journey. This exhibit portrays the careers and experiences of African-American congressmen from 1870 to the present. Reproductions of documents and photographs primarily from the National Archives, and to a lesser degree, from the Library of Congress, the Moorland-Spingarn Research Center, and other private sources, are included in this exhibition. A poster and brochure accompany the exhibit. Teachers of high school history and government courses will find this exhibit a valuable resource.

5.128   **Powell, Lawrence.** *New Masters: Northern Planters During the Civil War and Reconstruction.* New Haven, Conn.: Yale University Press, 1980.

Powell's study explores the role of the northern planter-missionaries who went south to invest in and raise cotton after the Civil War, and who introduced their own form of free labor in the South. Powell argues that this study of the estimated twenty thousand to fifty thousand northerners who left the North and settled in the South between 1860 and 1870 "illuminates important aspects of the Old South's metamorphosis into the New South . . . [as well as painting a fuller picture] of North–South relations."

In the first two of the seven thematically arranged chapters, Powell reveals who the new masters were and why they came south. In addition to the primary reason of making money in the cotton industry, they were also convinced they could introduce new methods of agriculture that would guarantee greater profits. Powell makes it clear that these northerners were and intended to be temporary settlers or "absentee landlords."

In the third and fourth chapters, Powell explores the attitudes of the southern planters toward their northern counterparts, including expectations of how northern planters were to treat ex-slaves. What united them, of course, was their common preoccupation with making large profits.

In chapter 5, "The New Dispensation," Powell explains that the most popular justification for the northern planter was the argument that only Yankees could provide ex-slaves with humane and intelligent supervision. However, the confidence in ex-slaves' ability to adjust to the new free labor system was not universal among northern planters, according to Powell, who then devotes the remainder of the chapter to a discussion of the few differences between the systems of labor created by the new masters and those practiced by the old masters. One of the most-common differences was the use of a task system by the new masters as opposed to a gang-labor system. Most important, the interest of northern planters in educating the freedmen set them apart from their southern counterparts.

In chapter 6, Powell explores the complex relationship between the northern planter and the ex-slave. He asserts that northern planters had unrealistic expectations about the ease of managing the ex-slaves and making them work harder to turn over a larger profit. The freed people had their own concrete notions of what freedom meant in terms of material advantages and, most of all, greater personal autonomy. Northern planters, then, had to balance their own concept of how ex-slaves should be "controlled" with the freed people's need and desire to exercise some independence over their time and lives. In the end, the new masters encountered considerable resistance from the freedmen.

In the final chapter, Powell traces the demise of the relationship between northern and southern planters to the failure of northern and southern business interests due to drought and falling cotton prices. Southern suspicion of northern interests in social equality and education for freedmen, coupled with historic sectional hostilities, economic ruin, and the enfranchisement of former slaves, further deteriorated any sense of goodwill that may have existed initially between the two groups.

Following chapter 7, Powell includes an epilogue, an appendix, footnotes, a bibliographical essay, and an index. The appendix includes a series of charts on the demographics of northern planters.

This book is an important work that is especially appealing to undergraduate history instructors and students.

5.129 Stampp, Kenneth. *The Era of Reconstruction, 1865–1877.*
New York: Alfred A. Knopf, 1970.

In this classic collection of enlightening lectures, originally delivered at
the University of London in 1960, Stampp analyzes the Reconstruction
period by incorporating political history written in the last two decades.
Through historical analysis, Stampp systematically repudiates the late-
nineteenth-century interpretation of Reconstruction written by William
A. Dunning, James Ford Rhodes, and their contemporaries.

Stampp charges that Dunning's characters were only one-dimen-
sional—good or evil—and that rather than relying on historical documents, facts, and objectivity, his writings were discolored by myth, racist
attitudes, and legend. For example, in the first chapter, Stampp states
that Dunning falsely accuses radical Republicans of punishing white
southern officers for their disloyalty to the Union. In reality, Confederate officers were only required to take an oath of allegiance to be
pardoned and to regain their right to vote and hold public office. With
the exception of Jefferson Davis (who was released within a few
months), no Confederates were ever brought to trial. Stampp also accuses Dunning of neglecting the accomplishments of radical Reconstruction, such as the organization of freedmen's aid societies and the
passage of the Fourteenth and Fifteenth Amendments. Finally, Stampp
traces the misinterpretation of the Reconstruction period to racist
stereotypes and theories that dominated nineteenth-century thought.
As these theories were challenged by twentieth-century sociologists and
anthropologists, revisionist historians have reinterpreted this period.

The remaining six chapters are arranged chronologically and reflect a revisionist view of Reconstruction. In chapter 2, on the politics
of Lincoln, Stampp examines Lincoln's philosophy and plan for the
Civil War, Reconstruction, and the Negro by analyzing his actions in
light of his background and political agenda. According to Stampp,
Lincoln's goal for Reconstruction was to restore the relationship between the southern states and the Union, which he saw as a task of
the president, not Congress. The radical Republicans insisted that the
problem belonged to Congress.

Stampp, like John Hope Franklin and other historians, indicates
that Lincoln approached the Reconstruction problem with several assumptions regarding the Negro: (1) emancipation must be gradual, (2)
colonization was the ideal solution to the race problem, and (3) if
colonization failed, the Negro had to accept an inferior status in American society. Consequently, Lincoln's conservative plan for restoring
southern states to the Union with maximum speed and minimum federal
intervention was disrupted by the radical Republicans and northern

humanitarians. Yet by 1870, conservative whites gained control of southern state governments and the South became solidly Democratic.

In chapter 3, on Andrew Johnson, Stampp traces Johnson's failure to get his Reconstruction policies past Congress to his underestimation of the tension between the southern yeomen and the southern aristocracy. The radical Republicans put Johnson in office because they hoped he would sympathize with their views on Reconstruction, yet when he changed his ideas about Reconstruction—the planter politicians convinced him to grant them amnesty—the radicals could not support him. Under Johnson, the Black Codes were passed to control and restrict the civil rights of blacks. It was Johnson, then, who introduced a pattern of disfranchisement, discrimination, and segregation into the postwar South.

In chapter 4, Stampp explains the victory of the radical Republicans and counters Dunning's claims that radicals wanted to exploit the Negro to punish the southern white man. Although Congress was dominated by moderate Republicans in 1865, they joined with the radicals to defeat the Democrats. The moderates feared that through the southern governments, Johnson would lose peace and that rebels were regaining control of the South and reestablishing slavery. Stampp paints a picture of idealistic radicals who were uncompromising on the subject of human rights. These radicals, including Charles Sumner, Thaddeus Stevens, George Julian, and Henry Wilson, were all antislavery crusaders whom Stampp refers to as the last group of nineteenth-century romantic reformers.

In chapter 5, "Radical Rule in the South," Stampp challenges Dunning's view that the radical governments expelled the South's natural leaders from power and replaced them with corrupt carpetbaggers and scalawags. Stampp insists that the conservatives criticized the radical governments because of their attempt to organize Negroes for political action and their easy acceptance of civil and political rights for blacks. He explains that although masses of Negroes joined the radicals, and Negroes *had influence* in all the radical governments, they certainly did not *control* them. Stampp suggests that one of the shortcomings of the radical governments was in not recognizing the need for the general education of the white masses, which led to social disorganization after the Civil War. He concludes that the radical governments were by far the most democratic the South had ever known. "Radicals were the only ones to extend to Negroes complete civil and political equality and try to protect them. The overthrow of these governments was hardly a victory for political democracy."

Chapter 6 is an analysis of radical Reconstruction. Stampp contends that the failure of the land reform program "made inevitable the ultimate failure of the whole radical program." The radicals proposed that confiscated lands from southern rebels be redistributed to freed people to ensure their independence and self-sufficiency. Lincoln, however, permitted the return of confiscated lands to the heirs of southern planters who had joined the Confederacy. In spite of successful experiments—for example, in the Georgia Sea Islands where black farmers were provided lands and in one year made $159,200 in profits—Johnson returned the land to the original plantation owners. Moderate Republicans would not support land reform, and, according to Stampp, many radicals did not understand the need to provide economic emancipation for the Negro, so land reform was defeated. Finally, Stampp documents the role and successes of the Freedmen's Bureau and the passage of the Fourteenth Amendment and the Civil Rights Act of 1868.

In the final chapter, "The Triumph of the Conservatives," Stampp documents the failures and successes of the radical Republican's Reconstruction. He concludes the greatest failure of the radicals was their inability to transform the South into a truly democratic society by providing for the civil and political rights of Negroes. The sharecropping system replaced slavery and reduced Negroes to second-class citizenship by failing to provide land reform. However, Foner (see entry 5.124) agrees with Stampp's assessment that the Fourteenth and Fifteenth Amendments were now part of the Constitution and could have been adopted only under the conditions of radical Reconstruction.

Following the main text are a twelve-page bibliographic essay and an index.

This classic work should be read by all students and teachers of American and African-American history at the undergraduate level. High school teachers and general readers who have an interest in this period will find this book highly readable and illuminating.

5.130 **Williamson, Joel.** *After Slavery: The Negro in South Carolina after Reconstruction, 1861–1877.* Chapel Hill: University of North Carolina Press, 1965.

This revisionist study of Reconstruction in South Carolina in many ways serves as a case study of Litwack's work. Again, freed people are portrayed as shaping the meaning of freedom. Common themes echoed in Litwack's work include the mass exodus of domestics and mechanics from plantations; freed people's desire to work for themselves, especially to grow food, not cotton; the freedom to move freely and express themselves in new forms of dress; the ability to speak freely and candidly to whites; and freed people's resistance to an unfair contract labor system imposed by whites.

In the thirteen chapters, Williamson explores the meaning of freedom to former slaves as laborers and in religion, education, race relations, the community, and politics. He describes how blacks worked harder for planters who had reputations of dealing fairly with laborers. (Agricultural production in South Carolina rose steadily during Reconstruction.) He also discusses the role blacks played in forming their own associations to purchase lands and describes the work of non-agricultural black laborers in South Carolina—domestics, artisans, carpenters, blacksmiths, masons, plasterers, mechanics, and engineers—who functioned as free economic agents. In summarizing the economic progress of blacks, Williamson states that the majority of blacks during this period made some improvement in their material situations and actively supported cooperative organizations such as reading clubs, burial and insurance companies, and fraternal associations.

The withdrawal of blacks from predominantly white congregations began with emancipation in South Carolina. Williamson's discussion of the various churches blacks established reveals that their decision to form their own churches was based on a need and desire to worship in their own style.

Educational progress in South Carolina was slow. By 1870 the illiteracy rate for blacks was only reduced from 95 percent to 85 percent due to the curtailment of benevolent societies' work, the termination of the Freedmen's Bureau's education activities, and the delay in the organization of a public school system. Negro teachers reduced the illiteracy rate from 78.5 percent in 1880 to 64 percent in 1890 and then to 52.8 percent in 1900.

Racist attitudes toward blacks did not die with emancipation. The basic assumption of whites, according to Williamson, was that the "Negro race was inherently and immutably inferior to their own." These attitudes led to the rise of racist organizations such as the Ku Klux Klan and gun clubs founded by whites to terrorize black communities and discourage Negro voters. Yet, blacks were able to exercise their political power during Reconstruction with the election of black politicians from South Carolina.

A bibliography of primary and secondary sources and an index are provided. By functioning as a case study on the effects of emancipation and Reconstruction on the state of South Carolina, this book serves an important purpose. It is recommended for undergraduate students and faculty in American history.

Documentary Histories

5.131   Berlin, Ira, ed. *Free at Last: A Documentary History of Slavery, Freedom, and the Civil War.* New York: The New Press, 1992.

Drawing from a selection of documents located in the National Archives and included in the four-volume study entitled *Freedom: A Documentary History of Emancipation, 1861–1867*, this single-volume work "unravels the history of emancipation and explains how a people with little power and few weapons secured its freedom against the will of those with great power and many weapons." An important theme that unites these original source materials is the black role in transforming the Civil War into a war against slavery and for freedom.

Many voices are represented in these 539 pages of letters, telegrams, and other documents. There is correspondence between black soldiers and their families and between relatives who were separated during slavery. There are also letters from slaveholders, Union soldiers, and officers, politicians, and ordinary citizens, which together help explain the events and changes in the nation that proclaimed a new social order.

The six chapters are arranged by subject and preceded by a concise but useful chronology of primarily Union activity, from the election of Abraham Lincoln in 1860 to the ratification of the Thirteenth Amendment on December 18, 1865. There is also an introduction by the editors. Each document or group of related documents includes revealing editorial commentary to explain the context, events, or personalities in greater detail.

A sampling of documents from the first chapter, entitled "A War for the Union," includes a letter from a slave who escaped to a Union regiment looking for his wife, instructions from Union officers requiring troops to treat fugitive slaves as persons rather than chattel, the District of Columbia Emancipation Act, letters from slaves who accompanied their owners into the Confederate army informing loved ones of the federal emancipation policies, and letters from Union officers explaining the need for black men to bear arms against the Confederacy to save the Union.

In chapter 2, "A War for Freedom," which includes documents written after the Emancipation Proclamation issued in 1863, the range of documents includes black soldiers setting out to free other slaves; a letter from a slave in Tennessee telling of brutal, inhumane treatment by his slaveholder; letters from former slaves requesting aid in locating and reuniting with their families; letters from southern planters to President Jefferson Davis advising him of the need to enlist slave men into the Confederate army to win the war; and a letter from a slave in South Carolina who secretly aided the Union effort.

In the chapter "Life and Labor within Union Lines," the editors include documents that question the status of slaves and their families who escaped to the Union army before the North committed itself to emancipation. The struggle to organize free labor agreements—largely based on northern models—for the liberated slaves is explored in the chapter "Free Labor in the Midst of the War." Conflicts over the terms and conditions of labor, the extent of discipline and supervision, and the amount and form of compensation are documented here.

The precarious status of slaves from the loyal slave states of Maryland, Missouri, and Kentucky (which were excluded from the Emancipation Proclamation) is explored in a chapter entitled "Slavery within the Union." In the final chapter, "Soldiers and Citizens," the documents reveal the complex experiences of former slaves. On the one hand, former slaves were ill treated in the Union army, assigned to hard labor, and paid less than their white counterparts. On the other hand, the world of former slaves was broadened by the war experience since many learned to read and write, which "laid the foundation for a new world of freedom."

The book concludes with a section of footnotes arranged by chapter, a bibliographical essay of suggestions for further reading, and an extensive index. History teachers in colleges and secondary schools across the United States assisted in the construction of this volume by lobbying for documents that "had to be included." Therefore, the resulting volume of rich primary source materials is especially useful for this group. Editors of this volume include Ira Berlin, Barbara Fields, Steven Miller, Joseph Reidy, and Leslie Rowland, whose editorial commentary provides valuable insight into the interpretation of the broad range of documents selected for the volume.

5.132   McPherson, James M. *The Negro's Civil War: How American Negroes Felt and Acted during the War for the Union.* New York: Pantheon Books, 1965.

This documentary collection of speeches, letters, and articles presenting all aspects of the Negro's role in the war is told primarily in the words of blacks. The purpose of the book is to document the contributions, achievements, hopes, aspirations, and opinions of blacks as active participants in the war effort and in the shaping of their own freedom.

Unlike *Free at Last* (entry 5.131), McPherson includes only excerpts of documents created by blacks. Like *Free at Last*, he supplies thoughtful commentary at the beginning of each of the twenty-two chapters and between all sets of documents.

The chapters are arranged chronologically from the election of Abraham Lincoln in 1860 through the end of the war. The documents included here articulate the views and opinions of black leaders such as Frederick Douglass, Henry Highland Garnet, Susie King Taylor and Charlotte Forten, William Wells Brown, Martin Delany, and countless less-renowned blacks. Excerpts from editorials in black newspapers are also presented here.

Topics covered include the black response to the war, black and white attitudes about black participation in the war effort, black response to race riots in the north, experiences of black teachers in educating the children of contraband and freed people, black response to Lincoln's colonization plan, organization of relief efforts and the establishment of black churches and educational institutions after the Emancipation Proclamation, Negro participation in the Union army, the struggle for equal pay, the controversy over land ownership, and Negro attitudes toward Lincoln near the end of the war.

The chapters are followed by two appendixes—general Negro and white population statistics in 1860, and Negro and white population statistics in selected American cities in 1860. A section of footnotes arranged by chapter, a bibliographical essay on sources, and an index are provided.

Specifically designed for the general reader, this book is well suited for high school and lower-division undergraduate history courses.

5.133 **Ripley, C. Peter, ed.** *Black Abolitionist Papers, 1830–1865.* Vol. 1, *The British Isles, 1830–1865.* Vol. 2, *Canada, 1830–1865.* Vol. 3, *The United States, 1830–1846.* Vol. 4, *The United States, 1847–1858.* Vol. 5, *The United States, 1859–1865.* Chapel Hill: University of North Carolina Press, 1985.

The purpose of the Black Abolitionist Papers project was to collect and make available to the public writings of black Americans involved in the abolitionist movement from 1830 to 1865. The international search for primary documents including letters, speeches, diaries, newspaper articles, editorials, sermons, and essays took approximately four years. The search yielded more than 14,000 documents written by nearly 300 men and women, which editors located in 200 libraries and 110 newspapers.

The selection criteria included documents that "fairly represent the goals, ideas, and actions of black abolitionists," as well as documents that reveal race relations in the free states, black churches and schools in northern cities, black family life, African missionary work, and other aspects of African-American life and culture during this time period. Both renowned and lesser-known black abolitionists' works are included. The editorial board includes many of the historians whose works are represented in this book: Earl Thorpe, John Blassingame, John Hope Franklin, Leon Litwack, Benjamin Quarles, and Dorothy Porter.

The five-volume series covers the British Isles, Canada, and three volumes on the United States: 1830–1846, 1847–1848, and 1859–1865. The published volumes include edited and annotated representative documents—only about 10 percent of the total. The microfilmed edition contains the 14,000 unedited documents.

Each volume begins with an extensive introduction that provides historical context for the documents. Information on each document includes place and date, recipient's name and address, salutation, closing, signature, marginal notes, and postscripts. To enhance the reader's understanding of the documents, headnotes precede each document provided. Extensive document notes are also included, especially for subjects on which there is little or no available information. The introduction to the U.S. series (volumes 3 through 5) traces the evolution of black abolitionist activity and organizations including moral reform, racial advancement, temperance, the role of the black press, the Underground Railroad, and the role of the American Missionary Association. The documents are followed by an index.

These important volumes are better suited for upper-division and graduate history classes, while high school history instructors and students will find Ripley's *Witness for Freedom* (entry 5.134) more appropriate for their use.

5.134   **Ripley, C. Peter, ed.** *Witness for Freedom: African-American Voices on Race, Slavery, and Emancipation.* Chapel Hill and London: The University of North Carolina Press, 1993.

With the exception of seven documents, all documents included in this book were drawn from the four-volume series the *Black Abolitionist Papers* (entry 5.133), including introductory essays and full annotations. A chronology from 1619 to 1865 precedes an extensive introduction to the history of the abolitionist movement. The editors credit black abolitionists with serving as a persistent voice for racial equality, and insisting that racial prejudice was inseparable from the slavery question.

The five chapters are arranged chronologically; each chapter and each topic within a chapter includes an introduction. Chapter 1 focuses on the rise of black abolitionism and covers documents related to moral reform and prejudice. Chapter 2 provides documents on African Americans and the antislavery movement, which includes slave narratives, black women abolitionists, antislavery and the black community, and problems in the movement. Chapter 3 explores themes of black independence: the African-American press, antislavery politics, and black antislavery tactics. Chapter 4 is entitled "Black Abolitionists and the National Crisis." The Fugitive Slave Act, black emigration, black nationality, and blacks and John Brown are topics highlighted in this chapter. The last chapter covers documents on or relating to the Civil War: the Emancipation Proclamation, the black military experience, and Reconstruction.

David Walker, Samuel Cornish, Ellen Craft, William Wells Brown, Henry Highland Garnet, Samuel Ward, David Ruggles, Sarah Forten, Sojourner Truth, Emily Allen, and Charles Ray are but a few of the abolitionists whose compelling stories and perspectives are represented here. For each document, the original source is provided, as is a citation to the volume and page numbers where the document appears in the *Black Abolitionist Papers* (entry 5.133).

A useful glossary, complete with short biographical sketches of individuals who either created the documents or were mentioned in the documents, is provided. Also included are a bibliographical essay and an index.

This accessible source can easily be incorporated into the curriculum for high school and lower-division undergraduate history courses.

5.135 **Sterling, Dorothy, ed.** *We Are Your Sisters: Black Women in the Nineteenth Century.* New York and London: W. W. Norton, 1984.

This documentary history of black women depicts the lives of women during slavery, Reconstruction, and emancipation by drawing upon ex-slaves' oral-history interviews, letters, diaries, autobiographies, and newspaper accounts. Due to the growing interest in black women's history and the availability of a wider range of primary documents, Sterling, unlike Lerner (entry 4.97) twenty years earlier, was able to include a more representative sample of women, both renowned and lesser-known, from all walks of life—washerwomen and domestics to teachers, lecturers, and writers—who lived between 1800 and the 1880s. Sterling does not include formal writings, sermons, or speeches that can be found in other works; instead she chooses to present this work as a "sourcebook sampler."

The six chapters are arranged chronologically and provide a rich documentary record of the experiences and activities of black women.

Sterling adds to Lerner's work in that she provides excerpts of personal letters written by black women to their families and friends. Topics in the first chapter on slavery include stories of work in the field, slaveholders' houses and slave quarters, relationships with husbands and children, the heartbreak of separation from families, rape and concubinage, and resistance and resettlement.

From documents on northern free women of color, presented in the second chapter, readers learn of their participation in organizations for mutual relief, self-education, and abolition. The personal challenges experienced by the wives and children of several abolitionist black men, Anna Douglass (wife of Frederick Douglass) and Rosetta Douglass (daughter of Frederick and Anna Douglass), as well as Elizabeth Brown (wife of William Wells Brown), are revealed through their letters.

In chapter 3, entitled "The War Years," black schoolteachers employed by the American Missionary Association describe their work and lives in the South where they were sent to educate the children of freed people. Letters of Charlotte Forten and Lucie Stanton Day and others provide valuable insight into their adjustment to the South and the children and families they taught. Chapter 4, on freedwomen, includes a portrait of the difficult but influential work and lives of several female members of the Fisk Jubilee Singers: Ella Sheppard and Maggie Porter.

Chapter 5, on the postwar North, contains excerpts from the documents of more renowned black women, such as Fannie Coppin, Frances Ellen Watkins Harper, Charlotte Forten Grimké, Anna Cooper, Susan B. McKinney Steward, and other prominent educators and doctors. The final chapter focuses on longer excerpts from the diaries of four black women: Frances Rollin, Mary Virginia Montgomery, Laura Hamilton, and Ida B. Wells-Barnett, to provide readers with an introduction to black women of the first free generation.

Special features in this book include an introductory historical overview of black women's history; a selected bibliography of books, articles, dissertations, manuscript sources, and periodicals; source notes arranged by chapter; and an index. Since Sterling's book is more limited in scope than Lerner's, the excerpts and introductory essays are more substantive.

Sterling's book provides a valuable sampling of primary documents used by both Jones and White in writing the histories of black women during slavery and Reconstruction. Teachers of women's history and black history at the upper-division high school and undergraduate levels will want to incorporate this rich source of women's history into the curriculum.

CHAPTER SIX

Sources by Chronological Period, from Migration to the Present

R APID SOCIETAL CHANGES OCCURRED IN THE 1890s THAT dramatically affected the lives of black Americans. The automobile was invented, which improved transportation for rural southerners, and almost a quarter of black farmers owned their land. In addition, major black organizations were founded during this period, including the National Business League (1900), The National Baptist Convention (1895), the National Medical Association (1895), and the National Association of Colored Women (1896). A black middle class was growing, and the black population in general was migrating from southern rural areas to southern urban areas.

In stark contrast to these developments, the resentment against black progress was also swelling. The 1890s were also characterized by the most brutal violence against blacks that the country had ever experienced. From 1889 to 1899, there was an average of 188 lynchings per year; most often the victims were successful blacks or those who refused to exhibit obsequious behavior toward whites. In spite of these attempts to frighten blacks into submission, a "New Negro" was indeed emerging as the black population continued to shift from the South to the North; gain political rights, greater educational, and more economic opportunities; and establish organizations to combat de facto and de jure segregation and discrimination.

Chapter 6 (entries 6.136–179) chronicles the African-American struggle for civil rights and economic equity. The chapter is divided into two parts: sources from the postemancipation period (including information on migration and urbanization) and sources on the Civil Rights movement and the struggle for economic equity.

Migration and Urbanization

With the passage of *Plessy* v. *Ferguson* in 1896, in which the Supreme Court upheld the doctrine of "separate but equal," racial hostility and violence intensified in the South. The decline of the cotton crop brought about by the boll weevil, the existence of an unfair sharecropping system that kept blacks in abject poverty, and the emergence of a caste system based on color, legal injustice, inferior schools, and denial of voting rights contributed to the general malaise and dissatisfaction of southern African Americans.

According to many historians, it was not only the dismal social and economic "push" of the South, but primarily the "pull" of the North that gave rise to the Great Migration during the period from 1916 to 1919. Economic opportunities in the North began to open up to blacks when World War I drained the pool of immigrant workers in industrial cities. From 1910 to 1920, more than a half million African Americans migrated from the South to the North, with the largest numbers migrating from 1916 to 1919.

The first section of chapter 6 (entries 6.136–156) reviews works on the migration and urbanization of blacks during the period from 1915 to the 1940s. Unlike earlier chapters, this one will include several relevant sociological works that have influenced historical works on this period—and without which no understanding of urbanization would be complete. Also annotated in this part are several seminal studies of migration to and urbanization of specific northern cities; these can be viewed as case studies.

Three of the standard works on Negro migration include W. E. B. Du Bois's classic *The Philadelphia Negro* (1899), Carter G. Woodson's *A Century of Negro Migration* (1918), and Emmett Scott's *Negro Migration during the War* (1920). The classic sociological study of urbanization is presented by St. Clair Drake and Horace Cayton in their groundbreaking work, *The Black Metropolis: A Study of Negro Life in a Northern City* (1945), and Gunnar Myrdal's *An American Dilemma* (1944). More recent general studies of migration include Florette Henri's *Black Migration: Movement North, 1900–1920* (1974) and Joe William Trotter's *The Great Migration in Historical Perspective: New Dimensions of Race, Class, and Gender* (1991). Books by Allan Spear (*Black Chicago*, 1967), Gilbert Osofsky (*Harlem*, 1968), and Nicholas Lemann (*The Promised Land*, 1991) are often-cited works that present a more pathological and hopeless view of urban black life during the Great Migration. Books by Kenneth Kusmer (*A Ghetto Takes Shape:*

Black Cleveland, 1976), James Grossman (*Land of Hope*, 1989), and James Borchert (*Alley Life in Washington*, 1980) study dynamic and complex communities created by internal and external forces in which the newly arrived black migrants cope with and respond creatively to adversity. Finally, works on two of the most prominent civil rights organizations of the period are annotated in this section: Nancy Weiss's *The National Urban League, 1910–1940* (1974), and Charles Kellogg's *NAACP* (1967). Together these studies indicate that although northern cities provided neither a haven from racism nor unlimited economic opportunities, the status of migrants after 1915 constituted an advance over their previous condition, albeit a mixed blessing.

Field to Factory, a groundbreaking National Museum of American History exhibit on the Great Migration, now offered as a traveling exhibit by SITES, recent videotapes on migration and civil rights, and photographic works by Richard Samuel Roberts and James Van DerZee also are reviewed here to assist teachers, students, and the general reader to experience this period through a variety of media.

6.136V Barron, Evelyn. *Uncommon Images: James Van DerZee.*
Videorecording, 22 min. New York: Distr. Filmmakers
Library, 1978.

This video portrays the life and work of the "dean of black photographers." Junior high through adult audiences will marvel at the artistic and historic value of Van DerZee's stunning photographs as well as his fascinating life.

Winner of the Black Film Festival, the CINE Golden Eagle, and the Silver Plaque (Chicago International Film Festival) awards, this video is visually and educationally rewarding and exciting.

6.137 Borchert, James. *Alley Life in Washington: Family,
Community, Religion, and Folklife in the City, 1850–1970.*
Urbana, Chicago, and London: University of Illinois Press,
1980.

Borchert's study examines creative strategies and institutions within migrant communities that assisted migrants to cope with and even enjoy their new urban environment. Borchert's objective is to "analyze the impact of the urban environment on folk migrants, examine the experiences of African-American migrants to determine whether the primary groups of folklife weakened or remained strong, and measure the extent to which migrants' lives were characterized by either order or disorder." Borchert's thesis is that migrants used primary groups and folk experiences to create strategies that enabled them to survive often harsh and difficult urban experiences. He further asserts that migrants modified their rural folk culture to the new urban environment without rejecting or dismissing their traditional patterns of behavior.

The book is arranged in six chapters. Chapter 1 provides an overview and context for the evolution of black residence patterns in Washington, D.C. Chapters 2 and 3 explore primary groups of family and community to determine the extent of social order and the persistence of traditional forms and adaptations to the urban environment. Chapter 4 examines childhood in the alleys to determine how external institutions and factors disrupted the socialization process. Chapter 5 describes occupational structure and work experiences of alley residents. The final chapter examines the roles played by religion and folklife in light of cultural breakdown.

In the first chapter, Borchert demonstrates how alley housing was originally designed for working-class whites but became ghettos for black residents after the Civil War, then recently was transformed and restored into expensive, high-demand residences for affluent Washingtonians.

In chapter 2, Borchert offers a new paradigm through which migrant family life can be viewed. Rather than concentrating on the merits of "stable and orderly" two-parent families among the migrant population, Borchert challenges assumptions and definitions inherent in census figures and reports. His approach is to pose questions about what constitutes family and which form is best, given the circumstances under which migrant families had to exist. He observes that there is much more equality between men and women among black urban families than in traditional white families, which prompted many sociologists to discuss the existence of a "pathological" black matriarchy among black migrant life. Furthermore, the extended family, composed of blood relatives and nonrelatives, demonstrated that migrant families were flexible and adjusted to severe economic stresses and the high cost of housing by creating a strong support system.

According to Borchert, this support system also extends to community life. Communal concerns expressed through mutual aid—especially during times of sickness, trouble, and death—friendship, protection, and concern for children were common among alley residents. In examining the socialization of children in chapter 4, Borchert observes that children were needed to work both inside and outside the home but turned work into play. He also examines the importance of songs, poems, and the traditional communal creation of story and song.

Employment data discussed in chapter 5 reveal that the majority of alley residents were concentrated in unskilled or service occupations that had not changed substantially by the 1950s. To make ends meet, families engaged in junking—collecting metal scraps and glass to sell, purchased clothes and furniture from second-hand stores, or took in boarders. Exploitation by alley store owners—who extended credit to residents at exorbitant interest rates—and landlords who refused to make repairs on their property may have influenced some residents to become involved in illegal businesses. While unacceptable by mainstream cultural standards, these businesses represented positive institutions within the alley. Borchert dispels the notion of a community plagued by crime and violence by revealing that most crimes were essentially petty and victimless.

In the final chapter on religion and folklife, Borchert examines limited sources that suggest the rural migrants' interaction with city life resulted in "the rise of more-formal institutions and activities, albeit ones which reflected traditional roles and functions." The importance of religious activity among alley residents is seen through church attendance, the singing of hymns and spirituals by children and adults, the prominent role of the Bible among family possessions, and alley funerals.

Four appendixes are included: sources and methodology, photographs, the 1880 manuscript census, and a bibliography of alley dwellings in other cities. An index follows the appendixes.

Urban or community history and social studies instructors at the high school and college levels will find this book valuable for challenging mainstream assumptions and interpretations of urban norms. Many will enjoy the three-dimensional people and lives Borchert describes.

6.138   Drake, St. Clair, and Horace R. Cayton. *Black Metropolis: A Study of Negro Life in a Northern City.* 2v. New York: Harcourt, Brace, and World, 1945. Reprint, 1970.

Black Metropolis was one of the first urban community studies of Negro life. It was also the first in a series of studies that focused on Chicago as a case study of the effects of the Great Migration on a typical large northern city. This classic book laid the groundwork for a series of studies that followed it in form and purpose, if not in content (see entry 6.141 by Grossman and entry 6.145 by Lemann). The purpose of Drake's study was to conduct a great social survey of a major community to point the way for reforming the conditions and lives of people living at or below poverty levels.

Although Drake, a sociologist, and Cayton, an anthropologist, skillfully weave the history of Chicago into the study, their reliance on survey research data and anthropological methodology is evident in their systematic analysis of social organizations. The authors hired students from the University of Chicago to assist them in conducting the research. In this respect and others, *Black Metropolis* is a more-comprehensive and analytical counterpart to Scott's work (entry 6.151). Charts, maps, census reports, statistics, and stories gathered from interviews and surveys permeate the study and guide the topics, analysis, and conclusions.

The work is divided into three parts. Part 1 provides historical background, context, and data for readers by discussing the history of Chicago, the reasons why southern Negroes decided to migrate to Chicago, the appeal of industrialized Chicago to them and to immigrants, and the causes and effects of the 1919 Chicago race riot. The authors describe Chicago as a city "characterized by a split into competing economic groups, social classes, ethnic groups, and religious and secular associations with their own sets of traditions that were divided into three groups: the white, wealthy few; the growing middle classes; and the poorer wage earners that included one-third of a million Negroes." This section also discusses the role of the immigrant population in Chicago and the great influence of John Abbott, a Negro migrant himself, and his newspaper, *The Chicago Defender*, in communicating job opportunities to Negroes in the South, beginning in the early 1900s.

Part 2 explores race relations; discrimination in housing, employment, and social life; the creation of the black ghetto; black workers and unions; and political participation. One of the results of the 1919 race riot was the formation of the Chicago Commission on Race Relations, which issued a report on the riots. In studying the problems, the commission in 1920 asked Negro migrants to explain what they liked about the North. The overwhelming responses were freedom in voting, a chance to make a living, and personal freedom. Optimism, expressed in the answer "opportunity to send their children to better schools and a sense of living without fear," was dissipated by the riots.

Perhaps even more revealing is a chart describing the areas of agreement and disagreement between Negroes and whites. Areas of agreement include intermarriage and membership in white cliques, churches, and social clubs. Areas of disagreement center around critical issues of economic and housing opportunities, such as white-collar employment outside the Black Belt (i.e., the black ghetto); membership in business and professional associations; use of hospital facilities outside the Black Belt; unrestricted use of beaches and parks throughout the city; and, most important, Negro residence throughout the city and white-collar employment outside the Black Belt.

Chapter 8, "The Black Ghetto," discusses residential segregation and real estate companies' widespread practice of "restrictive covenants"—arbitrary restrictions on living space of Negroes. Other topics discussed include limited employment opportunities that relegated the migrants to positions as domestics and as unskilled laborers, poverty and social disorganization in the Black Belt as measured by male juvenile delinquency and illegitimate births, and so on. On this latter point, the authors are quick to emphasize the reasons for poverty and disorganization in the Black Belt rather than merely criticize the phenomenon.

Chapter 9 in part 2 more fully explores the job status of Negro migrants after World War II: last hired and first fired employees in a labor-surplus economy. The origins of black poverty are readily defined as the authors cite statistics on unemployment and define reasons for the high unemployment of blacks: concentration in occupations that were the first to feel the economic crisis (e.g., service and unskilled laborers), last-hired first-fired policy set by white employers who preferred to maintain whites in jobs over Negroes, and the continued migration of Negroes to Chicago between 1930 and 1940 even though there were no jobs for them.

In one of the final chapters in part 2, the authors explore the pivotal role of labor unions, which helped break the job ceiling for Negro workers in the mid-1930s. The last chapter, on political expediency, discusses the emergence of black politicians and the voting patterns of the migrants who, the authors conclude, ". . . seldom supported reform against the Chicago political machine; they preferred to deal with realists who were trading political positions and favored legislation for votes." Politics became, then, the most important method by which Negroes sought to change their status.

Part 3 focuses entirely on the Bronzeville community in Chicago. Chapter 15 explores the overall influence of the black press and church; chapter 16 profiles Negro businesses; chapter 17 examines political machinery in Bronzeville; and chapters 18 through 23 are devoted to a discussion of internal relations within Bronzeville. In the final chapter, the authors call for a remedy to the problems confronting Negroes in Chicago and argue convincingly for the "progressive relaxation of discrimination and segregation, beginning immediately, and the strengthening of all social controls in the Black Belt."

The final chapter is followed by an explanation of the methodology used in the study, footnotes, and a bibliography.

High school and undergraduate history and sociology teachers will want to read this study for an understanding of the roots of present-day poverty among African Americans.

6.139   Du Bois, W. E. B. *The Philadelphia Negro: A Social Study.* Philadelphia: University of Pennsylvania Press, 1899.

The Philadelphia Negro, according to historian David Lewis, "virtually invented the field of urban sociology." The purpose of this pioneering study is similar to Drake and Cayton's study of Chicago: "to furnish local agencies and individuals interested in improving the conditions of the Negro population in Philadelphia a more comprehensive knowledge of the existing condition of Negroes." Du Bois's approach is based on the premise that to improve conditions, one must first study the problems, investigate the causes, and then explore solutions.

The study was done for the University of Pennsylvania and began in August 1896. It was completed in January 1898. A special report by Isabel Eaton on Negro domestic services, a companion study that utilizes similar research methodology, is provided at the end of this edition. Both studies use field research in addition to reviewing related research on the topic for historical context. Du Bois conducted house-to-house visitations and interviews and attended business, church, social, educational, and political meetings with more than 10,000 Negro residents in Philadelphia, especially in the Seventh Ward.

The eighteen chapters represent Du Bois's extensive report on the status and condition of Negroes in Philadelphia. The range of topics and issues covered includes a history of Negroes in Philadelphia; Negro population statistics and trends, education and literacy, occupations, health, family size, income, property, and family life; a review of institutions and organizations established by and for Negroes, such as the church, beneficial and secret societies, and businesses; criminal activity, poverty, and alcoholism; housing, racial prejudice, and racial intermarriage; and Negro suffrage.

Du Bois identifies major problems and factors contributing to some of the problems. Limited occupations open to Negro men and women, inadequate and expensive housing, lack of educational opportunities for children and adults, and class antagonism are a sampling of issues he delineates. In reporting that the positions held by most Negroes were in low-paid service occupations, Du Bois also explains that the causes were directly related to competition, industrial change, and racial prejudice against Negroes.

The report concludes with a chapter entitled "The Final Word," in which Du Bois summarizes the major findings and discusses the implications for improving the status of Negroes in Philadelphia. Three appendixes follow the chapters: schedules used in the house-to-house inquiry, legislation of Pennsylvania in regard to the Negro, and a bibliography.

This classic work, exemplary of Progressive-era writings, should be required reading for social studies instructors, urban historians, and sociologists at the high school and college levels.

6.140E *Field to Factory: Afro-American Migration, 1915–1940.* Spencer Crew, Curator. Smithsonian Institution Traveling Exhibition Service, 1993–1994.

This significant and popular SITES exhibit dramatically depicts real life stories of African-American families that migrated from the rural South to the urban North between 1915 and 1940. The exhibit combines photographs, personal objects, primary documents, and oral histories to document the forces that influenced blacks to venture north, the lives and families they left behind, the new life they encountered in the North, the jobs they found, the places they lived, the new communities they fashioned, and the hopes and disappointments they experienced. Based on the permanent exhibit hall installed in the National Museum of American History in 1985, the museum catalog by the same title was written by curator Spencer Crew, director of the National Museum of American History. The catalog serves as an appealing and vital resource for classroom use and contains reproductions of many of the photographs and excerpts of the oral histories included in the permanent exhibition. *Field to Factory* provides an invaluable history lesson for junior high through adult readers and viewers.

6.141 Grossman, James R. *Land of Hope: Chicago, Black Southerners, and the Great Migration.* Chicago and London: University of Chicago Press, 1989.

Grossman's history of the Great Migration examines the meaning of the movement, using the perspectives of its participants and focusing on their adjustment to a northern industrial city and their perceptions of their place in that city. Unlike Drake and Cayton's and Lemann's studies of Chicago (entries 6.138 and 6.145, respectively), Grossman explores the interactions among "the structural forces in the South, migration experiences, structural forces in the North, racial attitudes, and migrants' perceptions of each of these." To identify and explicate these forces and perceptions, Grossman draws upon a full range of migrants' letters, newspaper files, and government records—a much wider range of sources than were utilized by Lemann (entry 6.145).

The book is arranged in two parts. The first part, which includes four chapters, provides a narrative and analytical foundation for understanding what black southerners did and thought after they arrived in the North and how their experiences as black southerners shaped the ways in which they approached urban schools, politics, work places, and unions. Part 2, which includes five chapters, explores the experiences of migrants in Chicago and the ways in which the migrants' backgrounds and experiences affected their perceptions of and responses to the Chicago environment.

Grossman unveils a sophisticated network of migration clubs in explaining the ways in which black southerners learned of conditions and opportunities in the North. In these clubs, letters were passed along to blacks in Chicago, who in turn responded with reliable information about the North. Migrants used the information and the network to plan and execute the process. Once migrants arrived, they tapped into the networks of people who had assisted them. Therefore, in most cases, the move was calculated and the risks understood.

In part 2, Grossman turns to migrants' experiences in Chicago and focuses on their methods of adapting to the industrial North, themes not touched upon in Drake and Cayton's (entry 6.138) or Lemann's studies. Grossman characterizes black institutional development within Chicago as a dynamic of choice and constraint. State legislation prohibited segregation in public schools and accommodations, but de facto segregation in housing and schools was very much alive, as was discrimination in employment. Grossman describes a more thriving middle class—as defined by those with stable incomes—of African Americans who were businesspeople, postal workers, and Pullman porters. He also counters Lemann's descriptions of the immorality of lower-class blacks in Chicago. Grossman indicates that most African Americans had little time to lead dissolute, immoral lives; in fact, more than one-half of black women worked outside the home, compared with one-fourth of white women.

Grossman's assessment of the migrants' bleak housing situation was partly offset by a network of kin and good friends who helped them solve this problem, at least temporarily. Other important social and welfare organizations established by African Americans are discussed. These institutions included the Phillis Wheatley Association, which helped female migrants to adjust and locate jobs. The Negro Fellowship League, founded by antilynching crusader Ida B. Wells-Barnett in 1911, provided a lodging house, employment agency, and reading room. The work of the YMCA and the National Urban League, which were well supported by white philanthropists, is also discussed.

In chapter six, on race relations in Chicago, Grossman notes that although discrimination against African Americans could not be avoided in Chicago during this period, it was not ubiquitous. Whites seldom aggressively displayed attitudes in impersonal contacts with the migrants. This meant that migrants could leave behind most of their fears of whites in this context.

Grossman also details the experiences and hopes migrants had in educating their children and themselves. According to him, blacks entered schools in greater numbers than either immigrants or native-born whites of mixed or foreign parentage. Problems encountered by black students in Chicago schools will not be new to the present-day reader: African-American children were frequently labeled as retarded or of low mental capacity by white teachers and administrators who did not challenge existing racial stereotypes. Therefore, African-American children were not motivated to achieve, and if they did achieve, the payoff usually was not a better-paying job.

Grossman concludes that the rights to vote and gain access to educational and employment opportunities were offered by the industrial northern city, but migrants did not have the freedom to become involved in an ongoing process of full participation in the city's economic and political life.

Comprehensive footnotes to each of the nine chapters, a selected bibliography, and an index follow the main text.

This highly readable book is valuable for high school and undergraduate history instructors. It provides an important balance to Lemann's more recent work.

6.142 Henri, Florette. *Black Migration: Movement North, 1900–1920.* Garden City, N.Y.: Anchor Press, 1975.

Black Migration: Movement North documents the demographic, geographic, economic, political, social, and psychological changes blacks underwent between 1900 and 1920. Henri aims to reveal the stories of black men and women who were active participants in shaping their own destiny. She describes them as "choosers, makers, and doers . . ." and notes that "many blacks changed themselves, their world, and their children's future" by leaving the South to seek better opportunities in the North.

The eleven chapters of this book are arranged chronologically. The first chapter describes events that warned of bleak prospects for blacks at the turn of the century: the *Plessy* v. *Ferguson* decision,

Booker T. Washington's Atlanta Exposition speech denying black equality, and the resurgence of the solid Democratic South. Chapter 2 explores how blacks made the conscious, courageous, well-organized decision to venture from their homes to settle in northern cities. Chapters 3 and 4 explain the economic and social conditions blacks found and defined in the inner cities. Employment opportunities and wages for Negroes are explored in chapter 5. Henri explains that even with the problems encountered in northern ghettos, blacks could get better jobs and could live, dress, and eat better in the northern cities than they could in the South.

In chapter 6, "Paths to a Place in the Society," Henri discusses the impact of education, the church, a developing black middle class, and political power on moving blacks toward more-equal ground. Chapter 7 investigates the national causes that encouraged racism and racist ideology during the first two decades of the twentieth century. The position of the Progressive movement on the race question is the subject of chapter 8, entitled "Prejudice in Action." The hopes and disappointments and the treatment of black soldiers during World War I are revealed in chapter 9. "The New Negro who returned to white America after the war was indeed a changed person, yet America's attitude toward black soldiers and blacks in general only worsened." The race riots of 1919 and blacks' reactions to the riots are explored in chapter 10.

The final chapter examines the work of black writers and artists who participated in creating a Negro Renaissance, and the emergence of the New Negro who took pride in the African heritage by joining Marcus Garvey's Back to Africa movement. The book concludes with footnotes to all the chapters, an extensive bibliography, and an index.

High school history and social studies teachers will enjoy reading this book, which provides an excellent overview of the Great Migration.

6.143 **Kellogg, Charles Flint.** *NAACP: A History of the National Association for the Advancement of Colored People, 1909–1920.* Vol. 1. Baltimore: Johns Hopkins University Press, 1967.

Kellogg's lively and interesting history of the National Association for the Advancement of Colored People (NAACP) dramatically records the founding, purpose, accomplishments, internal struggles, leadership, and activities of the NAACP during the first decade of its existence.

The event that solidified the need to establish such an organization was a series of race riots in 1908 in Springfield, Illinois, where white mobs terrorized Negro neighborhoods, burned homes, and forced more than two thousand Negroes to flee the city. Several white liberals, including William English Walling, Mary White Ovington, Oswald Garrison Villard, Harry Moskowitz, Lillian Wald, Florence Kelley, and two prominent Negro clergymen—Rev. William Henry Brooks and Bishop Alexander Walters—organized a conference on the Negro problem. Out of this conference, a formal, permanent organization was formed. Soon thereafter, W. E. B. Du Bois and Ida B. Wells-Barnett would become actively involved in the organization, with Du Bois being appointed director of publicity and research.

Readers learn that in these early years the objective of the NAACP was to fight for full equality and rights for Negro citizens through nonviolent, primarily legal action.

The twelve chapters are arranged in chronological order and cover the critical period when leadership passed from white to black hands; the birth of and increasing readership of the NAACP's official organ, the *Crisis*; the explosion of membership in 1918, especially in the southern states; and the effects of the leadership rivalry between Booker T. Washington and W. E. B. Du Bois on the organization. The activity of the NAACP in the fight for equality is chronicled and includes the organization's activities against lynching and mob violence (1911–1915), including the antilynching conference; the fight against segregation in housing, education, and professional organizations and against disfranchisement; efforts to address discrimination against Negro troops in World War I; three successful court victories; and involvement in international affairs.

Kellogg's history reads much like an eyewitness account due to his extensive use of primary documents including NAACP board meeting minutes and correspondence, editorials in newspapers and magazines, personal papers of W. E. B. Du Bois and Booker T. Washington, and personal interviews with members at the national office of the NAACP. The appendixes include the following documents: "The Call: A Lincoln Emancipation Conference to Discuss Means for Securing Political and Civil Equality for the Negro"; The National Negro Committee, 1909; resolutions adopted by the National Negro Committee; NAACP Officers, Executive Committee, and General Committee, December 1910; First Board of Directors; Secretaries and Acting Secretaries, 1909–1920; and Board Chairmen and Acting Chairmen, 1909–1920. The book concludes with a bibliographic essay and an index.

Senior high school and undergraduate history teachers and students will find this book critical reading about the history of one of the premier civil rights organizations. The text provides many insights into organizational structure and leadership.

6.144 Kusmer, Kenneth L. *A Ghetto Takes Shape: Black Cleveland: 1870–1930.* Chicago: University of Chicago Press, 1976.

Kusmer's comprehensive comparative study of black urban history focuses on tracing "aspects of black life: economic, political, social, cultural in a single city over 60–100 years." Kusmer's purpose is to show how the changes in each aspect of black life in Cleveland are related to the developing ghetto.

Unlike urban studies by Drake and Cayton (entry 6.138), Lemann (entry 6.145), and Osofsky (entry 6.149), Kusmer hypothesizes that each city's development is unique and therefore one cannot make generalizations. He explores questions about the differences among cities and the different times and rates at which the northern ghettos developed. He also looks at differences among cities in patterns of property ownership, occupational mobility, family structure, and political participation. To that end, Kusmer compares Cleveland's development to that of other large northern cities, such as Chicago, New York, Philadelphia, and Detroit. He also compares immigrant and native white experiences in Cleveland with the experiences of African Americans to provide a richer context and understanding of the forces that helped shape the ghetto.

The book is arranged in three parts. Part 1 explores the historical development, conditions, and status of the black population in Cleveland prior to 1879. Part 2, which includes five chapters, examines the changing racial climate, residential patterns, and economic opportunities and the internal cultural and social environment that developed between the years 1870 and 1915. Part 3, which also includes five chapters, focuses on the consolidation of the ghetto from 1915 to 1930.

In part 1, Kusmer describes the differences between the development of Cleveland, which, unlike New York and Chicago, had no real black ghetto prior to the 1890s. The overall economic standing of the black population in Cleveland was higher than that of most black communities in the nineteenth century, with the exception of New Orleans. Kusmer describes the forces that began to shape the Cleveland ghetto, including the new modes of transportation that facilitated the physical exodus of whites to the suburbs and the influx of white immigrants that motivated native-born whites to leave the city. Unlike the native-born whites and immigrants, black migrants before World War I were predominantly young males without children who migrated from Virginia, Maryland, and North Carolina. The use of restrictive covenants by white real estate companies relegated the migrants to specific neighborhoods with poor housing and high rents.

151

Yet, educational opportunities for blacks to attend college in Cleveland were unsurpassed by any city, with the exception of Boston. The tradition of integrated education established by Oberlin College and Western Reserve University contributed to this environment in Cleveland years before wartime migration. In spite of these opportunities, Kusmer cites signs of the growing inferior status of blacks: occupational decline, restriction from apprenticeship training, exclusionary union policies, the decline in black entrepreneurs serving elite white clientele, the gap between black workers and the rest of the population, a higher proportion of black women working (36 percent, compared with 23 percent for all women), and a decline in property ownership (even though the percentage still exceeded that of blacks in the nation's ten largest cities).

In part 2's enlightening final chapter, Kusmer examines the dynamics of leadership, politics, and institutions in the black community by exploring the lives of several of its more prominent and diverse leaders: John Patterson Green, an accommodationist in his public life; Jere Brown, a militant who tempered his advocacy in later years; Charles Waddell Chesnutt, a novelist and attorney who advocated Negro rights but believed discrimination could be overcome if the Negro elevated his economic status; and Harry C. Smith, a militant who openly and vociferously attacked segregation, discrimination, and racial prejudice. Most of the city's black leaders assumed a more conservative view of social change. Kusmer concludes that due to the small size of the black community in Cleveland, social change remained more dependent on white institutions and financial support than did black communities in other cities, such as Chicago, New York, and Philadelphia.

In part 3, Kusmer explores consolidation of the ghetto; the reasons for the Great Migration; and racism in Cleveland, which took the form of exclusion of blacks from restaurants, theaters, hotels, recreational facilities, hospitals, and schools. He contends that a system of "racial etiquette" did not become established in northern cities due to de facto segregation that accomplished a goal similar to that of Jim Crow laws in the South.

The chapter on occupational flux describes the occupational status of black males in 1920 and 1930 compared with black women, native-born white men and women, and foreign-born white men and women. The declining status of black women compared with any other group is pronounced. The percentage of black women in domestic service in 1930 returned to the same high level it had reached in 1910, although the occupational status of black males had improved since the Great Migration even though job security was precarious.

In an illuminating chapter on poverty and progress in the black community, Kusmer explores the contradictory effects of racism on intensifying class distinctions, on the one hand, and promoting racial pride and unity, on the other. Black churches, black cultural institutions such as Karamu House (which was founded by two white social workers), and black family organization in the ghetto are discussed. By comparing the percentage of female-headed households in urban northern black communities with those in southern rural and urban communities and northern white communities, Kusmer effectively counters Franklin Frazier's assertion that the move north resulted in the disintegration of black family life.

The final chapter, "Toward the New Negro," traces the careers of three black leaders to demonstrate the different variations possible in response to the postwar situation. Kusmer also analyzes the contributions and activities of black organizations in Cleveland: the Negro Welfare Association, an affiliate of the National Urban League; the Phillis Wheatley Association, founded by Jane Edna Hunter for migrant girls; the NAACP; and the YMCA. These institutions illustrate the black community's responses in combating racism and improving the quality of life.

The chapters are followed by two appendixes, a comprehensive bibliographical essay, and an index.

This meticulous work presents a dynamic, complex, and interesting study of an urban city. The insights offered by Kusmer and his comparative analysis with similar cities provide a foundation for understanding the causes of contemporary urban problems. For this reason, it should be required reading for all high school social studies and history teachers and undergraduate sociology and history students.

6.145   Lemann, Nicholas. *The Promised Land: The Great Black Migration and How It Changed America.* New York: Alfred A. Knopf, 1991.

This book is perhaps the first comprehensive investigation into the second migration of African Americans from the rural South to the urban North, which occurred between 1940 and 1970. Lemann chronicles the meaning of this important historical phenomenon for black migrants, the southern community they left, the political machine they encountered in Chicago, and policies of the war on poverty that affected them.

Instead of telling the story of the second Great Migration in a traditional chronological style, Lemann, who is a journalist, uses an engaging narrative account to convey the facts and feelings of the people whose stories are unveiled through oral interviews. The first chapter focuses on people living in Clarksdale, Mississippi, where they work as sharecroppers in a system that is destined to maintain them in poverty. The second chapter follows them as they migrate north to the South Side of Chicago and encounter a different but similarly devastating life of Jim Crowism, segregation, racism, job discrimination, and welfare dependency.

In the third chapter, Lemann turns his attention to Washington, D.C., during the Kennedy, Johnson, and Nixon years and delivers his views on the war on poverty and its effect on his narrators. In the fourth chapter, the setting is inner-city Chicago again, but the time period is the 1960s and 1970s. The final chapter returns to a different but still racially divided Clarksdale, Mississippi, during the 1980s.

Following the five chapters are an afterword, acknowledgments, a note on sources, footnotes arranged by chapter, and an index.

Lemann's book emphasizes the need for government intervention in the lives of people like his narrators. By devising a new social policy agenda, the government can improve the quality of these people's lives. Yet, perhaps due to his need to convince readers of the tragic lives of black migrants, he paints a disturbing and unbalanced view of dysfunctional family life in a pathological and welfare-dependent ghetto of crime, poverty, and hopelessness. Lemann draws heavily upon the research and perspectives of sociologists and historians such as E. Franklin Frazier (*The Negro Family in Chicago*, 1932), Gilbert Osofsky (entry 6.149), and Allan H. Spear (entry 6.152). These works focus on migrants as victims of an unjust system without fully exploring the dynamic role of the African-American community in creating positive institutions, businesses, and role models that have strengthened the community and helped it adapt to a new environment.

Despite this controversial portrait of the lives of black migrants, Lemann's book is an important popular history of the period. High school and undergraduate history instructors and general readers will find this book captivating but should also balance it with the works of James Grossman (entry 6.141), James Borchert (entry 6.137), or Kenneth Kusmer (entry 6.144).

6.146   Myrdal, Gunnar. *An American Dilemma: The Negro Problem and Modern Democracy.* 2v. New York: Harper and Row, 1944. Reprint, New York: Pantheon Books, 1975.

During World War II, the Carnegie Corporation financed a comprehensive study of the "Negro problem," which was directed by Gunnar Myrdal, a Swedish political economist. The purpose of the study was to collect, analyze, and interpret the existing knowledge on the Negro in the United States to form the basis for a rational policy. The Carnegie Corporation funded educational and social projects and programs to benefit Negro institutions and commissioned the study to help it decide how to distribute its funds intelligently.

Myrdal hired a staff and drew heavily upon the work of other scholars from many disciplines—economics, sociology, political science, anthropology, and history—to synthesize existing knowledge on the Negro. He describes his tasks in undertaking the study as to depict the real-life conditions of Negroes, to describe who the American Negro is, and to attempt to discover and dissect the doctrines and beliefs held by white and Negro Americans.

The study was intended to be an objective and dispassionate, but thorough, study of an important moral and social phenomenon. The volumes are arranged in eleven parts and forty-five chapters; volume 1 includes parts 1 through 5. Part 1, entitled "The Approach," explores American ideals, the Negro problem as it exists in the minds of whites and Negroes, and the origins of color caste and discrimination. Part 2 deals with the subject of race and ancestry and racial characteristics.

Part 3 concentrates on population and migration. Myrdal gives significant attention to how and why black migration changed over time and persisted, even during times of high unemployment in the North. Part 4 examines economic issues including the roots of Negro poverty; economic exploitation during slavery; the sharecropping system and agricultural trends; urbanization and employment; the Negro in business, the professions, and public service; discrimination in employment; public assistance and social security; income and housing conditions; prewar labor market controls; and the Negro participation in war production and industries. Part 5 focuses on politics and Negro suffrage.

Volume 2 begins with part 6, which analyzes the justice system and the treatment of Negroes. Issues of social inequality including social segregation and discrimination and the effects of social inequality on the Negro are examined in part 7. Caste and class dimensions and structure are explored in part 8, while part 9 analyzes patterns and types of Negro leadership, individual and organizational, including the Negro church, press, and school. Part 10, on the Negro community, examines the impact of the family, education, and other institutions on the Negro community. The title of Part 11 is "An American Dilemma"; it summarizes and analyzes recent social trends, Negroes in the war crisis, and America's opportunity to "choose whether the Negro shall remain her liability or become her opportunity." The book concludes with ten appendixes on methodology and research. An extensive bibliography, footnotes, and an index are provided.

Myrdal's study focuses on the pathological nature of Negro life and culture in analyzing the causes of then-present conditions of Negroes. According to Joe Trotter (entry 6.153), the historical perspective provided by Myrdal is weak because Myrdal used history merely to illuminate present situations and trends. However, the study focused national attention on the conditions and lives of Negroes and emphasized the gap between America's promise of equality and practice of racial discrimination. Therefore, this study deserves to be examined by students and teachers in urban history and sociology courses at the undergraduate level.

6.147V   Nelson, Stanley. *Two Dollars and a Dream.*
Videorecording, 56 min. New York: Distr. Filmmakers
Library, 1989.

This biography of self-made millionaire Madame C. J. Walker chronicles her life and career from her birth in Delta, Louisiana, to the beauty school she established in New York City in 1913. Madame C. J. Walker's invention of a metal heating comb and conditioner for straightening black women's hair led her to peddle her wares door-to-door and eventually to build a manufacturing plant in Indianapolis, Indiana. The video features interviews, historical stills, and film footage to document the lives of Walker and her daughter, A'Lelia, in New York. Also included are scenes from Harlem's famous Cotton Club, featuring the music of Cab Calloway and Duke Ellington.

Audiences from high school students through adult general viewers will find this award-winning video both entertaining and educational. It was the winner of the following awards: Best of the Decade by the Black Filmmakers Foundation, the CINE Golden Eagle, and the Bronze Apple (National Educational Film Festival), among others.

6.148V   Nelson, Stanley, and Elizabeth Clark-Lewis. *Freedom
Bags.* Videorecording, 32 min. New York: Distr.
Filmmakers Library, 1990.

Freedom Bags tells the dramatic story of African-American women who migrated from the South to the North between 1900 and 1930. The film portrays their lives as domestics, where they were often exploited and sexually harassed, and contrasts these images with positive times shared with family and friends.

Winner of the American Film and Video Festival, the Gold Apple Award, and the Best Nonfiction Film (Black Filmmakers Hall of Fame), this video is highly recommended for high school through adult audiences.

6.149   **Osofsky, Gilbert.** *Harlem, The Making of a Ghetto: Negro New York, 1890–1930.* New York: Harper and Row, 1966.

Osofsky devotes a major portion of this book to explaining the forces that transformed Harlem from a black community, to a ghetto, to a slum. The book is divided into three parts. Part 1 describes the rapid growth of Negroes in New York and the racial and social problems resulting from this growth. Part 2 explains how and why an upper-middle-class community became segregated; part 3 discusses how the ghetto became a slum.

The critical forces that shaped Negro Harlem into an "incredible slum" Osofsky describes as a new course of building activity and property and land speculation; a surplus of houses constructed at one time, with rents too high for the general population; the rapid growth of the Negro population due to the Great Migration; the subsequent migration of whites from Manhattan to other boroughs that was further facilitated by an increase in modes of transportation; discrimination in housing that restricted Negroes to Harlem; the high rents charged Negro Harlem dwellers (for example, Negroes spent 40 percent or more of their earnings on rent compared with whites, who used only 20 percent on rent); and discrimination in employment.

Osofsky also discusses a range of related social conditions and problems that contributed to Harlem's transformation into a slum. Many of these, he suggests, were caused by the migrants themselves: poor health due, in part, to churches espousing "Jesus as the healer" and the Negroes' tendency to go to quack doctors; vice and gambling in the Negro community; juvenile delinquency; and a lack of educational readiness of Negro school children. Osofsky, unlike Kusmer (entry 6.144), Borchert (entry 6.137), and Grossman (entry 6.141), does not attempt to explain the causes of these problems or provide specific statistics on related problems in white communities or in southern Negro communities. Although Osofsky includes a brief discussion of urban reformers and reform organizations, such as the NAACP, the National Urban League, and the lesser-known National League for the Protection of Colored Women, readers learn little about other ways in which migrants coped with and fought against discriminatory conditions and racism.

In later chapters, Osofsky identifies several experimental programs—designed to improve housing for poor tenants—that were thwarted by the Great Depression when many Negroes lost their jobs. Negroes fared better in the political arena, according to Osofsky, in that they were able to wield greater political clout due to their concentration in two districts. As a result, by the 1920s, Harlem had Negro police officers and firefighters.

Finally, in an epilogue on the Harlem Renaissance, Osofsky asserts that this awakening of interest in Negro cultural and intellectual life was not the dominant thought among whites. Osofsky indicates that whites viewed the "New Negro culture" as the opposite of, and perhaps inferior to, white American culture. Again, Osofsky's emphasis is on the perspective of whites as opposed to the impact on and contributions of this movement to Negro life, culture, and history.

Although few new perspectives are included here, this work should be compared and contrasted with similar studies of Chicago (Grossman, entry 6.141) and Cleveland (Kusmer, entry 6.144) in urban history courses at the upper-division college level.

6.150P   Roberts, Richard Samuel. *A True Likeness: The Black South of Richard Samuel Roberts, 1920–1936.* Columbia, S.C.: Bruccoli Clark, 1986.

Richard Roberts, a self-taught photographer and a native Floridian, operated his own studio in Columbia, South Carolina, from 1920 until his death in 1936. Columbia was an educational center for blacks in the South and one of the two primary urban centers for black South Carolinians. The two hundred photographs included in this book were miraculously uncovered almost half a century after his death. The exquisite photographs provide a rare glimpse into black middle-class life in a southern city during the period of the Great Migration: portraits of the black families that were left behind or who perhaps chose not to migrate North.

The editors of this volume are Thomas L. Johnson, assistant director of the South Carolinian Library, and Phillip C. Dunn, associate professor in the department of art at the University of South Carolina. They describe Roberts as a "skilled pictorial artist, a master of the uses of light and shadow for purposes of photographic composition." Johnson's detailed and informative introduction vividly describes the dramatic discovery of the photographs and the subsequent development of the negatives, the life and work of Roberts, and publication of the book.

The rich, lifelike portraits contained in these pages portray the dignity of a people and the range of occupations, activities, and important events in which they participated. Most of the images were identified through the assistance of dozens of residents of the community and their descendants. These descriptions are in many cases detailed biographical sketches of the individuals and families portrayed in the photographs. Individual men, women, and children as well as families, mothers and children, friends, brothers and sisters, high school and college graduation classes, and a small number of buildings, homes, and black-owned businesses are depicted in the book. These images are so realistic that to browse the pages of this book is to step back into history and experience another time and place.

Children, young people, and adults will readily identify with the photographs of their counterparts, although they may be amused by the style of dress. However, the descriptions of individuals included in the photographs will naturally pique students' interest in the historical period, customs, lives, and professions and occupations of blacks in the urban South.

6.151   Scott, Emmett. *Negro Migration during the War.* New York and London: Oxford University Press, 1920.

This early study of Negro migration explores the causes for the migration and the effect the movement had on the South. The author was assisted in the study by Monroe Work (see entry 1.22) and Charles Johnson, at the time a graduate student at the University of Chicago, who would later become one of the most-respected black sociologists of the twentieth century.

Chapter 1 discusses the causes of the migration, including labor depression in the South caused by a decline in the cotton crop and exacerbated by the floods of 1915, the decrease in foreign immigration and subsequent demand for laborers in the North, unemployment and low wages in the South, poor treatment of Negroes in southern courts, inability to educate children properly in the South, and the opportunity to earn a living in the North.

In chapter 2, Scott explores the communication mechanisms that spread the news about the migration in the South: the role of the *Chicago Defender* and of labor agents, discussions in barber shops and beauty parlors, and stories from migrants who returned to the South to visit relatives. Chapter 3 describes the spread of the movement through the South. In chapter 4, Scott explores limitations for Negro laborers in the North, while chapters 6 through 8 discuss the effects of migration and of "draining the Black Belt."

The remaining four chapters report on the status of migrants in various parts of the North. Housing conditions, employment opportunities in industries, wages, social welfare agencies, discrimination in public places, and the general state of race relations are discussed in these reports that were compiled by research assistants assigned to specific geographic regions. The final chapter provides an overview of national organizations such as the National Urban League, Home Missions Council, and the African Methodist Episcopal Church, which were founded to help migrants adjust to their new environment. Following the thirteen chapters is a bibliography and an index.

This classic book provides an excellent introduction and overview of the causes and effects of the Great Migration from the perspective of those who were living through it. Contemporary works by Grossman, Drake, and others draw upon Scott's work; therefore, high school and undergraduate history instructors will want to familiarize themselves with this study.

6.152 Spear, Allan H. *Black Chicago: The Making of a Negro Ghetto, 1890–1920.* Chicago and London: University of Chicago Press, 1967.

Spear's book on the first black migration concentrates on the forces that shaped the physical, sociological, and psychological ghetto of Chicago. The issues he discusses include external forces such as labor tension, political corruption, discrimination in employment and housing, segregation in public accommodations, and education. The internal forces explored in the book focus on the institutions, businesses, churches, and social clubs established by blacks in their communities as a response to exclusionary and hostile attitudes and practices of the white community.

The book is divided into two parts: part 1, entitled "The Rise of the Ghetto, 1890–1915," and part 2, entitled "The Migration Years, 1915–1920." In the first section, the author examines and discusses the physical ghetto, Jim Crow laws, Chicago's Negro elite, new leadership, the institutional ghetto, and business and politics. In the second section of the book, Spear describes the impact of migration on the struggle for jobs and homes, Negro community life, business and politics, and the white response. Spear's image of the black community in Chicago is not unlike the image portrayed by Lemann (entry 6.145) in that the newly arrived migrants, the activities in which they are engaged, their interactions with one another, and the institutions they built are not viewed as dynamic, positive, and adaptive but rather as poor imitations of those in the white community. Particularly useful, however, are Spear's insights into the reasons why and from where blacks migrated to Chicago during this period, statistical data on the Negro population in Chicago by wards, a general history of Chicago, and an overview of black businesses and entrepreneurs in Chicago.

Following the eleven chapters are a conclusion, a note on sources, and an index. This book is suitable for lower-division college students as supplemental reading, but it should be studied in conjunction with sources that present a more balanced view of the shaping of northern ghettos.

6.153   Trotter, Joe William, ed. *The Great Migration in Historical Perspective: New Dimensions of Race, Class, and Gender.* Bloomington and Indianapolis: Indiana University Press, 1991.

This collection of essays emphasizes the role African Americans played in shaping their own migration experiences. It explores the sources and impact of black migration on different cities. The introduction by Trotter reviews the literature on the Great Migration according to three models of black urban history: the race relations, ghetto, and proletarian approaches. The review begins with Du Bois's *The Philadephia Negro* (entry 6.139) and ends with contemporary works by Gilbert Osofsky, Allan Spear, Kenneth Kusmer, James Borchert, and Florette Henri (entries 6.149, 6.152, 6.144, 6.137, and 6.142, respectively).

According to Trotter, the essays in this book address the relationship between changes in southern black rural life and subsequent patterns of community change in southern, northern, and western cities. In the first essay, Earl Lewis explores black migration, work, and community in Norfolk, Virginia, between 1910 and 1945, a geographic area in which migration has not been studied. In his essay entitled "Black Migration to Southern West Virginia, 1915–1932," Trotter focuses on the migration from a rural to an industrial setting. Peter Gottlieb examines the migration of southern blacks to Pittsburgh as "a process of self-transformation." In his essay on black migration to Chicago, James Grossman documents the migration as a grass-roots social movement.

Shirley Ann Moore analyzes black migration to the urban west before the 1940s in her essay on migration to Richmond, California. Darlene Clark Hine's essay, "Black Migration to the Urban Midwest: The Gender Dimension, 1915–1945," critiques the existing literature on black migration and challenges readers to document not only gender-specific causes of the black migration but class and race dimensions as well. In a final essay, Trotter emphasizes the importance of analyzing the black migration from a historical perspective so that ". . . we will be able to fully understand the formation and transformation of the black community in urban America." The book concludes with a note on contributors and an index.

Undergraduate and graduate faculty will find this book invaluable reading because of its comprehensive overview of the black migration period.

6.154 Weiss, Nancy. *National Urban League, 1910–1940.* New
York: Oxford University Press, 1974.

In documenting the history, purpose, programs, and services of the
National Urban League (NUL) in the first thirty years of its existence,
Weiss demonstrates how the league provided employment and welfare
services to blacks and assisted new migrants to adjust to life in large
urban cities. The history also illuminates the organization's national
role in shaping racial reform and labor practices, addressing Depression-
era problems, and working for the participation of minorities in politics.

Weiss's work is limited to the available source material on the
NUL. Unfortunately, some of the official records were destroyed when
the league moved its headquarters in the early 1950s. The personal
correspondence of one of the league's cofounders, Ruth Standish Baldwin, was lost in a flood in the 1950s. The papers of Charles S. Johnson,
the first director of research and editor of *Opportunity*, reveal little
about the role of the league. Similarly, the league's early records of its
affiliates were either destroyed or lost. The existing records show where
the league "pioneered and refined tools of interracial teamwork, research and investigation, and professional social work training to help
reach some sort of rapprochement between blacks and the cities." In
her study, Weiss emphasizes the changing context of the league's concerns and the continuity of the organization's efforts.

The book is divided into two parts of nine chapters each. Part 1
covers the years from 1910 to 1918; part 2 spans the years from 1918
to 1929. Within each part, the chapters are arranged by topic. The early
chapters discuss the origins of racial protest and the forerunners of the
Urban League including the National League for the Protection of
Colored Women and the Committee for Improving the Industrial Condition of Negroes in New York. The chapter on the league's founding
reflects a structure and composition similar to the NAACP in that
women, blacks, and whites were instrumental in establishing the organization.

The relationship between the NAACP and the NUL and their
roles as Progressive-era products and racial reformers is the subject of
the fourth chapter. The mandate of the league, "to promote, encourage,
assist, and engage in any and all kinds of work for improving the industrial, economic, social, and spiritual conditions among Negroes,"
translated into the need to train personnel. The league's efforts and
programs to train personnel and subsequent efforts to define and set
priorities and structure its operations are discussed in several chapters.

The league's focus and priorities became clearer during the Great
Migration, at which time the league was challenged to meet the im-

162

mediate and long-term needs of black migrants. Migrants encountered housing and employment problems, and a threatening moral and social environment in northern cities, which the league addressed through its professional social work programs. The struggle to further define how the league would focus its resources and efforts is explored in chapter 9. Weiss explains that once the league began to emphasize employment opportunities, it started to function as a truly national organization.

Chapter 10 discusses the league's response to postwar pressures and racial disturbances: to strengthen and encourage the growth of its affiliates, sponsor research and scientific fact-finding activities, and prepare Negroes to take advantage of industrial opportunities. The next several chapters focus on the league's expanded social service projects and its efforts to create new areas of employment for Negroes, in part by negotiating policy changes with labor unions.

In chapters 14 through 17, readers learn that the league's commitment to American capitalism, integration, and interracial cooperation shaped its response to the economic crisis of the Depression. During the New Deal era, the league concentrated on ensuring that blacks reaped the benefits of the promises. The league accomplished this by supplying President Franklin D. Roosevelt with facts and recommendations for policies and programs. The league's record in influencing organized labor to integrate its trade unions is examined in chapter 18. The final chapter of the book assesses the internal organization, leadership, and overall effectiveness of the league in its third decade of existence. Extensive footnotes, several appendixes, and an index are also provided.

Weiss's study deserves to be included as required reading in undergraduate American and African-American history survey courses. Together, Weiss's and Kellogg's (6.143) books are important companion histories of two of the most important Progressive-era organizations, the NAACP and the National Urban League.

6.155P   Willis-Braithwaite, Deborah. *Van DerZee: Photographer, 1886–1983.* New York: Barry N. Abrams, 1993.

Van DerZee, a self-taught photographer, is recognized as the "dean emeritus of African-American photographers and Harlem's most significant photographic biographer." Van DerZee is best known for his photographs of Harlem life from the 1920s to 1945, including moving portraits of black soldiers, celebrities, entertainers, community leaders, children and families, brides and grooms, and social and literary organizations.

This book is the first survey of his work in more than twenty years. *The World of James Van DerZee*, the first book on the famous photographer and his work, was published in 1969. Although Van DerZee was one of the most successful portrait photographers in the 1920s through the 1940s, his work was not recognized nationally until the 1970s when his first one-man show opened at Lenox Library in Massachusetts. The first retrospective exhibition was launched at the Studio Museum of Harlem in 1971.

Van DerZee: Photographer was written in association with the National Portrait Gallery of the Smithsonian Institution. The two substantive and enlightening essays in the book discuss Van DerZee's formidable technical and artistic vision and his fascinating life. They were written by Deborah Willis-Braithwaite and Rodger C. Birt, respectively. The remainder of the book contains more than seventy black-and-white images. Lengthy descriptions, including biographical notes and dates, are provided for each photograph.

The book contains photographs of earlier figures such as Father Divine, Adam Clayton Powell, Adam Clayton Powell Jr., Bill "Bojangles" Robinson, the Mills Brothers, Florence Mills, Madame C. J. Walker, Marcus Garvey, and Eubie Blake, in addition to more-contemporary images of Bill Cosby, Lou Rawls, Max Robinson, Ossie Davis and Ruby Dee, and Muhammad Ali. All the images reflect Van DerZee's efforts "to get as much life and expression as I can into the picture."

Following the black-and-white plates are footnotes and a bibliography. Photography students and history lovers will want to use this book for its visual images of black life during the Harlem Renaissance and beyond.

A traveling exhibit of eighty framed photographs from the National Portrait Gallery exhibition is available for rental from SITES. Van DerZee's early photographs from the turn of the century and his last portraits from the 1980s, as well as the images from the 1920s and 1930s that made him famous, are included.

6.156 **Woodson, Carter G.** *A Century of Negro Migration.*
Washington, D.C.: Association for the Study of Negro Life and History, 1918.

Woodson's classic study of Negro migration presents a historical chronology from the struggle to flee from slavery and oppression through the beginning of the Great Migration. While only the last two chapters actually cover the period of the Great Migration, the beginning chapters, arranged in chronological order, provide readers with a useful context for understanding the forced and voluntary migration of Negroes and the factors that precipitated their movement away from the South.

The first chapter, for example, explores the interest of some white antislavery groups in colonizing blacks, the black settlements set up by Quakers in Ohio and Michigan for escaped slaves, and a review of Underground Railroad routes (including the migration of many African Americans to Canada). Subsequent chapters describe migratory patterns before, during, and after the Civil War, which included migration from rural to urban southern communities, and the exodus from Louisiana and Mississippi to Kansas, Indian territory, and Oklahoma.

In the penultimate chapter, Woodson explains the "migration of the talented tenth." Here, he discusses the migration to the largest northern cities of Negro politicians, educated Negroes, and the laboring classes. In the final chapter, on the exodus during World War I, Woodson delineates the common reasons for the migration northward. He presents the advantages and disadvantages of leaving the South as if he were talking directly to blacks who have been contemplating the move but have not yet decided. Woodson describes the housing conditions of the migrants in the North, the importance of migrants participating in the political process, the role of the National Urban League, and the occupations of Negroes who settled in the North. He concludes that the North offers Negroes the best chance to secure their rights as American citizens.

An extensive bibliography of almost twenty pages and an index follow the nine chapters.

A Century of Negro Migration was one of the first books on the Great Migration, and while not as thorough or as comprehensive as Scott's work (entry 6.151), it is useful because of the historical perspective it provides. Therefore, high school history and social studies teachers will want to review this work.

Civil Rights and the Struggle for Full Equality

After fighting for America in World War II, African Americans became more insistent on exercising their rights as citizens of the United States. In 1946, the Ku Klux Klan killed two black soldiers and their wives in Monroe, Georgia—one of several violent attacks against black veterans who had defended their country against fascism only to confront segregation and racism at home. Since local and state officials did nothing to protect them, black leaders pressured President Harry S. Truman to intervene on behalf of African Americans. President Truman appointed a Committee on Civil Rights, which issued its report, *To Secure These Rights*, in 1947. The report offered specific remedies for giving African Americans their full rights, but justice would not be won without a major struggle initiated by African Americans. This struggle culminated in the modern Civil Rights movement.

The Civil Rights movement was made possible, in part, by the political power gained by newly arrived black migrants to northern and southern cities. This second section of chapter 6 (entries 6.157–179) documents the movement and the struggle for economic equity. Harvard Sitkoff, in his book *A New Deal for Blacks*, traces the origins of the national issue of civil rights to the 1930s. A second book by Sitkoff, *The Struggle for Black Equality*, serves as an interpretive history of the Civil Rights movement, beginning with the 1954 *Brown* v. *Board of Education* decision. In his *Origins of the Civil Rights Movement*, Aldon Morris explains how the movement was not a sporadic and disjointed chain of events but rather a structured network of grass-roots and church-affiliated organizations that already existed in the South. A powerful visual story of the Civil Rights movement, beginning in 1954, is eloquently portrayed in the nationally acclaimed videotape series by PBS, *Eyes on the Prize*. Disturbing and revealing still photographs of and commentary on the movement are captured by Michael S. Durham in *Powerful Days: the Civil Rights Photography of Charles Moore*.

The pivotal but neglected role of women in the Montgomery bus boycott is poignantly told by Jo Ann Gibson Robinson in *The Montgomery Bus Boycott and the Women Who Started It*. The internal and external operations, the leaders, and achievements of two civil rights organizations are documented in four different books: Clayborne Carson's *In Struggle: SNCC and the Black Awakening of the 1960s*, James Forman's *The Making of a Black Revolutionary*, Stokely Carmichael and Charles Hamilton's *Black Power*, and August Meier and Elliott Rudwick's *CORE*. Joe Feagin's *Ghetto Revolts* explores the history, causes, emergence, evolution of, and the reaction of government authorities to, the urban riots. And, of course, no discussion of the civil rights era would be complete without including *The Autobiography of Malcolm X*.

The struggle for economic equity, the role of race and class in determining economic success, and the emergence of a permanent underclass are analyzed and discussed in four more contemporary works: Alphonso Pinkney's *The Myth of Black Progress*, William Julius Wilson's *The Declining Significance of Race* and *The Truly Disadvantaged*, and a book edited by Bill Lawson, entitled *The Underclass*

Question. Documents or excerpts of documents from the Civil Rights movement are included in *Eyes on the Prize Reader* and *Voices of Freedom.*

With the end of the Civil Rights movement, the struggle for economic equality emerges as a major issue that was not adequately addressed by the movement or government programs. In a study based on 1980 census data, Reynolds Farley reported a staggering finding: "if the growth rates of 1959–1982 persist without interruption, the median incomes of black and white families in the United States will be equal in about three centuries." (*Blacks and Whites: Narrowing the Gap,* Cambridge, Massachusetts, 1984.)

The struggle indeed continues. . . .

6.157V   Blackside, Inc. *Eyes on the Prize.* Videorecording, 6 tapes, 60 min. each. Alexandria, Va., Distr. PBS Video, 1987.

Part 1 of this comprehensive documentary and multiple-award-winning series on the Civil Rights movement is divided into six segments: "Awakenings" (1954–1956), "Fighting Back" (1957–1962), "Ain't Scared of Your Jails" (1960–1961), "Mississippi: Is This America?" (1962–1964), "No Easy Walk" (1962–1966), and "Bridge to Freedom" (1965). Utilizing archival footage and interviews, part 1 takes viewers back to the forces that shaped the beginning of the movement, including the activities of existing local organizations and individuals, the lynching of fourteen-year-old Emmett Till, and Rosa Parks's act of defiance on a city bus in Montgomery. The contributions and actions of college students in the protest movement, the founding of the Student Nonviolent Coordinating Committee, voting rights campaigns in Mississippi, and nonviolent protests in Albany, Georgia, through the Selma, Alabama, march are chronicled in this segment. The entire series should be mandatory viewing for high school students and adults of all ages.

6.158V   Blackside, Inc. *Eyes on the Prize, Part II.* Videorecording, 8 tapes. 60 min. each. Alexandria, Va.: Distr. PBS Video, 1990.

Part II includes eight segments: "The Time Has Come" (1964–1965), "Two Societies" (1965–1968), "The Promised Land" (1967–1968), "Power!" (1966–1968), "Ain't Gonna Shuffle No More" (1964–1972), "A Nation of Law?" (1968–1971), "The Keys to the Kingdom" (1974–1980), and "Back to the Movement" (1979–mid-1980s).

This second portion examines the ways in which the Civil Rights movement of the South was transplanted to the North: community power in the schools, black power in the neighborhoods, police confrontations and violence, political confrontation in city halls, black pride and awareness, and urban poverty. The series concludes with a contrasting profile of two cities: Miami and Chicago.

6.159   Carmichael, Stokely, and Charles V. Hamilton. *Black Power: The Politics of Liberation in America.* New York: Random House, 1967.

The authors describe the purpose of this book as a framework and guidelines for broad experimentation with the concept of black power. It further aims to encourage a new consciousness and an attitude of communal responsibility among blacks. The authors are unequivocal about their position; they demand that blacks define themselves and their own roles and adopt their own methods for liberation through unconciliatory tactics.

The seven chapters of the book are organized around themes and examples of experimentation with black power. The first chapter discusses white power within the context of colonialism. The authors define racism in its various forms: overt, covert, individual, and institutional. The authors further discuss how the colonial status of black Americans operates in three areas: political, economic, and social.

Chapter 2 defines the need for a new consciousness among black people and describes the substance of this concept called "black power." According to the authors, black power empowers blacks to lead and run their own organizations, to consolidate and support their own leaders in order to bargain from a position of strength, and to fully participate in the decision-making processes affecting their lives. The authors repudiate the notion by whites that black power advocates are racists or black supremacists and explain why black power advocates reject the notion of integration.

In chapter 3, "The Myths of Coalition," the authors explore the shortcomings of the "traditional approach to ending racism." They refute the notions that the goals of white liberal groups are the same as those of black organizations and that white groups would be willing to condemn "racist institutions that exploit black people." The authors do offer grounds for viable coalitions.

Chapter 4 examines how the Mississippi Freedom Democratic Party "represents the kind of political action which black people must pursue." In the fifth chapter, the authors examine the Student Non-violent Coordinating Committee's work in helping form a political organization that was successful in registering more than 3,900 blacks, holding a nominating convention, and selecting a slate of seven members to run for county offices. The sixth chapter discusses Tuskegee, Alabama, and how in perpetuating a deferential society it lost its opportunity to serve as a model of black power.

The next two chapters focus on urban ghettos and attempt to explicate the reasons for urban unrest that erupted in major cities during the 1960s. The final chapter calls for a new approach to addressing problems in the black community through the formulation of independent political parties and the establishment of community rebate plans and tenants rights groups.

The book concludes with an afterword, a bibliography, an index, and a biographical note on the authors.

No course on the modern Civil Rights movement would be complete without the inclusion of this classic book on the philosophy of black power; therefore, it is highly recommended for high school and undergraduate courses.

6.160   **Carson, Clayborne.** *In Struggle: SNCC and the Black Awakening of the 1960s.* Cambridge, Mass.: Harvard University Press, 1981.

This study of the development of the Student Nonviolent Coordinating Committee (SNCC) follows the emergence of the organization in the midst of the modern Civil Rights movement of the 1950s through its dissolution in the 1970s. The book focuses on the evolution of SNCC's radicalism, which Carson describes as "a process of conflict as well as consensus. . . . SNCC staff members agreed that the goal of their struggle was to enhance human freedom, but they became increasingly aware of the limitations of individualist values as a guide for movements seeking collective goals."

The book explores the development of SNCC through three stages. In the first stage, civil rights activists adopted ideas from the Gandhian independence movement, from pacifism and Christian idealism practiced by the Congress on Racial Equality (CORE) and the Southern Christian Leadership Conference (SCLC). However, perhaps due to the different ages and backgrounds of its leaders, SNCC members were less likely than other civil rights groups to discourage southern black militancy. According to Carson, as SNCC's activities moved from desegregation to political rights, its commitment to nonviolent direct-action protest was replaced by a secular, humanistic radicalism influenced by Marx, Camus, Malcolm X, and by SNCC organizers' own experiences in southern black communities.

During the second stage of SNCC's development, the organizers began questioning the viability of their strategy to achieve the fundamental social changes they viewed as essential. Following the failed attempt of the Mississippi Freedom Democratic Party to unseat the all-white Democratic National Convention in 1974, SNCC workers questioned whether "their remaining goals could best be achieved through continued confrontation with existing institutions or through the building of alternative institutions controlled by the poor and powerless."

The third phase of SNCC's development was characterized by the members' efforts to address the need for black power and black consciousness by adopting a separatist ideology and by building black-controlled institutions. Stokely Carmichael was elected as the chairman of SNCC in 1966, but he and other workers were unable to articulate a set of ideas to unify blacks. Carson points out that SNCC workers became embroiled in factional battles and failed to sustain local black movements in the South. These battles reflected the struggles of black communities throughout the nation as they disagreed about the future direction of the movement.

The book is divided into three parts arranged in roughly chronological order. Part 1, entitled "Coming Together," discusses the evolution of the organization and its numerous activities, including sit-ins, freedom rides, and participation in the Albany, Georgia, march and the March on Washington. SNCC was created in 1960 to preserve the militancy of the sit-ins; it gained widespread support when the enthusiasm of the early protests subsided. The founding conference was called by Ella Baker, executive director of the SCLC. According to Carson, it was Ella Baker who encouraged the students to establish an independent organization free from adult control. Baker initiated the conference to prepare black students for the leadership roles they would assume within SNCC.

Part 2 of the book explores SNCC's task of reexamining its past work and future strategy. SNCC organizers planned a one-week retreat to identify the central issues and future strategies for the organization. New projects and initiatives adopted by SNCC, including an organization that was later to be known as the Black Panther Party, are discussed in a chapter entitled "Breaking New Ground." SNCC's new ideological focus classified it as part of the New Left. Its activities with Students for a Democratic Society, in addition to the radicalization of CORE and the SCLC, are revealed in chapter 12. SNCC's adoption of racial separatism and abandonment of the New Left dream of an interracial movement is presented in the final chapter of part 2.

Part 3, entitled "Falling Apart," chronicles the rise of Stokely

Carmichael, the newly elected chairman of SNCC, as an advocate and outspoken proponent of black power. Internal conflicts within SNCC over issues of leadership, militant rhetoric versus development of practical programs, and a shift from activities in the deep South to urban centers are explored in chapter 15. Chapter 16 follows efforts by the white establishment to repress the work of SNCC (through violent confrontation and racial conflict) and to blame the organization for urban racial violence. The final two chapters discuss SNCC's attempts to align itself with other human rights organizations under the leadership of Rap Brown, and the subsequent decline of black radicalism. The book concludes with footnotes to each chapter and an index.

Undergraduate students and faculty who are studying any protest organization or social movement, including the Civil Rights movement, will greatly benefit from reading this insightful book.

6.161P   Durham, Michael S. *Powerful Days: The Civil Rights Photography of Charles Moore.* New York: Stewart, Tabori and Chang, 1991.

This graphic and often disturbing visual record of the Civil Rights movement documents the actions, activities, interactions, and participation of both the organizers and supporters of the movement as well as those who fought desperately to destroy its efforts and the movement itself. Moore, a white photographer from Alabama, captured on film all the drama and violence of this momentous historical period.

The photographs cover the years from 1955 to 1965, which takes the viewer from the beginning of the Montgomery bus boycott through the march on Selma. Following a biographical essay on Charles Moore and his work, the book is divided into seven topics: Montgomery; Oxford, Mississippi; the freedom march; Birmingham; voter registration in Mississippi; the Ku Klux Klan in North Carolina; and the Selma march.

Each chapter begins with a brief introduction; the exquisite photographs are accompanied by often detailed captions. From tender moments between Martin Luther King Jr. and his wife, Coretta, to images of nonviolent protests by demonstrators, to pictures of police dogs and fire hoses, clubs, and baseball bats being hurled at marchers, Moore's photographs graphically portray the power and pain of the movement. The story is told through photos of renowned and unknown participants: civil rights leaders, U.S. marshals who defended James Meredith when he integrated the University of Mississippi, black and white demonstrators, Martin Luther King Jr., Ralph Abernathy, Dick Gregory,

Andrew Young, John Lewis, courageous voter-registration workers, men and women in full Ku Klux Klan attire, Governor George Wallace, and police officers with tear gas.

These images will surprise, enrage, and sadden those who did not live through the movement and fascinate those who did. School, public, and college libraries should own *Powerful Days*; instructors of American or African-American history should assign readings on the movement using this book as a visual resource.

6.162P   **Easter, Eric, D. Michael Cheers, and Dudley M. Brooks, eds.** *Songs of My People: African-Americans: A Self-Portrait.* Boston: Little, Brown, 1992.

This extraordinary collection of photographs by fifty-three of the nation's most talented black photojournalists documents the depth and breadth of the African-American experience. The lives of African Americans from all social, economic, and occupational strata are represented here, as are those from all geographic locations, ages, and cultures.

From sports figures, folk artists, dancers, musicians, clowns, gospel singers, preachers, and nuns, to college students at graduation, black families in a multitude of settings, lovers, cowboys, poets, children at play, politicians, prisoners, soldiers, and doctors, these images evoke feelings of joy, sorrow, inspiration, and hope. There are photographs of the famous, such as Colin Powell, Andrew Young, Mother Clare Hale, David Dinkins, Quincy Jones, Miles Davis, Thurgood Marshall, Sharon Pratt Dixon, Muhammad Ali, and Isiah Thomas; but most of the portraits are of African Americans whose faces are unrecognizable but whose lives are far from typical.

The book is arranged loosely in broad subjects. The first section includes a range of diverse images, while the second section focuses on the black male in a variety of professional and occupational environments, from a rodeo, construction site, New York stock exchange, doctor's office, and photography studio to a car race track. Other parts of this section present images of black men in prison, in the military, and in the medical profession. A third section of the book depicts a range of images focusing on the black community: renowned and obscure musicians, dancers, entertainers, artists, sports figures, church congregations, and politicians. A fourth section, on black women, illustrates the range of vocations these women have chosen, either voluntarily or involuntarily: actress, nun, author, single mother, dancer, college student, jazz singer, doctor, model, and beautician. The last section presents powerful images of family settings.

Four of the sections are preceded by carefully chosen essays that provide a historical context and a poignant literary complement to the photographic images. The four essays provided here are on the black male (by Sylvester Monroe), the black community (by Nelson George), black women (by Paula Giddings), and the black family (by Dr. Joyce Ladner).

Children, adults, and students of all ages should take the time to study this book, for the messages conveyed here cannot be replaced by words alone.

6.163V   Elwood, William A. *The Road to Brown.* Videorecording, 47 min. San Francisco: Distr. Resolution Inc., 1990.

During the 1930s, Charles Hamilton Houston, a brilliant civil rights attorney, waged a series of precedent-setting legal battles that led to the landmark 1954 *Brown* v. *Board of Education* Supreme Court decision. This video provides a concise history of Houston's role in the struggle for legal equality for African Americans. (See Genna Rae McNeil's article in *Black Leaders of the Twentieth Century*, entry 2.44, for an excellent biographical essay on Houston.)

This educational video is appropriate for high school students through adults.

6.164   Feagin, Joe R., and Harlan Hahn. *Ghetto Revolts: The Politics of Violence in American Cities.* New York: Macmillan, 1973.

The authors of this book explore the following issues related to the riots that occurred between 1962 and 1970: the history, the causes, the role of various factors, the emergence and evolution, and the reaction of government authorities to the riots. Feagin and Hahn admit that their analysis is necessarily tentative and exploratory.

In the introduction, the authors reveal that the literature on ghetto riots pays little attention to the number of riots, trends over time in the character of ghetto violence, and the specific types of action taken in the wake of rioting. Also omitted from the literature are the ghetto riots that occurred between 1969 and 1971 and those that took place after the assassination of Martin Luther King Jr.

The seven chapters are arranged thematically. Chapter 1 reviews the popular and social science theories that have been used in examining the collective violence that occurred in urban ghettos. The authors present an alternative view of riots that analyzes them in terms of a struggle between powerful groups and powerless blacks. Chapter 2 examines the historical emergence of collective violence in America, including the first instances of collective violence on the part of black Americans in the 1960s. Chapter 3 presents data on the number of riots, the definition of a riot, and the conditions underlying the emergence of riots. Chapter 4 focuses on the events that precipitated the rioting and the various stages the rioting went through. The reactions of authorities in riot situations are also examined. Chapter 5 begins a three-chapter examination of the effects of the rioting and analyzes the reaction to riots by federal, state, and local governments and agencies. Chapter 6 assesses the views on riots of black urbanites in several post-riot surveys, especially in the aftermath of the 1967 Detroit riot. The concluding chapter examines the consequences of ghetto revolts by looking at the emphasis in black communities on self-determination and black power.

This objective and well-researched study provides a useful perspective on a crucial period in American history. Sociology instructors at the undergraduate level and those individuals who seek to understand the causes and prevent the recurrence of this urban phenomenon will find this book resourceful and illuminating.

6.165   Forman, James. *The Making of a Black Revolutionary: A Personal Account.* New York: Macmillan, 1972.

Forman's autobiographical account describes in poignant detail his early family life; religious education and disappointing experiences with ministers; harassment and abuse by white police officers; discrimination in civilian and military life; exposure to the writings of black and white intellectuals, socialists, and revolutionaries; and subsequent involvement in the Civil Rights movement as a voter-registration worker and then as an active member of the Student Nonviolent Coordinating Committee (SNCC).

Fully two-thirds of the autobiography is devoted to the Civil Rights movement and to Forman's gradual but steady evolution into a black revolutionary. The book is divided into two parts. Part 1 is entitled "A Constant Struggle" and follows Forman's early life and experiences through his initial involvement in the Civil Rights movement. Part 2, "A Band of Sisters and Brothers in a Circle of Trust," documents Forman's life, work, and revolutionary development from his membership in SNCC to his relationship with the Black Panther Party.

Of particular interest and historical value are Forman's detailed accounts, interactions, and reflections on the internal organization, structure, and leaders of SNCC, and to a lesser degree the Congress on Racial Equality (CORE) and the Southern Christian Leadership Conference (SCLC). Forman's personal stories and excerpts from the writings of other civil rights workers and his own diary of his work in the South augment the more prosaic histories of civil rights organizations by breathing life into the players and their activities. For example, there is a full chapter on Forman's interaction with Ella Baker, primary organizer of the SNCC and a dedicated, well-respected activist. This chapter highlights Baker's organizational skills and the effects of her infectious, inspirational spirit on SNCC members.

Readers also learn about Forman's life-threatening experiences in the South as a freedom rider and the violence he and other civil rights workers endured, the organization of the March on Washington in 1963, the relationship and tensions that developed between SNCC and the more mainstream and leader-centered civil rights organizations, the internal conflict within SNCC, and the evolution of SNCC into an organization that advocated and adopted a doctrine of black power. The last several chapters focus on liberation for the black community, the emergence of the Black Panther Party, and the Black Manifesto (a list of demands that addressed "the human misery of black people under capitalism and imperialism").

The book concludes with a short postscript and an index. Forman's autobiography provides an insightful analysis into his own personal struggles and development as well as into SNCC and other major civil rights and black power organizations, their activities, and their leaders. He writes in a riveting style that is sure to hold the interest of the general adult reader and college-level students.

6.166V   Helios Productions. *My Past Is My Own.* Videorecording, 47 min. Santa Monica, Calif.: Distr. Pyramid Films and Video, 1989.

In this enlightening video, two contemporary black teenagers are "transported" back to the days of the Civil Rights movement, where they encounter a segregated world fiercely divided by racial tensions. Whoopi Goldberg plays the role of the aunt frustrated by her niece and nephew who seem oblivious to their history. The lessons they learn are memorable and important ones for high school students.

6.167V   Landau, Kaplan, and Martin Luther King Jr. Foundation. *King: Montgomery to Memphis.* Videorecording, 103 min. Chicago: Distr. Films, Inc., 1970.

Of the numerous films on the life and work of Martin Luther King Jr., this one is perhaps the most popular. The film follows King's career from the Montgomery bus boycott through his assassination. Excerpts from his speeches and interviews with civil rights leaders and members of his family revive the passion and power of the man and the movement. Junior high school students through adults will be inspired by this video.

6.168   **Lawson, Bill E., ed.** *The Underclass Question.* Philadelphia, Pa.: Temple University Press, 1992.

This collection of contemporary essays resulted from "Meditations on Integration: Philosophy and the Black Underclass," a conference held at the University of Delaware in 1989. The conference focused on critiquing William Julius Wilson's *The Truly Disadvantaged* (6.177). *The Underclass Question* and the conference sought to analyze philosophical questions regarding (1) conceptualizing poor urban blacks as a class, (2) the relationship between values formation and social progress, (3) affirmative action and the underclass, (4) conception of the political and legal rights of the underclass, and (5) intragroup values and obligations.

According to Lawson's introduction, the ten authors represented in this book share common perspectives on the black underclass. First, they believe that a segment of the black population may never be able to experience the American dream and that this segment is often plagued by factors that are cited as group characteristics (for example, high incidence of unemployment, welfare dependency, crime, violence, etc.). Second, they agree that since the existence of this "class" is a by-product of the normal functioning of a capitalist economy, the remedies that do not address fundamental social change are destined to fail and may reinforce racism and political oppression. The authors also emphasize the importance of understanding the difference between the poor and the underclass.

The book is divided into three parts: part 1, entitled "Class Analysis"; part 2, "Urban Values"; and part 3, "Social Policy." The book concludes with an epilogue entitled "Back on the Block" by Cornel West, professor at Harvard University. Part 1 includes two essays that explore the questions of whether class-specific programs eliminate urban poverty, what the role of race is in the emergence and maintenance of the underclass, and whether the underclass is really a class. One of the authors, Bernard Boxill, argues against William Julius Wilson's claim that social policy must appeal to the self-interest of whites.

Part 2 focuses on the values held by some members of the urban poor. The first of the three essays in this section examines the claim of laziness that is often made against members of the urban poor. A second essay analyzes the values of urban black youth—whom the author argues possess values similar to those of mainstream America—through rap music. Lawson examines the assertion that middle-class blacks are in some sense responsible for the continuation of the urban underclass.

Part 3 explores the relationship between racism and social policy. Anita Allen, the author of one essay in this section, argues that the conception of legal rights has worked along with racism and politics to further black inequality. A second author, Albert Mosely, counters the "culture of poverty" thesis of black conservatives Thomas Sowell and Glenn Loury. The final essay by Frank Kirkland summarizes many of the points made throughout the volume. Kirkland concludes that any programs directed toward improving the lives of the underclass must address cultural, economic, and political concerns. In the epilogue, Cornel West discusses the issues involved in being a black philosopher and doing research on the underclass.

These essays greatly contribute to advancing the concepts and philosophy on the black underclass that will be especially appealing to professors and students of sociology, political science, and public policy. This work should be read in conjunction with Wilson's *The Truly Disadvantaged* and *The Declining Significance of Race* (entries 6.177 and 6.176).

6.169   Little, Malcolm. *The Autobiography of Malcolm X.* New York: Grove Press, 1965.

Interest in the life of Malcolm X, one of the most renowned and intriguing leaders of the twentieth century, continues to grow; a feature-length film on this charismatic man, produced by Spike Lee, was released in 1992.

This riveting autobiography traces the life of Malcolm X: his frightening introduction to white supremacy in Omaha, Nebraska; his life as a slick hustler and finally a prisoner; his conversion to a black Muslim, pilgrimage to Mecca, and conversion to Islam; and his disillusionment and break with the Honorable Elijah Muhammad.

The nineteen chapters of the book are arranged chronologically. An introduction and epilogue by Alex Haley describe the character, abilities, personality, and resolve of a man who was "committed to the cause of liberating the black man in American society rather than integrating the black man into that society."

Malcolm's memoirs poignantly portray his transformation from a street hustler to a powerful national spokesman, orator, and leader and from a man who unequivocally believed in and preached about the monolithic white man as "the devil" to a man who, once he embraced Islam, began to abandon racism, separatism, and hatred. The autobiography also reveals Malcolm's relationship and tensions with civil rights leaders such as Martin Luther King Jr. and the "mainstream" civil rights organizations and discusses the influence and attraction of the masses of blacks to the black Muslims, as well as the divisions within that organization.

Suitable for high school and college-level students, this book should be required reading for any course on the Civil Rights movement, American history, or American literature. Adults will also want to add this book to their reading list.

6.170   **Meier, August, and Elliott Rudwick.** *CORE: A Study in the Civil Rights Movement, 1942-1968.* New York: Oxford University Press, 1973.

Meier and Rudwick's comprehensive history of the Congress on Racial Equality (CORE) describes the origins, development, successes, failures, and contributions of one of the most prominent civil rights organizations. The authors note that particular attention is given to the tactics, strategies, ideologies, organizational structure, and major activities of CORE.

Unlike Kellogg's study of the NAACP (entry 6.143), Meier and Rudwick devote considerable attention to the activities of CORE's autonomous affiliates, especially those that were important in the organization. Sources used by the authors to write this study include organizational records in archives as well as newspaper articles, manuscript collections held by individuals, and more than two hundred personal interviews.

The book is divided into five chronological parts: "The Pioneers, 1942-1959," "CORE and the Sit-ins Come of Age, 1960," "Ride Toward Freedom, 1961-1963," "CORE at Its Zenith, 1963-1964," and "CORE in Decline: The Road Toward Black Power, 1964-1966."

In part 1, the authors provide a detailed description of the formation of CORE and its founders, James Farmer, George Houser, Bernice Fisher, Homer Jack, Joe Guinn, and James R. Robinson. CORE's major contributions to the Civil Rights movement included the initiation of freedom rides, an active role in the southern voter-registration drive of 1962 through 1964, and participation in demonstrations in the South during 1963. More than any other civil rights organization, the authors credit CORE with being "responsible for the massive outpouring of direct action against housing, employment, and educational discrimination in the North."

CORE was founded in Chicago in 1942 by a group of dedicated pacifists who were interested in applying Gandhian principles to racial problems. However, by 1959, the national office's efforts to set up affiliates in other major cities was disappointing to its founding members. Its expansion into southern states would propel CORE into the black student movement of the 1960s.

The second part of the book analyzes CORE's growth and active participation in student sit-ins, jail-ins, and training of students in nonviolent direct action. The effects of the student demonstrations on the Civil Rights movement propelled CORE into the front ranks of protest organizations, which created some tension among CORE, the NAACP, and the Southern Christian Leadership Conference.

Part 3 begins with James Farmer as the national director of CORE, and follows CORE's search for a major campaign. The freedom ride of 1961 was chosen. The freedom ride served to invigorate old concepts and stimulate new ones. CORE's voter registration activities in the South (which were met with fierce resistance and violence) and its efforts to attack housing discrimination, police brutality, and de facto segregated schools in the North are discussed. The authors also delve into CORE's internal struggle between the "means-oriented idealists" and the "ends-oriented militants," which posed new challenges to its leadership.

Part 4 explores the activities and internal organizational change of CORE during its peak years and just before its decline. Meier and Rudwick indicate that in the spring of 1963, the Negro protest movement was infused with a new militancy. CORE played only a supporting role in the Birmingham demonstrations of 1963, the March on Washington (1963), and the Mississippi Freedom Democratic Party's challenge to the seating of the states' "regular" Democratic National Convention in 1964. According to the authors, this latter event crystallized the disillusionment with CORE's traditional strategy. Although CORE's membership expanded following the Birmingham demonstrations, these new members were increasingly overt in their skepticism of CORE's nonviolent tactics.

Part 5 examines CORE in its decline as black power ideology became more pronounced. Black revolutionaries and militants became more demanding in their call for a separatist movement as civil disorders erupted in major urban areas. CORE's response was to direct its focus toward community organization and political action, which met with mixed success despite valiant efforts. CORE, like many other civil rights organizations, experienced a growing sense of isolation from American society as protest efforts became more fragmented. The membership was further divided by those who wanted CORE to condemn the Vietnam War and those who felt the organization should not publicly oppose the war. Due to a lack of financial resources and an inability to address the problems of low-income urban blacks, the decline of CORE was complete in 1966.

In the epilogue, the authors analyze CORE's successes and failures and contributions to the Civil Rights movement. Following the epilogue is a bibliographic note on sources, including interviews. Extensive footnotes, arranged by chapter, and an index are also provided. This important work, along with the studies of the NAACP by Kellogg (entry 6.143) and the SNCC by Carson (entry 6.160) provide a comprehensive understanding of the major civil rights organizations and their contributions to the modern Civil Rights movement. Therefore, this book on CORE should be included in the syllabus of any undergraduate American history course on this period.

6.171 Morris, Aldon. *Origins of the Civil Rights Movement: Black Communities Organizing for Change.* New York: Free Press, 1984.

Morris's highly acclaimed and well-respected study of the origins and development of the modern Civil Rights movement begins with the 1953 bus boycott in Baton Rouge, Louisiana, and ends in 1963. Morris argues convincingly that only through a well-developed indigenous base of institutions, organizations, leaders, communication networks, and money was the movement able to "gather momentum and endure in the face of state power and widespread repression." This sociological study explores the connection between the local indigenous church and the movement in order to demonstrate how blacks organized and sustained the movement. The resources used by Morris are formal interviews with leaders and participants, the documents these people generated, and secondary sources.

In the introduction, Morris places the modern Civil Rights movement within the tradition of black protest and confrontation—from slave ships to the Underground Railroad to the March on Washington. However, he identifies the distinctive qualities of the modern movement as (1) the first time masses of blacks directly confronted and disrupted normal functioning of groups and institutions responsible for their oppression and (2) the first time in American history that blacks used nonviolent tactics en masse to affect social change.

To provide a context for understanding how it functioned within the movement, the role of the urban southern black church is explored in the first chapter. Morris describes the urban black church as a social power due to its organized but nonbureaucratic base, well-defined division of labor, and the charismatic relationship between the minister and the congregation. The NAACP began to spread to southern cities around 1918 and was closely aligned with the church in the South since the church was the primary independent black organization. Members of the congregation, then, became active members of the local NAACP chapters and developed strong working relationships with its officers. Conversely, the NAACP provided opportunities for local church leaders to acquire leadership skills and develop networks.

In chapter 2, Morris provides a valuable organizational analysis of the effectiveness of the Baton Rouge bus boycott, which served as a model for subsequent boycotts. Reverend Jemison, the pastor of the large, prestigious Mt. Zion Baptist Church, emerged as the leader of the bus boycott. Through interviews with Reverend Jemison and others, Morris discovers that Jemison evolved as a leader of the boycott in a large part due to his sincere commitment to the community. In a brilliant tactical move, Jemison established a coalition of community organizations, the United Defense League, which was composed of leaders of black community organizations speaking and acting as "one voice." The boycott involved organizing a free car lift to transport workers to and from work; this activity was financed by black churches in Baton Rouge, as were Jemison's bodyguards. Jemison then made his blueprint for the boycott available to other southern ministers. He served as a consultant to Martin Luther King Jr. and Ralph Abernathy in organizing the Montgomery bus boycott, Reverend Steele in planning a bus boycott in Tallahassee, Florida, and Reverend A. L. Davis in New Orleans.

Morris further contends that the attack on the NAACP by the southern white power structure after the 1954 *Brown* v. *Board of Education* decision opened the door for tactics other than legal redress. Black ministers took this opportunity to organize church-related direct-action organizations, which gave rise to the modern Civil Rights movement.

In an insightful final chapter, Morris presents his conclusions within a theoretical framework. Two key conclusions deserve discussion here. In analyzing Max Weber's theory of charismatic movements, Morris suggests that Weber's theory did not go far enough. Weber postulates that people follow leaders not because of leaders' organizing abilities but because people identify closely with leaders' visions, missions, and magnetic personalities. In applying the theory to the leaders in the Civil Rights movement, Morris insists that King and other leaders were successful due to their charisma *and* the organizational backing provided by already existing institutions and locally organized groups. He states, "Churches, colleges, and movement organizations, reinforced

181

by charismatic leadership, provided resources essential to the development of the movement. The charisma already existed in black church leadership."

Morris's own analysis explains the endurance of the Civil Rights movement and supports his thesis. According to Morris's theory, sustained movements depend on basic resources, social activists with strong ties to mass-based indigenous institutions, and tactics and strategies that can be employed effectively against a system of domination. He describes the critical role of local movement centers, which enable activism to spread rapidly and sustain innovations. These local movement centers, such as the Southern Christian Leadership Conference, the Mississippi Improvement Association, and the Student Nonviolent Coordinating Committee, were loosely organized but nonbureaucratic. The leaders were active *before* the beginning of the movement; they were newcomers—as were Jemison and King—but not identified with conflicting factions.

Morris's book, then, assists readers to understand the organizational dynamics of protest movements as well as important dimensions of leadership. By clarifying the roles of King and other leaders in the movement and focusing readers' attention on the powerful influence of locally based organizations, community and church organizers and sociologists are provided valuable models of social protest movements.

The eleven chapters are followed by four useful appendixes, including a list of interviewees, a sample interview questionnaire, and sample fundraising statements. A bibliography and an index also are provided.

6.172   Pinkney, Alphonso. *The Myth of Black Progress.* New York: Cambridge University Press, 1984.

The purpose of this book is to evaluate the current (1984) status of African Americans in the United States compared with that of whites. The author was motivated to write the book in response to what he calls the newest wave of conservatism: Patrick Moynihan's *The Negro Family: The Case for National Action* (1965), in which the black family is blamed for the lack of economic progress; William J. Wilson's *The Declining Significance of Race* (entry 6.176); and the work of other social scientists and economists who claim that the income gap between blacks and whites is closing, that class is more important than race in determining economic success, and that affirmative action is no longer needed as a remedy to counter the effects of past discrimination. Pinkney insists that these individuals have based their findings on "distorted statistics and erroneous data."

The ten concise chapters of the book present data and discuss the myth of black progress. In the introduction, Pinkney provides an instructive analysis of civil rights legislation between 1954 and 1968, beginning with *Brown* v. *Board of Education* and ending with the Civil Rights Act of 1968. The second chapter, by Walter Stafford, explores the factors that contributed to the economic decline and the rise of new conservatism. He identifies the dissolution of civil rights organizations and the change in black leadership, demands of developing nations for substantive resources from the United States, and the decline in U.S. productivity as factors that contributed to this decline. He also discusses the efforts of the New Right, including the so-called Religious Right, to influence public policy issues, and outlines the deleterious effects of their positions on African Americans.

The third chapter explores dimensions of class and race in America. The author concludes that class conflict is much broader than racial conflict, and while the two are linked and thrive on each other, racism is the dominant factor in explaining why blacks fare less well than, for example, immigrants. In the fourth chapter, Pinkney examines the difference between prejudicial attitudes and discriminatory behavior. Most enlightening is a discussion of surveys on white attitudes toward blacks. In 1978 one survey revealed that one-fourth of American whites felt that blacks have less native intelligence than whites. Other important studies and statistics on discrimination are discussed, including discrimination in housing, employment, and health care.

The fifth chapter presents data from federal sources on income, occupation, and unemployment. The author's purpose here is to analyze and interpret the comparative data between blacks and whites in these three areas and to counter the claims that gaps between the incomes of blacks and whites are closing rapidly. In chapter 6, Pinkney reviews various definitions of what middle-class status means in the black community. He attempts to dispel the myth that the black middle class is in conflict with lower-class blacks and vice-versa.

Pinkney acknowledges that there has been an increase in the percentage of blacks in the middle class, but in chapter 7 he discusses the growth, characteristics, lifestyle, and plight of the black underclass. Educational issues are examined in chapter 8, as education historically has been viewed by African Americans as the most important avenue for social and economic advancement. Pinkney reviews the current status of black education, desegregation of public schools, and open-admissions policies in higher education.

In chapter 9, "Bakke, Weber, and the Myth of Reverse Discrimination," Pinkney analyzes the facts, conclusions, and effects of the Bakke and Weber cases. In the final chapter, "Black Equity in White

America," Pinkney briefly assesses American presidents from John F. Kennedy through Ronald Reagan regarding their recommendations for funding of social and educational programs crucial to black progress. He concludes that economics, one of the most serious problems facing black Americans, was not addressed by the Civil Rights movement or affirmative action.

Extensive footnotes, arranged by chapter, and an index complete this book. *The Myth of Black Progress* is a highly readable book that brings an important balance and perspective to the discussion of economic progress and equity for African Americans. For a more recent review of the underclass in general, see *The Underclass Question* (entry 6.168) and Wilson's *The Truly Disadvantaged* (entry 6.177).

College students, high school instructors, and college professors in almost any discipline—but especially sociology, urban history, political science, and economics—and the general reader will find this book provides an analysis of contemporary social issues in America.

6.173   **Robinson, Jo Ann Gibson.** *The Montgomery Bus Boycott and the Women Who Started It: The Memoir of Jo Ann Gibson Robinson.* Knoxville: University of Tennessee Press, 1987.

Readers will find this engaging and personal story of the role of the Women's Political Council (WPC)—a black women's organization active in Montgomery long before the 1955 bus boycott—a crucial but heretofore missing link to their knowledge and understanding of the Civil Rights movement. The book, written by the woman who was president of the WPC from 1950 until 1958, chronicles the role of the WPC in bringing about the Montgomery bus boycott. In the words of Robinson, ". . . it was during the period of 1949–1955 that the WPC of Montgomery prepared to stage a bus boycott when the time was ripe and the people were ready. The right time came in 1955."

Robinson begins her memoir by recounting a personal incident that compelled her to become active in the WPC. On route to the train station in a bus, Robinson was aggressively and almost violently ordered by the white bus driver to sit in the seat designated for Negroes. It was a humiliating and dehumanizing experience she would never forget. Her outrage added to the chorus of complaints brought by other blacks in the community against the bus company.

In the first of nine chapters in the book, readers learn that the WPC—under the leadership of its founder, Dr. Mary Fair Burks, chairperson of the English department at Alabama State College and a colleague of Robinson's—was organized for the purpose of inspiring Negroes to improve their status as a group and to fight against injustice. When the bus company requested permission from the city commission to increase bus fares, a public hearing was held and members of the WPC attended to protest the indignities suffered by Montgomery blacks. They itemized a list of complaints against the company and met with the bus company manager to discuss them. Although the company agreed to treat its 70 percent Negro ridership better, the drivers soon resumed their demoralizing and inhumane treatment of Montgomery's black citizens.

The second chapter documents the little-known stories of Claudette Colvin, a young woman who was arrested and found guilty of violating Alabama state law by riding the bus in a white-only section, and Mary Louise Smith, an eighteen-year-old citizen of Montgomery who was arrested and fined for refusing to move to the rear of the bus. These incidents predated the well-publicized and historic actions of Rosa Parks on December 1, 1955, but were closely related to Mrs. Parks's brave efforts.

In the remaining seven chapters, the behind-the-scenes work of the WPC in assisting to organize the Montgomery bus boycott and participating in negotiations with the city and in the ensuing legal battle is poignantly told by Robinson. Robinson concludes the book with a glossary of individuals involved in the WPC, a useful chronology of events, and an index.

Robinson's work makes a monumental contribution to the history of the modern Civil Rights movement and black women's history by uncovering the true story of the Montgomery bus boycott. For this reason, high school and undergraduate American history and women's studies teachers and students should be exposed to this work and incorporate it into the curriculum.

6.174   **Sitkoff, Harvard.** *A New Deal for Blacks: The Emergence of Civil Rights as a National Issue.* Vol. 1: *The Depression Decade.* New York: Oxford University Press, 1978.

In this first volume on the emergence of civil rights as a national issue, Sitkoff defines the 1930s as the time when the seeds of the modern Civil Rights movement were planted. Sitkoff identifies a range of fundamental changes in the status of race relations during the Depression decade that set it apart from preceding decades. Governmental action was responsible for some of that change, but many other important outside forces, individuals, institutions, and events converged simultaneously to set the stage for the modern civil rights era.

Sitkoff credits Eleanor Roosevelt with positively influencing Franklin D. Roosevelt's policies, including the creation of a "Black Cabinet," that began advancing civil rights. Other forces Sitkoff identifies include ". . . Negro voters, southern liberals, egalitarian unionists, anti-fascist scholars, the transformation of southern agriculture, the shock of Hitlerism, and the nationalization of American culture." Indeed the focus of the New Deal on the forgotten and downtrodden contributed to an atmosphere of reform that resonated with the civil rights struggle.

New Deal policies ushered in economic assistance to the black community, and a new sense of hopefulness was bolstered by the unabashed advocacy of civil rights by prominent New Dealers. Each of the twelve chapters, then, explores the impact and contribution of the forces that precipitated this change.

The importance of the Negro vote in influencing politicians to strive for racial justice is discussed in chapter 4. Division in the Democratic Party, a decline in the popularity of white supremacy, and conservative southern politicians are examined in chapter 5, "A Rift in the Coalition." Chapter 6 analyzes how the American Left, socialists, communists, and others were successful in making civil rights a part of their Progressive agenda.

The policies of organized labor, which needed the support of Negroes to succeed, are explored in chapter 7. Cultural and intellectual developments that rejected the notion of the inferiority of the black race and aided the struggle for civil rights are discussed in chapter 8. The role of the judiciary in deciding important cases in favor of civil rights is addressed in chapter 9. In a chapter entitled "The Struggle," Sitkoff identifies numerous civil rights organizations that struggled tirelessly for racial equality in the 1930s. The NAACP and the National Urban League, among others, established special committees and councils to advocate for the rights of blacks. Chapter 11 describes the critical role of the antilynching crusade in fueling the black struggle.

In a concluding chapter, Sitkoff argues that the unprecedented public outcry against the Daughters of the American Revolution for barring Marian Anderson—a world-renowned mezzo-soprano—from giving a recital in its Constitution Hall in 1939 symbolized the changes that occurred during the 1930s. The final chapter is followed by footnotes and an index.

Undergraduate instructors of history and public policy studies will find this book critical reading.

6.175   Sitkoff, Harvard. *The Struggle for Black Equality: 1954–1992.* New York: Hill and Wang, 1993.

First published in 1980, this revised, updated book provides a narrative interpretation of the Civil Rights movement. Using an engaging style, Sitkoff's book begins with the *Brown* v. *Board of Education* decision outlawing separate but equal educational facilities and takes the reader through the 1990s.

The eight chapters are arranged chronologically. Beginning with slavery, the first chapter, "Up from Slavery," provides a concise historical overview of civil rights. The second chapter documents the Montgomery bus boycott beginning with Rosa Parks's act of defiance. The third chapter, cleverly entitled "Bigger than a Hamburger," tells the story of the student sit-ins started by black students at North Carolina A and T University in Greensboro, and the establishment and work of the Congress on Racial Equality (CORE) and the Student Nonviolent Coordinating Committee (SNCC). In the chapter entitled "The Long Journey," Sitkoff portrays the struggles, obstacles, and violence encountered by the freedom riders from CORE who traveled south to dismantle and test Jim Crow laws in restaurants, waiting rooms, and rest rooms.

The Civil Rights movement took a decided turn in Birmingham in 1963. Under the leadership of Martin Luther King Jr., a massive wave of nonviolent action was launched, which eventually resulted in the passage of the most comprehensive antidiscrimination legislation in American history. Chapter 5, "We Shall Overcome," is devoted to examining the Birmingham demonstrations, the impact of Malcolm X's philosophy on the movement, mainstream movement leaders like King, and the 1963 March on Washington.

In chapter 6, the forces that led to the passage of major voting rights legislation are discussed. An interpretation of the causes and significance of urban violence that erupted in major northern cities in the 1960s is explored in chapter 7, "Heirs of Malcolm X." In the final chapter, "A Dream Deferred: The Struggle Continues," Sitkoff takes the reader to contemporary America and discusses the effects of government policies and programs and affirmative action legislation on the economic condition of African Americans. The book concludes with a comprehensive bibliographic essay on civil rights. An index is included.

Teachers of high school and lower-division history, government, and public policy courses will want to assign this highly readable book to their students.

6.176   **Wilson, William Julius.** *The Declining Significance of Race: Blacks and Changing American Institutions.* Chicago: University of Chicago Press, 1978.

Wilson's controversial book was criticized by many in the black scholarly community for his thesis that in the modern industrial era, class has become more important than race in determining black opportunities. His thesis is that due to the historical consequences of racial oppression, blacks are disproportionately represented in the underclass population, which is continuing to grow. Therefore, public policy programs directed toward ameliorating class subordination may be more effective than those just limited to racial and ethnic discrimination.

In this book, Wilson traces the major periods of American race relations to different systems of production. He readily acknowledges that racial oppression was a characteristic in both the preindustrial and industrial periods of American race relations. But after World War II, he contends, the black class structure started to assume some of the characteristics of the white class structure. "Access to the means of production is increasingly based on educational criteria ... the labor market currently provides vastly different mobility opportunities for different segments of the black population." According to Wilson, this phenomenon was brought about by both the expansion of salaried white-collar positions and the pressures of affirmative action programs. Wilson would, then, agree with Pinkney's statement that affirmative action does not address the problem of equity and access for lower-class blacks.

The seven chapters are arranged in roughly chronological order. Chapter 1 presents a broad theoretical framework that examines the relationship between race and class. Chapter 2 analyzes the effect of a preindustrial system of production on the pattern of race relations in the South and examines the changing relations between slaveholder and slave. In chapter 3, Wilson focuses on different forms of racial antagonism in the preindustrial and early industrial periods in relation to issues of class and race conflicts. Chapter 4 looks at the effects of industrialization on the changing patterns of race and class relations in the North from 1900 to World War II.

Chapter 5 analyzes the modern industrial period of race relations, focusing especially on the role of changes in the economy and political changes of the government in creating mobility opportunities for different segments of the black population. Chapter 6 shows the connection between social class and different types of black protest movements and examines the importance of black urban political power in declining urban cities. The final chapter discusses the declining significance of race and attempts to redefine some of the problems that often are perceived as racial in nature.

Wilson's arguments are compelling and thoughtful, although in the current economic and social climate, he might be less optimistic about the ability of educated blacks to "continue to enjoy the advantages and privileges of their class status." College and university professors and students in sociology, political science, and economics should be required to read this book along with Pinkney's *The Myth of Black Progress* (entry 6.172).

6.177   Wilson, William Julius. *The Truly Disadvantaged: The Inner City, the Underclass, and Public Policy.* Chicago: University of Chicago Press, 1987.

Wilson expands upon his arguments in *The Declining Significance of Race* (6.176) by challenging mainstream, liberal analyses of inner-city problems and neighborhoods that have deteriorated rapidly since the 1960s. Wilson also discusses "the social pathologies of the inner city, and proposes a public policy agenda designed to improve the opportunities of the truly disadvantaged groups by emphasizing programs to which the more advantaged groups of all races can positively relate."

The book is divided into two parts, "The Ghetto Underclass, Poverty, and Social Dislocations" and "The Ghetto Underclass and Public Policy." The four chapters in the first section describe and critically examine the social changes and class structure in inner-city neighborhoods; the idea that the problems of violent crime, out-of-wedlock births, female-headed households, and welfare dependency cannot be accounted for by racism alone; and the popular welfare state explanations of the rise of the ghetto underclass and its relation to joblessness and rates of female-headed families.

The essays in part 2 analyze and examine public policy approaches to the problems of the ghetto underclass, including (1) shortcomings of race-specific policies, such as affirmative action, in addressing problems of the ghetto underclass and (2) the limitations of the race-relations model and the War on Poverty model in explaining the problems of the ghetto underclass and in proposing public policy solutions. The final chapter summarizes the basic arguments presented in earlier chapters and makes recommendations for a comprehensive public policy agenda to improve the opportunities and life chances for the ghetto underclass.

Wilson's provocative arguments have been and continue to be challenged by the academic community, but they will focus the debate on issues critical to public policymakers and to the nation. Therefore, this book is highly recommended for upper-division economics, political science, and public-policy students and professors. It should be read in conjunction with Lawson's *The Underclass Question* (6.168).

Documentary Histories

6.178   **Carson, Clayborne, David J. Garrow, Gerald Gill, Vincent Harding, and Darlene Clark Hine, eds.** *The Eyes on the Prize Civil Rights Reader: Documents, Speeches, and Firsthand Accounts from the Black Freedom Struggle, 1954–1990.* New York: Penguin Books, 1991.

One of several books written in conjunction with the PBS documentary series *Eyes on the Prize* (entries 6.157 and 6.158), the fourteen chapter titles and documents in this text correspond with the fourteen-part video series. The book is introduced by historian Vincent Harding's thirty-four-page historical and inspirational overview of the struggle for freedom, entitled "We the People: The Long Journey Toward a More Perfect Union." Each chapter is then preceded by an introduction. Excerpts—one-half page to three pages in length—of speeches, editorials, newspaper articles, letters, reports, and books follow the introductory statements.

The voices of leaders and participants in the Civil Rights movement represented in these pages include both the renowned and the obscure: Rosa Parks, Martin Luther King Jr., Ella Baker, John Lewis, Bayard Rustin, Daisy Bates, Emmett Till, Anne Moody, James Forman, Malcolm X, Sonia Sanchez, Stokely Carmichael, Geraldine Wilson, Bobby Seale, Huey P. Newton, Ralph Abernathy, Charlayne Hunter, Paula Giddings, Richard Hatcher, Angela Davis, Harold Washington, Maynard Jackson, and Nelson Mandela.

Instructors of high school and lower-division undergraduate American and African-American history courses will find this book an indispensable source.

6.179   **Hampton, Henry, and Steve Fayer, eds.** *Voices of Freedom: An Oral History of the Civil Rights Movement from the 1950s through the 1980s.* New York: Bantam Books, 1990.

An outgrowth of the *Eyes on the Prize* (entries 6.157 and 6.158) television series, *Voices of Freedom* is a powerful collection of oral-history interviews with individuals who participated in the movement. More than one thousand interviews were conducted in the late 1970s for the television series, but due to time constraints, only a few of the stories could be used. The transcripts were edited and compiled into this valuable collection.

According to the editors, this book is an event-driven oral history. Interviewers did not attempt to gather life histories of the movement; instead, people were asked to tell what they saw, heard, did, or felt at specific periods in civil rights history. In the words of one of the publishers, "We have tried to let the voices speak for themselves. . . ." Although not a comprehensive history of the Civil Rights movement, the stories told here illuminate themes of the movement as told by movement participants.

In each of the thirty-one chapters, which are arranged in chronological order, the interviewees are introduced by a short description of who they are in relation to the story being told. Interviewees were asked to take themselves back mentally and emotionally to the time of the event and reflect upon what happened and how they felt. The result is a fascinating and dramatic story of specific events from the point of view of actual participants.

Several of the events that come alive for readers include the tragic beating and killing of fourteen-year-old Emmett Till, which brought the United States international disgrace in 1955; the Montgomery bus boycott, 1955; the Little Rock school desegregation crisis, 1957–1958; student sit-ins in Nashville, 1960; James Meredith's desegregation of the University of Mississippi, 1962; the 1963 March on Washington; the rise of Malcolm X and the black Muslims, 1965; King and Vietnam, 1965–1967; the birth of the Black Panther Party, 1966-1967; Detroit riots in 1967; the election of Carl Stokes, the first black mayor of Cleveland, Ohio, in 1967; Attica and prisoners' rights, 1971; the Gary, Indiana, Convention, 1972; and Atlanta and affirmative action, 1973–1980.

Each chapter represents a specific event and is introduced with a brief historical overview. Like all the companion volumes for the *Eyes on the Prize* television series, the voices are those of famous leaders and of the countless civil rights volunteers and participants whose names will not be familiar to most readers, but whose courage and contributions now are being recognized and appreciated. The voices readers will hear include those of Emmett Till's brave grandfather, who identified his grandson's killers; Rosa Parks, whose single action sparked the Montgomery bus boycott; Coretta Scott King; Myrlie Evers, widow of slain civil rights leader Medgar Evers; and James Hicks, journalist for the *Amsterdam News*, a New York–based black weekly. Other personalities include Marion Berry, Julian Bond, James Farmer, John Lewis, Andrew Young, Bernice Johnson Reagon, Ralph Abernathy,

Fred Shuttlesworth, Unita Blackwell, Stokely Carmichael, Alex Haley, Ossie Davis, Marian Wright Edelman, Harry Belafonte, Sonia Sanchez, Bobby Seale and Huey Newton of the Black Panther Party, Delores Torres, Jesse Jackson, Angela Davis, Tom Wicker, Ben Chavis, Mary Frances Berry, and countless others.

An epilogue, "From Miami to America's Future," concludes the book. A bibliography, a list of the *Eyes on the Prize* project staff and funders, and an index are provided.

Instructors of high school and college American and African-American history and American studies classes will want to read these poignant stories to themselves and to their students in addition to assigning selected chapters as required reading.

SOURCES CONSULTED

Du Bois, W. E. B. *A Select Bibliography of the American Negro.* Atlanta: Atlanta University Press, 1905.

Glover, Denise M. "Academic Library Support for Black Studies Programs: A Plea to Black Studies Faculty and Administrators." *Journal of Negro Education* 53 (Summer 1984): 312–21.

———. "A Study of the Relationship between Academic Institutional Commitment to Minority Studies Programs and Minority Studies Libraries and Collections." Ph.D. diss., University of Michigan, 1982.

Gubert, Betty Kaplan. *Early Black Bibliographies, 1863–1918.* New York and London: Garland Publishing, 1982.

Johnson, Daniel M., and Rex R. Campbell. *Black Migration in America: A Social Demographic History.* Durham, N.C.: Duke University Press, 1981.

Katz, William Loren. *Teachers' Guide to American Negro History.* New York: New Viewpoints, 1974.

McPherson, James M., Laurence B. Holland, James Banner Jr., Nancy J. Weiss, and Michael D. Bell. *Blacks in America: Bibliographic Essays.* Garden City, N.Y.: Doubleday and Company, 1971.

Newman, Richard. *Black Access: A Bibliography of Afro-American Bibliographies.* Westport, Conn.: Greenwood Press, 1983.

Porter, Dorothy B. "Bibliography and Research in Afro-American Scholarship." *Journal of Academic Librarianship* 2 (1976): 77–81.

———. *The Negro in the United States: A Selected Bibliography.* Washington, D.C.: Library of Congress, 1970.

Smith, Dwight Z., ed. *Afro-American History: A Bibliography.* 2v. Santa Barbara, Calif.: Clio Bibliography Service, 1974, 1982.

Spradling, Mary Mace, ed. *In Black and White: A Guide to Magazine Articles, Newspaper Articles, and Books Concerning More Than 15,000 Black Individuals and Groups.* Detroit: Gale Research Co., 1980.

Stevenson, Rosemary. *Index to Afro-American Reference Resources.* Westport, Conn.: Greenwood Press, 1988.

Work, Monroe. *A Bibliography of the Negro in Africa and America.* New York: H. W. Wilson, 1928. Reprint, New York: Octagon Press, 1965.

AUTHOR-TITLE INDEX

SUBJECT INDEX

Denise Glover is currently an education/training specialist at the Federal Judicial Center in Washington, D.C. Her former positions include director of library services at the University of Maryland, University College; assistant director, Amistad Research Center at Tulane University in New Orleans; and head librarian/archivist at the National Afro-American Museum and Cultural Center in Wilberforce, Ohio. Glover received her master's and Ph.D. degrees in library science from the University of Michigan.